A
COURSE
IN APL
WITH APPLICATIONS

SECOND EDITION

A
COURSE
IN APL
WITH APPLICATIONS

SECOND EDITION

LOUIS D. GREY
Perkin/Elmer Corporation

ADDISON–WESLEY PUBLISHING COMPANY
Reading, Massachusetts
Menlo Park, California
London · Amsterdam · Don Mills, Ontario · Sydney

ISBN 0-201-02563-9
.BCDEFGHIJ-AL-79

To my wife Betty

PREFACE TO THE SECOND EDITION

In the three years since the original text was published, a number of events have occurred which make a revision desirable. Perhaps the most important of these was the release by IBM in August 1973 of the APL Shared Variable System (APLSV) with its capabilities for handling large files of data, powerful new primitive functions, a new system-command structure, and many other features. These features considerably expand the range of applications which are feasible with APL and will undoubtedly have a significant impact in promoting the growth of the APL user community. Many installations where APL\360 is already in operation will certainly convert to APLSV. To accommodate these changes, an entirely new section (Part 4) has been written describing in detail the features available under APLSV.

Other important changes have also been made. The features described in Chapter 19 of the first edition have for the most part become standard and they are now described in the appropriate chapter. The exercises and problems at the end of most of the chapters have been revised. The body of the text is relatively free from applications--this should make for easier reading. The appendices have been thoroughly revised and in come cases changed. The bibliography has also been updated to reflect the rapid growth of the literature. Last, but certainly not least, a serious attempt has been made to remove all typographical errors as well as mistakes and omissions. All terminal examples have been carefully reworked and checked.

For their critical comments and suggestions, I am particularly indebted to Professor David Gomberg of the State University of New York at Buffalo, to Professor Garth Foster and J. Wilson at Syracuse University, and to Professor Edward A. Feustel of Rice University. Finally, thanks are due to Ms. Helen Geraghty for her help in typing the manuscript.

Norwalk, Connecticut   L. D. G.
July 1976

This text is an introduction to APL, an acronym for A Programming Language, invented by Dr. Kenneth Iverson of IBM. In speaking of APL we really mean APL\360, the version of APL currently implemented for the IBM System 360 series of computers. The text is intended for both the experienced computer user familiar with at least one general-purpose language, such as FORTRAN IV, ALGOL, PL-1, etc., who wants to gain an understanding of APL, and the novice who has had no previous experience with a programming language.

The student is taught to use a computer rapidly and efficiently without having to learn the laborious details and mechanics of how computers operate. The exposition is aimed at showing that APL is a refinement and enhancement of mathematics. For this reason, the student does not have to learn a new jargon dictated solely by the whims of a computer. Emphasis is placed on the use of APL as an ideal language for developing and formulating algorithms.

Part 1 of the book provides the user with sufficient information to begin doing useful work on his own. Chapters 1-5 deal with various aspects of the APL language. Emphasis is placed on the concept of a primitive function. The treatment of the APL\360 System as a powerful desk calculator allows the student to explore and gain familiarity with the more elementary primitive functions.

Part 2 (Chapters 6-12) shows how the scope of the primitive functions is enlarged to permit complex operations on arrays of data. The more sophisticated primitive functions are introduced. Finally, the student is led to the concept of a program or user-defined function as a simple extension of the concept of primitive function.

Part 3 (Chapters 13-19) is concerned with new primitive functions, input-output, error diagnostics, system commands, and the direction of current research.

The organization of the text reflects the author's belief that the student will get the most out of APL if he concerns himself initially with the language and with the way it views the world rather than with its implementation.

To derive the most from this book, the student should have access to a remote typewriter terminal connected to the APL\360 System. A number of commercial time-sharing organizations are devoted exclusively to providing this service. In learning APL there is no substitute for doing and the surest way to gain facility is to carry out the calculations described.

The text developed from first-hand teaching experiences at the Perkin-Elmer Corporation, where the author has lectured and taught courses in APL to engineers, programmers, and other users.

Applications which form an integral part of the book are treated in the problem section at the end of each chapter. Problems are given in such areas as Fourier analysis, least square methods, numerical integration, the solution of Laplace's equation by numerical methods, the three-body problem, eigenvalue problems, the functions of mathematical physics, and many others. To reinforce the learning process, answers have been provided so that students may monitor their progress.

The organization and topics included allow the text to be used as a primer for the beginning student and as a reference manual for the more experienced student.

Much useful information has been provided in five appendices. Appendix A contains a summary with examples of all the primitive functions. Appendix B summarizes the system commands. Appendix C describes commercially available sources of APL\360, including prices. Appendix D describes the implementation of APL on computers other than IBM, and finally, Appendix E describes user groups and publications. The appendices are preceded by a comprehensive bibliography listing the important publications which have appeared on APL.

My debt to various individuals for their assistance is gratefully acknowledged. I am grateful to APL Service, Inc., and in particular to Mr. Ken David for providing me with computer time. My colleagues at Perkin-Elmer Corporation, Roger Arguello, Dr. Heinrich Kessler, Harvey Sellner, Ed Kob, Michael Crockett, and Dr. Martin Yellin, have made me aware of the uses of APL in the areas of Fourier optics and picture processing. With respect to the applications, specific acknowledgments are made in the body of the book. Mrs. Marjorie Knapp provided excellent secretarial support in the typing of the manuscript. I am grateful to all my students for providing the laboratory where ideas could be field-tested. Thanks are due to my daughters, Susan, Ronna, and Margery, who have encouraged me from the beginning. Above all, thanks are due to my wife, Betty, whose help and understanding have made this book possible.

Norwalk, Connecticut   L.D.G.
January 1973

CONTENTS

Contents   xv

Contents

APL (A Programming Language) is a significant step forward in the development of a general-purpose algebraic language. Although its symbols are like those of mathematics, there are at least two important respects in which it improves on mathematics. The first is in consistency of notation, the second in the capability it offers for formulating and structuring algorithms. APL represents a milestone in the realization of that goal. The language was first defined by Dr. Kenneth Iverson in his book A Programming Language (John Wiley, 1962). APL\360, which is the implementation of APL for the IBM System 360 series of computers, is the work of Iverson, A. Falkoff, L. M. Breed, R. H. Lathwell, R. D. Moore, and others.

For the physical scientist and engineer, APL is an ideal application language because in a sense it is not a new language at all. Although the notation at first sight appears awesome and unfamiliar, it takes only a short time to see that the symbols used are names for some of the most elementary algebraic and logical functions. Given the power and elegance of mathematical notation and structure, the user can concentrate on formulating his problem advantageously without any concern about how the computer solves it internally.

Fortunately, the virtues of APL are not confined to the physical sciences and engineering. As the social sciences become more quantitatively and mathematically oriented, the likelihood is ever greater that the social scientist will find himself involved with computers. The social scientist is likely to be on shakier ground in his understanding of how a computer works than either the physical scientist or engineer. Whether the computer is to be an effective tool for him or just an intellectual curiosity depends on the facilities available for communicating with the computer. He must have a language which is easy to learn. Such a language must relieve him of any need to know what is happening internally in the computer. It must be precise and economical enough to make practical computations which might otherwise take too long to program. In addition, it must provide the

facility for dealing with non—numeric data. In all these respects APL
is admirably qualified to do the job.

Still another domain in which APL is likely to exert a profound in-
fluence is education. Computer—assisted instruction is not a novel
idea, but one of the chief difficulties plaguing it has been the lack of
any language both simple enough and powerful enough to be used by
students and teachers. The implementation of APL\360 as a conver-
sational time—sharing language makes it ideal for testing the feasi-
bility of algorithms, for exploring mathematical functions, and for
gaining greater insight into all those activities that have come to be
associated with learning.

Remarkable as the applications of computers have been over the
past 20 years, they are slight compared with what has been envisioned
for them. Whether those visions remain visions or whether they can
be transformed to reality depends not so much on faster, cheaper, or
more reliable computers as on more effective ways of communicating
with them. The ultimate step in enlarging the community of computer
users is to give the capability of programming lucidly to everyone who
has the capacity to do so. Surely this is what APL is intended to do.

PART ONE
APL BASICS

PRELIMINARIES

1.1 INTRODUCTION

The student should have the opportunity to experiment and try things
for himself as soon as he can obtain access to an APL\360 system.
This chapter is intended to provide him with the necessary prerequi-
sites.

Although Part 1 of the text concentrates on the APL language,
we must remember that the language is embodied in a system, a minimum understanding of which is required even at the outset. Because
APL\360 is a time-sharing system, we will need to point out the distinguishing characteristics of such systems. In particular, we will
explain how to use the remote typewriter terminal, since for most
users that will be the only way of communicating with the system.

We shall discuss the mechanics of signing on and off, the APL
alphabet, the correction of typing errors, a way to interrupt the computer, etc. For the most part, these techniques are best learned in
practice sessions at the terminal.

1.2 TIME-SHARING

Our purpose here is not to give a definitive view of time-sharing but
rather to show what the essential characteristics of such a system are
from the user's point of view. An overall view of a time-sharing system is shown in Figure 1.2.1.

Each user communicates with the system through a terminal,
i.e., a typewriter with a communications interface. Since the users
of the system may be geographically remote from each other and from
the computer, the terminal is referred to as a remote terminal.
Communication between the terminals and the computer takes place
via telephone lines, microwaves, hard-wires, etc. Since information
is transmitted very rapidly, users are served on a real-time basis,
usually in a matter of seconds. The significance of the phrase 'time-

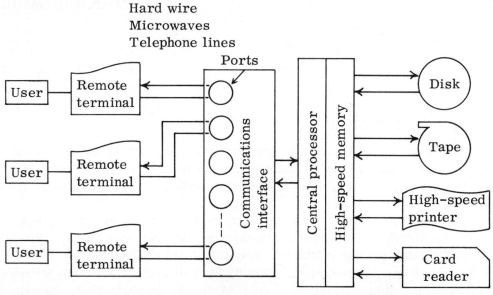

Fig. 1.2.1   An overall view of a time-sharing system

sharing' is that computer time is divided into discrete intervals, each interval being assigned to a user according to a scheduling discipline. Since the time interval between successive services is short, each user has the illusion that he has exclusive use of the computer. In addition to servicing many users simultaneously, a time-sharing system makes it possible to utilize the resources of the computer more efficiently. While the central processor is servicing one user, a second user may be retrieving a message on his terminal, and a third is obtaining information from a file. The capability of the system to carry out these complex functions stems from a highly sophisticated set of instructions called the executive program. This program, which includes the scheduling and priority functions, acts as the controlling element and is responsible for reliable continuous operation.

1.3   REMOTE TERMINAL

The remote terminal that will concern us is an electric typewriter with a communications interface. A number of manufacturers make terminals which will support the APL\360 system, but the best known is undoubtedly the IBM 2741.

Everything said in the text about the IBM 2741 will be applicable, with minor modifications, to the other terminals.

1.3.1 Operating the Terminal

In order to establish a connection with the APL\360 system, you must proceed as follows:

1. Make sure that the terminal has an APL typing element (golfball) and a keyboard with the APL character set shown in Figure 1.3.1. If the keytops have a different character set, they may be converted with a stick-on conversion kit or by means of an overlay or map. There are two kinds of terminals, commonly referred to as 'correspondence' and 'BCD'. Each one requires its own typing element.

2. Turn the typewriter power switch to the ON position and set the switch to the COM or communicate position. The keyboard will stay in a locked position. In the local position, LCL, the typewriter becomes an ordinary electric typewriter and nothing typed on it will be transmitted to the computer.

   If your terminal has a Dataset, proceed to step (3).

   If your terminal is linked via an acoustic coupler, proceed to step (4). If you have neither Dataset nor acoustic coupler, check the procedure with the installation manager.

3. Depress the TALK button and dial the number of the computer. When you hear the high-pitched beep, cradle the phone in the coupler.

   If noisy lines or other difficulties make it necessary to seek assistance from the telephone operator, be sure to tell her you are dialing a computer and that the high-pitched beep is what you expect.

1.4 GETTING STARTED

The instant your telephone link to the computer is established, your keyboard will unlock. You are now in a position to sign on and become an APL\360 user. In order to do this, however, you will need to obtain an account number from the installation servicing you. Let us

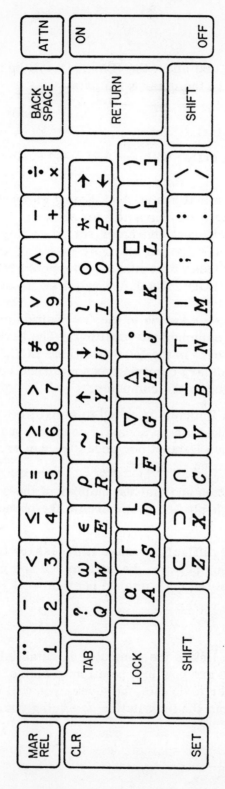

Fig. 1.3.1 APL\360 keyboard

assume that your account number is 106400. The sequence of events that might take place is shown in Figure 1.4.1.

```
)106400:GREY
OPR:  COPY PROBLEMS HAVE BEEN FIXED.
019)  11.26.35 05/04/70 APLPERKIN

   A P L \ 3 6 0
```

Fig. 1.4.1

Your sign-on is initiated by a right parenthesis followed immediately by your account number. All system commands, of which this is one, are initiated by typing a right parenthesis. The colon indicates that the information which follows is optional. In this case the name GREY is a password. We shall discuss the subject of passwords in Part 3 when we discuss the APL\360 system in much greater detail. At this point the sign-on is almost finished. In order to let the computer know that you have completed your sign-on, you strike the RETURN key. In general, when the computer detects the return key character, it knows that you have completed the current statement and that some action is required. The keyboard is locked to prevent you from interfering with the computer, and it remains locked until the computer has completed the calculations. At that point the carriage is returned to the left and moved up one line.

Line 2 of Figure 1.4.1 shows the message sent by the computer to the user at the time of sign-on. Such a message is optional and may or may not be sent. It is a means of passing on information which should be of interest to most users, e.g., changes in schedule, equipment problems, holiday greetings, etc.

Line 3 is also from the computer and the information it contains is always sent back. The characters 019) indicate that the user has reached Port 19. Each APL\360 system has a number of telephone extensions, or ports, to accommodate users. The number 11.26.35 denotes the time of day in hours, minutes, and seconds and ranges from 0.0 to 23.59.59. This information is followed by the date, i.e., month, day, and year. Following the characters APL, we have the system name for this particular account number, PERKIN, denoting Perkin-Elmer Corporation. The order of the information in line 3 may vary from one installation to another.

Following line 3 the computer skips a line, prints APL\360 or a similar title and releases the keyboard. The system is then ready to perform whatever computations are requested.

Let us briefly summarize the sign-on procedure. You initiate the sign-on by typing a right parenthesis and your account number, and then pressing the RETURN key. A broadcast message may or may not be received from the computer, but a line of information will be sent stating the port number reached, the time of day, the date, and the name by which the account is known to the system. This information will be followed by a line with the characters APL\360 or a similar title identifying the vendor's system.

1.5 TYPING

As we remarked earlier, when the computer is calculating or when it is printing out a message, the keyboard is locked so that the user cannot interfere with the computer's operation. When the keyboard is unlocked, it is the computer which must wait for the carriage return signal while the user types the information that the computer is to act on. Since a new line is initiated by the carriage return signal, it follows that each message typed by the user must fit in a single line. To a beginner this may appear to be a restriction but we shall see later that this really causes no difficulties.

In order to distinguish between your typing and the computer's typing, the computer will move the paper up one line when it has completed its operations and indent six spaces. Therefore, what the computer types starts at the left margin. What the user types is indented six spaces.

1.5.1 Correcting Typing Errors

In typing you are bound to make errors, and it is therefore important to know how errors are corrected. Suppose, e.g., you have typed the following sequence of characters:

$A \leftarrow B \div C$

You recognize that the character $\div$ should be $\times$. To correct your error, proceed as follows:

1. Backspace to the leftmost character that you want to correct.
2. Press the key marked ATTN. This key is sometimes marked INDEX or LINEFEED.

The computer will type the character ∨ under this letter and space the paper up. The character under which ∨ appears and all of the characters to the right of it have been erased. You can now proceed with your typing. Figure 1.5.1 depicts the sequence of events.

$$A \leftarrow B \div C$$
$$\vee$$
$$\times C$$

Fig. 1.5.1

Overstriking a character will usually result in an error when the RETURN key is depressed. For example, in Fig. 1.5.2 the character C has been overstruck with A, resulting in a character error. The character ∧ indicates where in the statement the error has been detected. This error could have been avoided by erasing the overstruck character before depressing the RETURN key. However, we shall see later that there are some very important exceptions to this rule, because certain functions are denoted by overstruck characters.

$$A \leftarrow B \times \blacksquare$$
$$CHARACTER\ ERROR$$
$$A \leftarrow B \times$$
$$\wedge$$

Fig. 1.5.2

The temporal order in which characters are typed is unimportant. You may skip ahead or back if you like because the order of the characters from left to right is what you see on paper at the same time the RETURN key is pressed.

1.6 INTERRUPTING THE COMPUTER

There will almost certainly be times when you will want to interrupt the computer. You may have begun a calculation which takes more time than you thought, or perhaps you recognize that the data you are working with is not what it should be. Whatever the reason, if your terminal is equipped with an ATTN key, you need only depress this key a few times. The computer will terminate its current operation, unlock the keyboard, move the paper up one line, and indent six spaces. You can now proceed as you wish.

If your terminal does not have the ATTN key, then you must adopt the following procedure.

1. Uncradle the telephone.
2. Press the TALK button for a few seconds (you'll hear the high-pitched tone again.)
3. Press the DATA button again.

The following additional step may be necessary.

4. If the carriage does not indent 6 spaces before unlocking, press the carriage return key repeatedly until it does.

1.7 THE APL CHARACTER SET

Let us take a closer look at the APL character set depicted in Figure 1.3.1. It is convenient to divide the set into four groups:

1. alphabetics
2. numerals
3. functions
4. miscellaneous

and to look at the distinguishing features of each group.

1.7.1 Alphabetics

Note that the alphabetics shown on the face of the keyboard print only in capitals, and they are always italicized.

ABCDEFGHIJKLMNOPQRSTUVWXYZ∆_

The primary use of the alphabetics is in naming variable quantities, which we shall say more about in the next chapter. The characters ∆ and _ are considered alphabetics because they also can be used to name variables as we shall see later.

1.7.2 Numerals

The numerals are always upright and shorter than the alphabetics, that is,

0 1 2 3 4 5 6 7 8 9

and have their usual meaning.

1.7.3 Functions

The characters which are used to define functions, with the exception of the Greek letters, are upright, that is,

○ | + − × ÷ ⌈ ⌊ ↑ ↓ ⊥ ⊤ ~ * → ← < ≤ = ≥ > ≠ ∨ ∧ / \ ∈ ρ ι ? ∘ ∇   (space and carriage return)

Some of the functions are formed by overstriking characters.

Although these characters may give the beginner the impression that the APL language is somewhat foreboding and ominous and most of them are unfamiliar at this stage, we shall see that by themselves or overstruck they denote various kinds of operations, just as the characters +, −, ÷, and × denote the basic arithmetic operations. As we proceed, we shall discover what each of these functions does and how they can be put together to form more complicated functions.

Because each group of characters has its distinguishing set of characteristics, no one character is easily mistaken for another.

In the design and layout of the keyboard, attention has been given to mnemonics. For example, the quotation mark appears above the K, the Greek letter iota, ι, above the I, the Greek letter rho, ρ, above the R, etc. This arrangement makes typing easier; after a little practice, many students are able to work with keyboards on which the APL characters are not shown.

1.7.4 Miscellaneous

⊃ ∩ ∪ α ω [ ] ( ) ⎕ ' . , ; : ¨ ‾

Some of these characters have not been defined. The others will be described in the appropriate place.

1.8 WORKSPACES AND THE LIBRARY

In order to understand the logical units in which computations are performed, we shall refer to Fig. 1.8.1. The logical unit in which each

user performs his computations is called his active workspace. From
a physical standpoint the active workspace is a portion of the computer'
primary storage, i.e., magnetic core, which is assigned to a user at
the time of sign-on. Its exact size will vary from installation to installation.

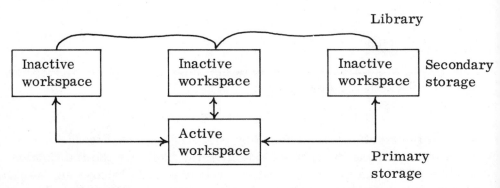

Fig. 1.8.1

At the time his account number is created, each user is also given
a block of secondary storage, i.e., magnetic disk, subdivided into
logical units, which we shall refer to as inactive workspaces. The
number of such units assigned to a user varies from installation to installation.

A portion of each active workspace is required by the system to
keep track of what is stored in the workspace, to determine how much
space is left, etc. This portion of the workspace is inaccessible to
the user. The remaining portion of the workspace is used for computation and for storing the results of various kinds of calculations.
Only the latter portion will be of concern to the user.

Normally, the active workspace assigned to a user at sign-on is a clear workspace, i.e., one which contains no previous computations. There are exceptions, but we shall not discuss them until Part 3, when we examine the workings of the system in great detail. As the user proceeds to compute, the contents of the active workspace will grow, and if nothing is done, ultimately there will be no space left. When the user decides to terminate his session, he has the option of assigning a name to his active workspace and saving it as one of his inactive workspaces, or he may elect to have the contents erased. At the next or any future session he may retrieve an inactive workspace that was previously saved and make it his active workspace, or he may elect to start with a clear workspace. Again, the mechanics of execution will be put off until Part 3.

The collection of workspaces assigned to a user is referred to as his library. Each of the workspaces in the library is a logically independent entity. Most installations also contain public libraries, i.e., collections of workspaces which may be accessed by any user. As a rule, these workspaces contain programs that have applicability to many different kinds of problems. It is a good idea to familiarize yourself with the public libraries at your own installation.

1.9 SIGNING OFF

When you decide that you would like to terminate your use of the computer, there are a number of different commands by which to do so. Here we shall indicate only the simplest way of signing off, by typing

)OFF

and depressing the RETURN key. A response in the form shown in Figure 1.9.1 will then be received.

```
      )106400:GREY
       002) 11.42.47 03/12/70 APLPERKIN
 CONNECTED     0.45.14    TO DATE   20.07.18
 CPU TIME      0.00.17    TO DATE    0.11.10
```

Fig. 1.9.1

The computer indicates the port number you have been occupying, the time of termination, the date, and the name by which the system identifies the user. The next two lines are accounting information for billing purposes. The first line indicates how long your terminal has been connected, i.e., the period between sign-on and sign-off and the total amount of connect time since the last billing period. The second line tells you the actual computer time you have used during this session and the total since the last billing period. (In general, your computer utilization will be only a small proportion of your connect time.) You therefore have a basis for keeping track of the charges accrued to your account.

EXERCISES

1. A. Familiarize yourself with the switches on the communication terminal.
   B. Study the APL keyboard and learn where the different function symbols are located.
   C. Make sure you understand the dialing procedure and practice signing on and off.
   D. Find out how many workspaces you have been allocated.

2. Correct the following typing errors. Type what is in Column 1 and then correct it so that it appears like Column 2.

Column 1	Column 2
$B \leftarrow 8 \div 15$	$B \leftarrow 8 \times 15$
$Z \leftarrow 20$	$Y \leftarrow 20$
$X \leftarrow 9 + 15 \div 7.21$	$X \leftarrow 9 + 15 \div 7.11E2$

3. Overstrike the characters H and Y and see what happens.

CONSTANTS AND VARIABLES

2.1 INTRODUCTION

This chapter begins with a discussion of how numbers are represented
in APL, i.e., the form that they must be in when they are entered
from the typewriter and the form that they are in when the computer
sends them back. We answer questions about such matters as precision, i.e., the quantity of significant digits that are obtainable and
the size range of a number. We then discuss variables, the rules for
naming them, and the way they are assigned values and displayed.
This leads to the very important concept of a primitive function. As
a final topic, we consider the representation of literal data.

2.2 REPRESENTATION OF DATA

For most problems numeric data entered into the computer will be in
either decimal or exponential form. In APL the two forms may be
mixed, and within each eategory there is some choice on the part of
the user. Other forms, e.g., Boolean, are possible, but here we
shall confine ourselves to the decimal and exponential forms.

Data typed out by the computer whose format is not explicitly
controlled by the user will also be in either decimal or exponential
form. The choice of form is made by the computer in accordance
with rules that we shall state in Section 2.8.1. In either case, the
computer prints the data in a standard format.

2.3 DECIMAL FORM FOR NUMERIC DATA

Numeric data may be entered in the usual decimal form. For example, the number twelve may be entered in any of the following forms.

    12.
    012
    12
    12.0

Leading or trailing zeros may be left out or included. In integral quantities the decimal need not be included. However, since commas and embedded blanks are not allowed, the following representations are not valid.

    22,000
    2 2 0 0 0

The format of a number typed out in decimal or exponential form can be controlled by the user, as we shall see in Chapter 16.

2.4 THE SIGN OF A NUMBER

The negative sign is denoted by the character ¯, which appears above the 2 on the keyboard of the typewriter. The negative sign, the decimal point, and the numerics are the only characters which may be used to represent a number in decimal form. It is important not to confuse the negative sign, ¯5, with the subtraction operation, −5. The operation of subtraction may result in a negative number, but it is not part of the representation of the number.

A number whose representation does not contain the negative sign is considered to be positive. For example, the positive number five is denoted by the character 5. The symbol + denotes the operation of addition and is not part of the representation of a positive number.

2.5 EXPONENTIAL FORM FOR DATA

It is often very convenient to represent numbers in exponential form. For instance, the sales of large companies are in the millions of dollars. If we think of a million dollars as being a unit of sales volume, then we can write a number like 2,506,000 as

    $2.506 \times 1,000,000$
or
    2.506×10^6.

Once it is understood what the units are, the quantity 10^6 need not be explicitly written each time.

In scientific work, units of 10^{19} and larger are common, thus writing numbers in decimal form would be a tedious chore.

In APL we can write 2,506,000 as:

$2.506E6$

or

$25.06E5.$

The letter E indicates that the quantity to the left, the mantissa, is to be multiplied by the power of 10 appearing to the right of E. We can position the decimal point in the mantissa as we choose, provided that we adjust the power of 10.

The exponential form makes it convenient to represent very small or very large numbers. The range of numbers which can be represented in APL\360 is approximately

$$1E^-75 \le X \le 1E75.$$

Any attempt to produce a number outside this range will result in an error.

2.6 PRECISION

By the precision of numeric data we mean the number of significant digits contained in the data. The exponential form is convenient as a means of expressing precision. In this form it is customary to specify the number of significant digits in the mantissa portion of the number. The power of 10 by which the mantissa is multiplied serves merely to position the decimal point and indicates the unit of measurement. When we say that a quantity X has a measured value of $2.81E2$ we mean that X satisfies the relationship

$$280.5 \le X \le 281.5$$

and we do not know what the next significant digit is.

Internally, the computer represents numbers with a precision of approximately 16 decimal digits. As we proceed to calculate, however, rounding and truncation errors may cause the final result to be good to only a few significant digits. The errors which arise in computation and the methods by which they can be analyzed are a part of that branch of mathematics called numerical analysis and cannot be dealt with here.

2.7 VARIABLES

Every branch of knowledge has a language peculiar to it. The physicist
talks about force, energy, power; the electrical engineer is concerned
with networks, currents, impedance; the mechanical engineer thinks in
terms of sheer, stress, and strain. The businessman talks about sales
volume, stockholder equity, profit margin; the psychologist talks about
personality, the unconscious, and mind. Variables are the language of
computing. From this standpoint, it is necessary to be able to introduce variables, to assign values to them, and to compute with them in
the same way that one would expect to compute with ordinary numbers.

2.7.1 Naming Variables

In APL\360 a name for a variable quantity must begin with an alphabetic character and may consist of any combination of alphabetic and
numeric characters, the delta charcter, $\triangle$, and the underscore character, _. No other character may be used as part of a name, and the
combination S $\triangle$ or T $\triangle$ may not be the first two characters of a name.
The length of the name is arbitrary, but only the first 77 characters
are significant.

EXAMPLE 1

The following are legitimate names for a variable:

MASS

MASS

*M*1

M$\triangle$

However,

M A S S

1*M*

S $\triangle$

are not legitimate names; they each violate one of the rules mentioned.

In choosing names, most users will rely on mnemonics, for example,

VELOCITY

VEL

VELOC

V

2.7.2 Specifying Values for Variables

Now that we know how to name variables, let us see how they are assigned values. To specify a value for a variable, we use the specification operator denoted by the character ← . In subsequent chapters we are going to be talking about different operators—or functions, as we shall call them. Here the specification operator, which is important in its own right, of course, also serves to illustrate some of the properties of functions we must be aware of.

EXAMPLE 1

To assign a value of 40 to a variable called PRICE, we write:

PRICE←40

Other assignments are:

SALES←2.6E6

The variable to the left of the operator is always given the value of the constant or variable to the right of the operator.

EXAMPLE 2

It is not possible to have a variable in our workspace to which no value has been assigned.

```
      VELOCITY←K
VALUE ERROR
      VELOCITY←K
          ∧
```

The variable VELOCITY cannot be specified by the variable K since
the latter has not been assigned a value. A VALUE error occurs
when a variable has not been specified.

2.8 FUNCTIONS AND THEIR PROPERTIES

Let us examine the function ← more closely. We say that it is a
primitive function, meaning that it is provided as part of the language.
In Chapter 9 we shall see how to define functions which are composed
or built up from primitive functions. Loosely speaking, primitive
functions are comparable to atoms, which cannot be logically subdivided into other kinds of operations. The user-defined function
must be built up from these primitives in accordance with certain
rules.

The specification function also requires a pair of arguments, or
operands, one operand appearing on each side. Because the function
always has two arguments, we refer to it as a dyadic function. In the
next chapter we shall discuss functions which take only a single argument and which are called monadic. In fact, we shall see that the
same function symbol may be used to represent both a monadic and a
dyadic function with entirely different meanings.

2.9 DISPLAYING VARIABLES

Whenever a statement contains the operator ←, the result of the calculation being performed is assigned to some variable. When the operator does not appear explicitly, the result of the calculation is printed.

EXAMPLE 1

Assume that variables called PRICE and SALES have been defined as
in Example 1 of Section 2.7.2. If we type the names of these variables, their values are printed out.

```
      PRICE
 40
      SALES
2600000
```

EXAMPLE 2

        SALES÷PRICE
65000

EXAMPLE 3

To save the result of a calculation and display it, assign the value to a variable and display the variable.

        UNITS←SALES÷PRICE
        UNITS
65000

    We said earlier that the computer carries numbers with a precision of about 16 decimal digits. However, all quantities will be displayed to 10 significant digits, and trailing zeros will be suppressed, unless you direct otherwise after signing on. You can display any number of digits between 1 and 16 by the system command

)DIGITS XX

where XX is a number between 1 and 16. When you issue this command, you will receive a response telling you the number of significant digits previously displayed. It is important also to note that displayed numbers are rounded off.

EXAMPLE 4

        VELOCITY←6.231598719246
        VELOCITY
6.231598719
)DIGITS 4
WAS 10
        VELOCITY
6.232
)DIGITS 8
WAS 4
        VELOCITY
6.2315987

2.9.1 Decimal and Exponential Form in Output

As mentioned earlier, when the format of a number that is to be displayed is not explicitly controlled by the user, the computer will determine whether the form is decimal or exponential. In APL any quantity may be displayed by naming it. The form it takes is determined by the following rules:

1. A number is displayed in exponential form if it is less than $1E^-5$ or greater than $1EN$, where N is the integer determining the number of significant digits displayed ($1 \le N \le 16$). At the time of sign-on, N is 10. In exponential form the mantissa portion is always given a magnitude X ($1 \le X < 10$).

```
      .000000739
7.39E⁻7
        920645318743
9.206453187E11
```

2. An integer greater than 1E10 is displayed in exponential form.

```
      36059234145
3.60592E10
```

3. In decimal form a number less than 1 in absolute value is always displayed with a leading zero.

```
      .09876
0.09876
      ⁻.987543
⁻0.987543
```

2.10 LITERAL DATA

By literal data we mean a string or sequence of APL characters. To specify the data as literal, we must enclose it in a pair of quote signs, for example,

'MASS'

'123'

'→+-'

It is important to recognize the difference between the number 123 and the string of characters '123'. The first represents a specific quantity. The second is a sequence of symbols, which may be used as a name for that number or which may have one of a variety of different meanings.

The first quote sign indicates that what follows is to be interpreted as literal data. All characters, including the space and carriage return, count as characters. Variables are assigned literal values in the same way that they are assigned numeric values.

EXAMPLE 1

```
        TITLE←'MASS COMPUTATIONS'
        TITLE
MASS COMPUTATIONS
```

When literal data is displayed, the initial and ending quotation marks are not printed.

EXAMPLE 2

When the carriage return character appears as literal data, it will cause the carriage of the typewriter to return and space up. Nothing is executed since the computer is waiting for the quotation mark signaling the end of the literal data.

```
        HEADING←'OPTICAL CALCULATIONS FOR PHY
SICISTS'
```

EXAMPLE 3

When a quotation mark (or apostrophe) is included as part of the literal data, it must appear as a pair of quotation marks.

```
        TITLE←'YOU CAN''T GO HOME'
        TITLE
YOU CAN'T GO HOME
```

When you are working with literal data, it is important to remember that everything following the first quotation mark is interpreted as literal data. Therefore, until the ending quotation mark appears, the computer accepts everything received without acting on it.

EXERCISES

1. Write the following numbers in exponential form with 1 significant digit to the left of the decimal point.

A.   296.853   B.   ‾1.07596

C.   16212.8   D.   .0007592

E.   ‾.095217

2. Some of the following numbers are incorrectly written as APL constants. Identify them and explain why.

A.   42,000   B. $6.9E^{-}5$

C.   1 1 3   D.   315.1

E.   62.9E81   F.   170.21987

G.   3185.2963475134568   H.   'MASS

3. Which of the following are improper names for APL variables and why?

A.   VELOCITY   B.   F O R C E

C.   T1   D.   1T

E.   SPRING   F.   ι

G.   V̲

THE PRIMITIVE FUNCTIONS
OF ARITHMETIC

3.1 INTRODUCTION

There are two modes in which all computations are performed: execution and definition. When the user has completed his sign-on, he is automatically placed in the execution mode, and he remains in that mode until some further action is taken. In this chapter we shall consider primarily the execution mode, deferring details of the definition mode, in which functions are defined (programs), to Chapter 9. Here we shall also discuss the use of function symbols to represent more than one function, the basic arithmetic functions and the way in which statements containing more than one function symbol are scanned and interpreted.

3.2 EXECUTION AND DEFINITION MODES

In the execution mode, each time the RETURN key is pressed, that action is interpreted by the computer as a signal to execute the statement just typed. Therefore we are limited to computing what can be typed in a single statement. This situation, analogous to using a desk calculator, is sometimes referred to as the desk calculator mode. As we progress, it will become clear that even within the framework of a single statement it is possible to do a good deal of computing. For the present the execution mode allows us to treat our terminal as a kind of scratchpad on which to doodle, to learn, and to explore.

The definition mode permits us to construct a sequence of statements that make up what we shall call a user-defined function. These user-defined functions work in the same way as the primitive functions. In the definition mode, pressing the RETURN key is interpreted as a signal to store but not execute the statement just typed. From the standpoint of practical applications, the definition mode is the one in which most computations are implemented. In Chapter 9, when we have completed the necessary preliminaries, we will examine this mode in detail.

3.3 FUNCTION SYMBOLS

In Sections 2.7 and 2.8 we examined the symbol ← , which denotes the assignment or specification function. We saw that this function symbol always requires two arguments and always has the same meaning. It therefore denotes a unique dyadic function. We shall see in the next section, however, that some APL function symbols may denote two entirely different functions. This is accomplished by using the symbol with either one or two arguments and assigning a different meaning in each case.

3.4 THE PRIMITIVE FUNCTIONS OF ARITHMETIC

Of all the functions which occur in mathematics the most familiar and best understood are the basic arithmetic functions. They are at the root of practically all calculations. It seems appropriate to begin our study with these functions. Reversing things a bit, we shall begin with multiplication rather than addition because it provides a good example of a function symbol with two distinct and unrelated meanings.

3.4.1 Multiplication and the Signum Function

The multiplication symbol, ×, has two different meanings. When it has two arguments, for example,

```
        A←2
        B←¯3
        A×B
¯6
        5×11E2
5500
```

it has its usual meaning, and we obtain the product of the arguments. We are also permitted to write

```
        ×¯3
¯1
        ×0
0
        ×7
1
```

Note the results returned by the computer. When × takes a single argument, it denotes an entirely different function, called the signum, or sign function, which is defined as follows (let A be a variable assigned a numeric value):

$$\times A \text{ is equal to } \begin{cases} 1 \text{ if A is greater than 0} \\ 0 \text{ if A is equal to 0} \\ {}^{-}1 \text{ if A is less than 0} \end{cases}$$

The signum function provides a convenient means of obtaining the sign of a number. In a monadic function, the single argument always appears to the right of the function symbol.

3.4.2 Division

The function denoted by ÷ may appear with either one or two arguments. With two arguments it has the usual meaning of division, for example,

```
      A←4
      B←2.6
      B÷A
0.65
```

In this case B is the dividend and A the divisor. In the monadic mode,

```
      ÷3
0.3333333333
```

we obtain the reciprocal of the argument. The two functions here have closely related meanings, but, in general, that need not be true. Division by 0 is not permitted except for the case 0 ÷ 0 which results in 1 as an answer.

3.4.3 Addition

The function denoted by + with two arguments has the usual meaning of addition, for example,

```
      A←3
      B←‾2
      A+B
```

1

The monadic mode,

$$+A$$
$$3$$
$$+\ ^-3$$
$$^-3$$

corresponds to addition with a left argument of zero.

3.4.4 Subtraction

The function symbol –, not to be confused with the negative sign, has the meaning of subtraction in the dyadic mode. If we write

$$A-B$$
$$5$$
$$1.6E1-8.2$$
$$7.8$$

we obtain the result of subtracting the right argument from the left. In the monadic mode,

$$-A$$
$$^-3$$
$$-\ ^-5$$
$$5$$

we obtain the negative of the argument. This is equivalent to dyadic subtraction with a left argument of zero.

3.5 SCANNING AN APL EXPRESSION

So far we have considered examples in which only one function symbol appears. In most applications we shall have to consider expressions in which more than one function appears. It is essential that our language be rich enough to specify any well-defined computation and at the same time be free of ambiguousness and vagueness. Consider the following expression.

$$A \div B \times C + D$$

Such an expression may have a number of different meanings. By the use of parentheses we can indicate some of the possible interpretations.

$(A \div B) \times (C + D)$

$A \div (B \times (C + D))$

$(A \div (B \times C)) + D$

If we let

$A \leftarrow 4$
$B \leftarrow 2$
$C \leftarrow 1$
$D \leftarrow 3$

then the value of the expressions is given by 8, .5, and 5. respectively.

In APL there are two simple rules for scanning an expression and determining its value.

1. Every expression is scanned <u>from right to left</u>, and each function takes for a right argument everything to the right of it.
2. Parentheses have their usual meaning. What is in parentheses cannot be used until the entire expression has been evaluated.

The first rule may seem rather strange, but we can easily see that it possesses certain advantages. For one thing, there is no hierarchy of functions with which we have to be concerned. Multiplication and division do not take precedence over addition and subtraction, as in conventional mathematical notation. There is therefore no need to scan back and forth. In APL there are no exceptions to the scanning rule. Let us illustrate the rule with some examples.

EXAMPLE 1

$A \leftarrow 2$
$B \leftarrow 3$
$C \leftarrow 5$
$D \leftarrow 2$
$\div 8 \times B + D$
0.025

This is how the result is obtained. In scanning from right to left, the computer detects the first function, +. Since there is a left argument, B, the computer interprets + as a dyadic function with the usual meaning of addition. This results in the evaluation of the expression B + D as 5. This value now becomes the right argument for the function ×. Since there is also a left argument, 8, the function × is interpreted to mean ordinary multiplication, and the expression 8 × 5 is evaluated as 40. The next function symbol encountered is ÷. Since there is no left argument, the function is interpreted as meaning "take the reciprocal of." This results in the value shown in Example 1.

EXAMPLE 2

Evaluate

$\div C \times \times B$

Proceeding from right to left, we find the sequence

$$
\begin{array}{ll}
 & \times B \\
1 & \\
 & C \times 1 \\
5 & \\
 & \div 5 \\
5 &
\end{array}
$$

The first occurrence of × is in the monadic mode since there is no left argument.

EXAMPLE 3

Evaluate

$(B \div C) \times \times - A + B$

Again proceeding from right to left, we scan the expression as follows:

$A+B$
5
                    -5
$^-5$
                    $\times ^-5$
$^-1$
          $6\div C$
0.6
          $.6\times ^-1$
$^-0.6$

Note that the right argument for the subtraction function is A+B, not A. Before the final multiplication can be carried out, the expression in parentheses must be evaluated. Omission of the parentheses would result in a different answer.

EXERCISES
_____

1. Evaluate the following expressions

   $\times 7$ $\times ^-4$ $^-45\div ^-9$ $-\ ^-5$ 9×8

   $7+^-10$ $^-5+^-1$ $+\ ^-10$ $^-5\times 6$ $\times 0$

   $2+6\div 2\times 3\times \times 2$ $2\div 6\times ^-1+5$ $\times 1+4+5\times 2.E1$

2. Let X $\leftarrow$ 7, Y $\leftarrow$ 8, and Z $\leftarrow$ 2. For each of the following mathematical expressions, write an equivalent APL expression and evaluate it.

A. $\dfrac{X \times Y}{Z}$ B. $\dfrac{Y}{Z} + X$ C. $(X + Y)^2$

3. Which of the following APL expressions are incorrect? Assume that all variables to the right of $\leftarrow$ have previously been assigned a value.

A. $Z\leftarrow 3\times$ B. $Y+5\times U\div V$

C. $X\leftarrow 3U+Y\div Z$ D. $Z\leftarrow 2\times U+4^-5H$

E. $Z\leftarrow (X+Y\div H$ F. $Y\leftarrow 2+H+Z$

4. In the following example assume that variables have been assigned values as follows:

$$X = 3; \ Y = 2; \ Z = -1$$

Compute values for the following expressions by hand and then check to see whether you understood the scan rule.

A. $W \leftarrow \times \times X + Y \times - Z$

B. $W \leftarrow Z + X \times Y \div Z$

C. $W \leftarrow 3 \times X - Y - Z$

D. $W \leftarrow X + Y + Z - 3 \div Z$

5. Assume that the rule for computing income tax is given by the following table for incomes up to $10,000.

First $1000 of income	3%
Next $3000 of income	2%
Next $4000 of income	1%
Next $2000 of income	1/2%

Write APL expressions to find the tax on
a) $7000   b) $10,000

4
THE PRIMITIVE FUNCTIONS
OF LOGIC

4.1 INTRODUCTION

In this chapter we are going to consider some primitive functions
which will enable us to deal with logical expressions, i.e., expressions which are characterized as true or false. We begin with a study
of mathematical equalities and inequalities and describe the primitive
APL functions which deal with these relations. We then go on to consider various other logical functions.

4.2 EQUALITIES AND INEQUALITIES

A logical relationship is one which we can think of as being either
true or false. For example, when we say 7 is less than 8, we are
expressing a relationship between two numbers concerning their magnitude, and the proposition expressed by the statement is true. On
the other hand, if we say 9 is equal to 7, the proposition expressed is
false. In APL a logical expression is given the numerical value 1
when true and 0 when false. Expressions in which logical functions
appear are still evaluated from right to left, and the value of the logical expression becomes the argument for the next operation in the
sequence. In Table 4.2.1 we have listed those logical functions which
are useful in expressing magnitude relationships between numbers.
The functions listed in Table 4.2.1 have only the dyadic form. Let
us illustrate how these functions work with some examples.

EXAMPLE 1

$$A \leftarrow 2$$
$$B \leftarrow 3$$
$$\times A < B+1 \geq 1$$

1

TABLE 4.2.1
The Logical Equalities and Inequalities

Function symbol	Meaning	
=	equal to	Whenever the relation holds, the result is 1. If the relation does not hold, the result is 0.
≤	less than or equal to	
<	less than	
≠	not equal to	
≥	greater than or equal to	
>	greater than	

This is how the result of Example 1 is obtained. The expression $1 \geq 1$ is evaluated as 1 and becomes the right argument for the function +. The expression B + 1 is evaluated as 4 and becomes the right argument of the function <. The expression A < 4 is evaluated as 1 and becomes the right argument for the × function. Since there is no left argument, the expression × 1 is evaluated as 1.

EXAMPLE 2

$A \leftarrow 2$
$B \leftarrow 3$
$B < (2 \times A) - B$
0

EXAMPLE 3

Two numbers which differ by less than 1 part in 1E13 are considered to be equal. The quantity 1E13 is called fuzz.

$A \leftarrow 10$
$B \leftarrow A + .9999 E^{-} 13$
$A = B$
1

The treatment of equality is motivated by the fact that in APL, although 16 significant digits are carried, the final digits are often meaningless because of loss of accuracy. It is important for the beginning student to remember that, although the variables A and B when displayed are identical to 10 digits, this fact does not ensure equality beyond the tenth digit.

EXAMPLE 4

The functions = and ≠ may be used with literal arguments.

$$('A')=('B')$$
0
$$('A')\neq('B')$$
1

4.3 BOOLEAN FUNCTIONS

We shall now consider an entirely different set of logical relationships, which occur in everyday discourse and which form part of what is called Boolean algebra. To introduce these relationships, we shall consider the following statements.

1. Two times two is four or I am going to the movies.
2. John is thirteen years old and the room is warm.
3. It is not snowing.

Ignoring the content of these statements and concerning ourselves only with their truth or falsity, we can rewrite them in a form which reveals their structure.

1. P or Q
2. P and Q
3. Not P

This form makes it apparent that the statements being analyzed are built up from simpler statements, i.e., those denoted by the letters P and Q, together with logical connectives, i.e., or, and, not. Clearly the truth or falsity of these statements will depend on the truth or falsity of the propositions expressed by P and Q and the meaning assigned to the logical connectives.

We may therefore think of these connectives as binary functions of binary arguments, i.e., functions which produce a 0 or a 1 and whose arguments are limited to 0 and 1. This makes it possible to exhibit these functions in the form of a table showing the value of each function for all possible combinations of its arguments. Such a table is known as a truth table. Before we examine the truth tables for the Boolean functions, we need to know the APL symbols which denote these functions. They are shown in Table 4.3.1. Since the functions $=$ and $\neq$ are also Boolean, they are repeated in the table.

TABLE 4.3.1
The APL Function Symbols for the Boolean Functions

Function	Meaning
$\vee$	or
$\wedge$	and
$\sim$	not
$=$	equal
$\neq$	not equal
$\barwedge$	not and (nand)
$\veebar$	not or (nor)

4.4 TRUTH TABLES

Consider Table 4.4.1, which shows the truth tables for each of our Boolean functions.

TABLE 4.4.1
Truth Table for the Logical Functions*

P	Q	P$\vee$Q	P$\wedge$Q	$\sim$P	P$=$Q	P$\neq$Q	P$\barwedge$Q	P$\veebar$Q
0	0	0	0	1	1	0	1	1
0	1	1	0	1	0	1	1	0
1	0	1	0	0	0	1	1	0
1	1	1	1	0	1	0	0	0

*P and Q are logical variables; i.e., they assume values of 0 or 1.

Let us examine Table 4.4.1 to see what can be inferred about each of these functions. The function ∨ yields a value of 0 only when both of its arguments are 0. The function is referred to as the 'inclusive or' because it is true when both arguments have the value 1, that is, are true.

In everyday discourse and in formal logic the use of the connective 'or' is often intended to convey the meaning that P and Q may not both be true simultaneously. This use of the function is often referred to as the 'exclusive or'. An example occurs in the statement "An integer is odd or it is even." The 'exclusive or' is equivalent to the function ≠ shown in Table 4.4.1.

The logical function ∧ has the value 1 if and only if both of its arguments are true.

The meaning of the logical function ~ is obvious. In addition to these functions there are two other primitive Boolean functions that we shall describe, called 'nand', denoted by the character ⩑, and 'nor', denoted by the character ⩒. The nand symbol is formed by overstriking the ∧ and ~ symbols, and the nor symbol is formed by overstriking ∨ and ~. The truth tables for these functions are shown in Table 4.4.1. Clearly P⩑Q is equivalent to ~(P∧Q) while P⩒Q is equivalent to ~(P∨Q). Let us illustrate how these functions work with some examples.

EXAMPLE 1

$P \leftarrow 1$
$Q \leftarrow 0$
$\sim P \leq P \wedge P \vee Q$

   0

EXAMPLE 2

$P \leftarrow 1$
$Q \leftarrow 1$
$0 = P \neq 2 \star \sim Q \wedge P$

   1

EXAMPLE 3

$P \leftarrow 1$
$Q \leftarrow 1$
$(\sim P \vee \sim Q) = \sim (P \wedge Q)$

   1

There is an important connection between the relational operators shown in Table 4.3.1 and the Boolean operators shown in Table 4.4.1. When P and Q are logical variables then each of the relational operators has an equivalent Boolean operator. This equivalence is shown in Table 4.4.2.

TABLE 4.4.2.
The Relational Operators and their Boolean Equivalents*

Relational Operator	Boolean Equivalent
$S \leftarrow P = Q$	$S \leftarrow (P \wedge \sim Q) \vee ((\sim P) \wedge Q)$
$S \leftarrow P \leq Q$	$S \leftarrow (\sim P) \vee Q)$
$S \leftarrow P < Q$	$S \leftarrow (\sim P) \wedge Q)$
$S \leftarrow P \neq Q$	$S \leftarrow (P \wedge \sim Q) \vee ((\sim P) \wedge Q)$
$S \leftarrow P \geq Q$	$S \leftarrow P \vee \sim Q$
$S \leftarrow P > Q$	$S \leftarrow P \wedge \sim Q$

Combining various logical functions and using the laws of Boolean algebra for showing the equivalence of different logical forms make it possible to design more sophisticated and complicated circuits.

---

* P and Q assume values of 0 or 1

EXERCISES

1. All of the variables which appear in these exercises are assumed to be logical, i.e., have a value of 0 or 1. Two logical expressions are equivalent if they yield the same value for all possible combinations of their arguments. Determine which of the following pairs are equivalent.

A. $\sim(A \wedge B)$ B. $A \wedge \sim(A \wedge \sim B)$ C. $A \wedge (B \vee C)$

     $\sim A \vee \sim B$ B $(A \wedge B) \vee (A \wedge C)$

D. $\sim(A \vee B)$ E. $(A \wedge B) \vee (\sim B)$

     $(\sim A) \wedge (\sim B)$ $A \vee \sim B$

2. A tautology is a logical expression which is true for all possible combinations of its arguments. A contradiction is a logical expression which is false for all possible combinations of its arguments. Determine whether each of the following expressions is a tautology, a contradiction, or neither.

A. $\sim(A = B) \wedge (B \neq A)$ B. $A \wedge (\sim(A \wedge B))$

C. $\sim(A \wedge B) \wedge A$ D. $A \wedge \sim A$

E. $A \vee \sim A$ F. $\sim(A = B) \wedge (B = C) \wedge (A \neq C)$

G. $\sim(A \vee B) \wedge (\sim A \vee \sim B)$ H. $\sim((A \vee B \wedge (\sim B)) \vee \sim A$

3. Write APL statements to accomplish the following.

     A. Assign a value of 10 to X if $Y < Z$, otherwise a value of 2.
     B. Assign a value of 1 to X if Y and Z have the same signs, otherwise a value of 3. Assume X and $Y \neq 0$.
     C. Assign a value of 6 to W if X and Y and Z are equal, otherwise a value of 3.
     D. Assign a value of $(.2 \times Z)$ to Y if $X < 1.7$ or a value of $(.25 \times Z)$ if $X \geq 1.7$.
     E. Let the four quadrants of the plane be numbered as in the following figure.

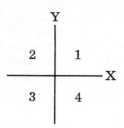

Let X and Y be the coordinates of a point in the plane not lying on a co-ordinate axis. Write a statement which assigns to the variable Z the number of the quadrant in which the point is located.

5. The Boolean functions play an important role in the design of switching circuits. The following figure shows two switches in parallel connected to a bulb. The bulb will be lit, if and only if, at least one of the switches is closed. If we designate the switches by variables P and Q and if we let the condition of being closed correspond to a value of 1 for the variable and the condition open correspond to a value of 0, then the circuit is represented by the truth table of $P \wedge Q$.

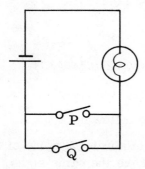

What logical function is represented by wiring the switches in series, as shown in the following figure.

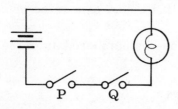

5. A customers account in a department store is assigned a number in in accordance with the following table:

Number Assigned	Meaning
1	Account is current.
2	Payment is 10–30 days late.
3	Payment is 31–60 days late.
4	Payment is 61–90 days late.

Let A1, A2, and A3 be the account numbers of three different customers. Write an APL expression to determine:

A. the lowest number assigned to any of these three accounts;

B. the highest number assigned to any of these three accounts.

5.1 INTRODUCTION

In this chapter we introduce some of the better known mathematical functions which are available in APL as primitive operators. We shall examine the exponential and logarithmic functions, the trigonometric and inverse trigonometric functions, the gamma function, a function for generating random numbers, and others. These functions are basic, and it is important for the student to understand and to master them. Adding these functions to our repertoire will enable us to consider more sophisticated problems and applications, many of which appear as exercises at the end of the chapter.

5.2 EXPONENTIAL FUNCTION

The exponential function is denoted by the symbol $*$, which has both monadic and dyadic form. In the dyadic form, A$*$B, the function returns the Bth power of A, written conventionally as A^B. In the monadic form, $*$A, the base is e, that is, the base of the natural logarithms. Here again, we see that a function symbol may have two different meanings.

EXAMPLE 1

```
        A←2
        B←5
        C←(1+A*2)*(2+A<B)
        C
125
```

EXAMPLE 2

Fractional powers are interpreted as roots.

```
      A←.5
      B←2
      C←B*A
      C
1.414213562
```

EXAMPLE 3

An attempt to extract an even root of a negative number will result in an error.

```
      A←.5
      B←¯2
      C←B*A
DOMAIN ERROR
      C←B*A
      ∧
```

EXAMPLE 4

```
      B←.5
      *B
1.648721271
```

EXAMPLE 5

```
      C←*2.6÷*1.1
      C
2.376110287
```

5.3 LOGARITHM FUNCTION

The logarithm function is denoted by the character ⍟ formed by over-striking the small circle o with the asterisk. The dyadic function A⍟B returns the logarithm of B to the base A, whereas the monadic function ⍟B returns the natural logarithm of B.

EXAMPLE 1

```
        A←10
        B←1000
        A⊛B
  3
```

EXAMPLE 2

```
        A←2
        B←128
        A⊛128
  7
```

EXAMPLE 3

The logarithm function and the exponential function are inverse functions since B is equal to $A \circledast (A*B)$.

```
        A←2
        B←5
        B=A⊛(A*B)
  1
```

EXAMPLE 4

The monadic function ⊛B is interpreted as the logarithm of B to the base e.

```
      B←3
      ⊛B+2
1.609437912
```

5.4 MINIMUM AND MAXIMUM

The function symbol ⌊ has both monadic and dyadic form. In the monadic form, ⌊A, the function returns the greatest integer less than or equal to A. Consider Figure 5.4.1, which depicts the real number line. If points A, B, and C are as indicated, then ⌊A, is equal to ¯1, ⌊B is equal to 0, and ⌊C is equal to 3. The function is appropriately described by the term 'floor'.

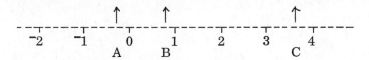

Fig. 5.4.1 The real number line

EXAMPLE 1

```
A ← 3
B ← 5
A ⌊ B
```
3

EXAMPLE 2

```
A ← 2
B ← 3
( ( B ⋆ 2 ) - 3 ) ⌊ ( ( A ⋆ 3 ) - 1 )
```
6

EXAMPLE 3

Successive applications of the function produce the minimum of a set of argument.

```
A ← 2
B ← 3
C ← 5
A ⌊ B ⌊ C
```
2

The monadic function ⌈A returns the smallest integer greater than or equal to A. Referring to Figure 5.4.1, we see that ⌈A is equal to 0, ⌈B is equal to 1, and ⌈C is equal to 4.

EXAMPLE 4

$$\lceil*2$$

8

EXAMPLE 5

$$A\leftarrow2$$
$$B\leftarrow3.5$$
$$\lceil(B*2)-(4\times A\times B)$$

¯15

In contrast to the floor function, this function is appropriately called the 'ceiling' function.

The dyadic function A⌈B returns the maximum of its arguments.

EXAMPLE 6

$$A\leftarrow3$$
$$B\leftarrow2$$
$$C\leftarrow5$$
$$((A\times B\times C)*(1\div3))\lceil(A+B+C)\div3$$

3.333333333

EXAMPLE 7

$$A\leftarrow7.5$$
$$B\leftarrow2.9$$
$$C\leftarrow3.6$$
$$A\lceil B\lceil C$$

7.5

5.5 ABSOLUTE VALUE FUNCTION

The absolute value of a real number X is defined as

$$\begin{cases} X & \text{if X is greater than or equal to zero,} \\ -X & \text{if X is less than zero.} \end{cases}$$

From this definition if follows that the absolute value is a non-negative
quantity.

In APL the absolute value function is denoted by the stroke character, |, which appears on the keyboard above the M.

EXAMPLE 1

```
      C←1
      A←2
      B←2
      |B*2-(4×A×C )
0.015625
```

EXAMPLE 2

```
      B←¯3.5
      |B
3.5
      C←0
      |0
0
```

5.6 RESIDUE FUNCTION

In carrying out the operation of division, we are often more concerned
with the remainder, or residue term, than with the quotient. For example, consider an angle, A, expressed in degrees. Dividing the
angle by 360 and taking the remainder, we obtain an angle, B, whose
trigonometric functions are equivalent to the given angle, A. In ordinary division the quotient and remainder are expressed as a single
number. In order to facilitate the remainder operation, we introduce
the dyadic residue function, A|B. We speak of the A residue of B, the
remainder when B is divided by A. Let us look at Figure 5.6.1.

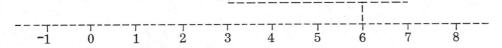

Fig. 5.6.1 Calculating the residue

In order to calculate 3|7, we mark off the points 3 and 7. Beginning at 3, we mark off multiples of 3 in the direction of 7, but we do not go beyond 7. The difference between 7 and the last point marked is the value of the function. In this case the value is 1.

EXAMPLE 1

```
        A←2
        7|A*5
    4
```

EXAMPLE 2

There is no need for either A or B to be integral.

```
        16.82|75.1
    7.82
```

EXAMPLE 3

```
         ¯7|16.5
    2.5
```

EXAMPLE 4

If A is equal to zero and B is greater than or equal to zero, then A|B is equal to B.

```
        A←0
        B←7
        A|B
    7
```

EXAMPLE 5

If A is equal to zero and B is less than zero, an error results.

```
        A←0
        B←¯7
        A|B
    DOMAIN ERROR
        A|B
        ∧
```

5.7 TRIGONOMETRIC AND INVERSE TRIGONOMETRIC FUNCTIONS

The trigonometric or circular functions are denoted by the function symbol $○$. The monadic function $○A$ is equivalent to $\pi \times A$.

EXAMPLE 1

```
      ○1
3.141592654
```

EXAMPLE 2

```
      (○2)|(○6.2)
0.6283185307
```

The trigonometric functions and their inverses are given by the dyadic function $I○A$, where I is an integer ranging from ⁻7 to 7 and A is an argument in the domain of the function selected by I.

The different trigonometric functions available as primitives are shown in Table 5.7.1.

TABLE 5.7.1
The Primitive Trigonometric Functions

Function	Meaning
0○B	(1−B*2)*.5
1○B	Sine B
⁻1○B	Arcsine B
2○B	Cos B
−2○B	Arccos B
3○B	Tan B
⁻3○B	Arctan B
4○B	(1+B*2)*.5
−4○B	(⁻1+B*2)*.5
5○B	Sinh B
−5○B	Arcsinh B
6○B	Cosh B
⁻6○B	Arccosh B
7○B	Tanh B
⁻7○B	Arctanh B

5.7.1[*]   Principal Values for the Inverse Trigonometric Functions

Since the inverse trigonometric functions are multivalued, their
principal values are given in Table 5.7.2.

TABLE 5.7.2
Principal Values of the Inverse Trigonometric Functions[1]

Principal values for $x \geqq 0$	Principal values for $x < 0$
$0 \leqq \sin^{-1} x \leqq \pi/2$	$-\pi/2 \leqq \sin^{-1} x < 0$
$0 \leqq \cos^{-1} x \leqq \pi/2$	$\pi/2 < \cos^{-1} x \leqq \pi$
$0 \leqq \tan^{-1} x < \pi/2$	$-\pi/2 < \tan^{-1} x < 0$
$0 < \cot^{-1} x \leqq \pi/2$	$\pi/2 < \cot^{-1} x < \pi$
$0 \leqq \sec^{-1} x < \pi/2$	$\pi/2 < \sec^{-1} x \leqq \pi$
$0 < \csc^{-1} x \leqq \pi/2$	$-\pi/2 \leqq \csc^{-1} x < 0$

5.7.2[*]   Hyperbolic Functions

The hyperbolic functions are defined as shown in Table 5.7.3

TABLE 5.7.3
The Hyperbolic Functions

Function	Meaning	Definition
5∘B	Sinh B	$((*B)-(*\bar{B})) \div 2$
6∘B	Cosh B	$((*B)+(*\bar{B})) \div 2$
7∘B	Tanh B	$((*B)-(*\bar{B})) \div ((*B)+(*\bar{B}))$

5.7.3[*]   Principal Values for the Inverse Hyperbolic Functions

Like their counterparts, the inverse hyperbolic functions are multivalued. We therefore restrict our attention to principal values for

(1) See Mathematical Handbook of Formulas and Tables, Murray R.
Spiegel, McGraw-Hill, 1968, p. 18.
*   Mathematical material which may be omitted.

which they can be considered single-valued. These values are shown in Table 5.7.4.

TABLE 5.7.4
The Principal Values of the Inverse Hyperbolic Functions

$$\text{Sinh}^{-1} x = \ln(x + \sqrt{x^2 + 1}) \quad -\infty < x < \infty$$

$$\text{Cosh}^{-1} x = \ln(x + \sqrt{x^2 - 1}) \quad x > 1$$

$$\text{Tanh}^{-1} x = \tfrac{1}{2} \ln\left(\frac{1+x}{1-x}\right) \quad -1 < x < 1$$

EXAMPLE 1

Since the trigonometric functions require that angles be expressed in radians, we must convert degrees to radians. For example, to obtain the sine of 45°, we write

```
      1○○(45÷180)
0.7071067812
```

EXAMPLE 2

```
      A←4
      B←5
      2○A÷((A*2)+(B*2))*.5
0.8111415086
```

EXAMPLE 3

The angle whose tangent is 1 is given by

```
      ‾3○1
0.7853981634
```

EXAMPLE 4

An improper argument results in an error.

```
      ‾1○2
DOMAIN ERROR
      ‾1○2
      ∧
```

5.8* GAMMA FUNCTION[2]

The next function to be examined is the classical gamma function, which plays an important role in both theoretical and applied mathematics. Before we discuss the representation of this function in APL, let us examine some of its properties. In conventional mathematical notation the gamma function is defined as

$$\Gamma(n) = \int_0^\infty t^{n-1} e^{-t} dt \qquad n > 0$$

It can be shown that it satisfies the following recursion formula.

$$\Gamma(n+1) = n\,\Gamma(n)$$

$$\Gamma(n+1) = n! \qquad \text{if } n = 0, 1, 2, \ldots \text{ where } 0! = 1$$

The standard factorial function is thus a special case of the gamma function.

If we were to graph the gamma function, it would appear as shown in Figure 5.8.1.

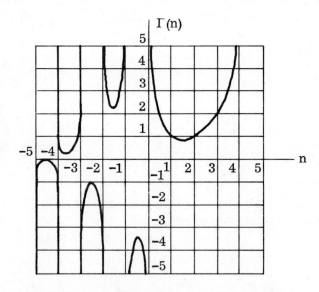

Fig. 5.8.1 Graph of the gamma function

---

(2) Ibid.
*   Mathematical material which may be omitted.

The following are frequently used values of the function.

$$\Gamma(\tfrac{1}{2}) \;=\; \sqrt{\pi}$$

$$\Gamma(m + \tfrac{1}{2}) \;=\; \frac{1 \cdot 3 \cdot 5 \cdots (2m-1)}{2^m}\sqrt{\pi} \qquad m = 1, 2, 3, \ldots$$

$$\Gamma(-m + \tfrac{1}{2}) \;=\; \frac{(-1)^m 2^m \sqrt{\pi}}{1 \cdot 3 \cdot 5 \cdots (2m-1)} \qquad m = 1, 2, 3, \ldots$$

$$\Gamma(n) \;=\; \frac{\Gamma(n+1)}{n}$$

In APL\360 the gamma function is denoted by the factorial symbol, !, formed by overstriking the quote sign with the period. With our definition of gamma function, !N is equal to $\Gamma(N+1)$.

EXAMPLE 1

For a non-negative integer N the function returns the product of the first N integers.

```
      !5
120
```

EXAMPLE 2

$\Gamma(.5) = \sqrt{\pi}$

```
      (!¯.5)
1.772453851
```

EXAMPLE 3

The function is not defined for negative integers

```
      !¯5
DOMAIN ERROR
      !¯5
      ∧
```

5.8.1* Binomial Coefficients

The dyadic function A!B returns the number of combinations of B things taken A at a time. These are the familiar coefficients which play an important role in probability theory and combinatorial analysis.

---

* Mathematical material which may be omitted.

EXAMPLE 1

```
        2!6
  15
```

EXAMPLE 2

A!N and (N-A)!N have the same value.

```
        A←2
        N←7
        2!7
  21
        5!7
  21
```

EXAMPLE 3

The sum of the binomial coefficients for a fixed N is 2*N.

```
        (0!3)+(1!3)+(2!3)+(3!3)
   8
```

5.9 ROLL FUNCTION

The monadic function ?B, where B is a non-negative integer, returns a randomly chosen integer from the integers 1,2,...,B or 0,1,2,..., B, depending on whether the origin (Section 6.9) is set at 1 or 0, respectively. One can think of the integer as having been produced by the roll of a die with B faces.

EXAMPLE 1

Assume the origin is set at 1.

```
        ?31
   5
```

EXAMPLE 2

```
        A←2
        ?(A*2)+7
   9
```

EXAMPLE 3

```
        A←4
        ?⌈*A
   8
```

EXERCISES

1. Evaluate the following expressions

$\lceil 0.5$ $^{-}6 \lfloor ^{-}3$ $^{-}6 \star 2$ $\star 0$

$3 | ^{-}10$ $20090 \div 180$ $| ^{-}5$ $\sim 1 \vee 30090 \div 360$

$! 6$ $4 ! 8$

2. Evaluate the following mathematical constants.

e^{π} e^{e} $\sqrt{\pi}$ $\log_{10} 3$ $\ln_{e} 3$

3. Write APL expressions for each of the following mathematical expressions.

A. z^{m+n}

B. $z - 1^{m-n}$

C. $\dfrac{c+d}{ax+y} - 3$

D. x^{-y}

E. $\dfrac{1}{\sqrt{x+1}}$

F. $(\sqrt{x-y}) \cdot \dfrac{1}{z}$

G. $\dfrac{\ln (x-y)}{\log (x+y)}$

H. An integer selected at random from the integers 1 through 100 (origin is 1)

4. In each of the following write the proper APL expression and assign the value to the variable Z.

A. The minimum of the variables U, V, W, and Y;
B. The remainder when X is divided by Y, $Y \neq 0$.
C. An integer chosen at random from the integers 1 to 51.

5. To convert temperatures from Fahrenheit to Centigrade, we use the formula

$$C = \frac{5}{9} (F - 32^{\circ})$$

where

C = temperature ($^{\circ}$Centigrade)
F = temperature ($^{\circ}$Fahrenheit).

Write an APL expression for the formula.

6. The formula for the area A of a triangle with sides a, b, and c is given by

$$A = \sqrt{s(s - a)(s - b)(s - c)}$$

where $s = \dfrac{a + b + c}{2}$.

Write an APL expression for the area and calculate the area of the triangles whose sides are given by:

A. 3, 4, 5

B. 1, 2, 2

C. 1, 11, 13

7. The distance S (ft.) that a freely falling body will travel after a time t (seconds) is given by the formula

$$S = 16t^2.$$

Write an APL expression for the formula and find out how far a body will have fallen after:

A. 3 seconds;

B. 6 seconds.

C. If a man jumps off a 1000 ft. building, can his life be saved by putting a net under him 8 seconds after he jumps.

8. A digital counter is used to record the number of vehicles which pass a given intersection. The counter is incremented by 1 each time a vehicle passes the intersection and automatically reset to zero by the count following 3296. Use the residue function to determine the counter reading after the following number of vehicles have passed the intersection. Assume the counter is initially zero.

A. 18,325

B.   6,594

C. 12,111

9. A lending institution uses the following formula to determine the monthly payment on a loan. The formula used is

$$P = A \cdot i \, \frac{(1 + i)^n}{(1 + i)^n - 1}$$

where

> P = monthly payment in dollars,
> A = total amount of the loan in dollars,
> i = the monthly interest rate (annual $\div$ 12 expressed as a decimal),
> n = the total number of monthly payments.

Write an APL expression for the formula.

10. The value of an investment A of a given principal P at an annual interest rate I (expressed as a decimal) with C conversions a year for n years is given by the formula

$$A = P(1 + \frac{I}{C})^n .$$

Assuming Manhattan Isle was purchased on January 1, 1610, for $24, how much would the $24 amount to if it had been invested in a bank paying 2% interest per year, compounded quarterly. Use December 31, 1975, as the current date.

PART TWO
OPERATIONS ON ARRAYS

6.1 INTRODUCTION

Up to this point numeric variables have had their values specified by assigning a single number to them. Such numbers are referred to as scalars, and variables to which they are assigned are called scalar variables. In numerous applications variables occur whose specification consists of an ordered array of data rather than a single number. This chapter opens with a discussion of the simplest array variable, namely, a vector. It then goes on to discuss the way in which vectors are represented in APL and the more important properties of vectors: dimension and rank. These concepts are then extended to matrices and more complex structures. Some primitive functions which generate arrays and provide information about their dimension and rank are examined in detail.

    As Part 2 unfolds, the student will see that the efficient and compact implementation of a problem in APL often depends on how the user chooses to organize and structure his data. Choosing one data structure rather than another will often allow him to employ fewer and more powerful primitive functions.

6.2 VECTORS

In the real world certain quantities cannot be specified by a single number. To the physicist, velocity is a quantity which has both magnitude and direction.

EXAMPLE 1

Suppose a particle is moving at a speed of 60 meters a second and at an angle of 30°, as shown in Figure 6.2.1.

    A convenient and useful way of describing its velocity is to separate the numbers representing its speed and direction by a space: 60 30. This notation emphasizes the fact that although velocity has two distinct components, it is nevertheless a single quantity.

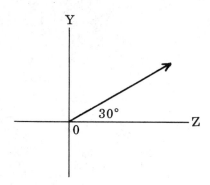

Fig. 6.2.1

EXAMPLE 2

Various deductions are made from an employee's bimonthly salary check as shown:

	Gross Salary	$1010.12
(1)	Withholding Tax	173.48
(2)	F.I.C.A.	63.25
(3)	Credit Union	50.00
(4)	Hospital Insurance	12.35
(5)	United Fund	1.25
(6)	Retirement	18.35
(7)	Stock	16.50

We may think of the different deductions as an ordered array of data.

6.2.1 Row and Column Vectors

All the previous examples illustrate the concept of a vector, an ordered linear array of numbers. The notion of ordering is crucial because rearranging the numbers within the vector gives it an entirely different meaning. The numbers within the array are called the components of the vector. Vectors are either row vectors or column vectors, depending on whether the components are represented as a horizontal or a vertical array. All the examples given have been instances of row vectors, but it would have been just as easy to think of them as column vectors.

6.2.2 Vector Variables

The variables described in the previous examples are called vector variables because they are specified by an array of numbers. Up till now, all our computations have been with scalar variables. From this point on, vectors will play a more fundamental role, so it is important to see how they are represented in APL.

6.2.3 Representation of Vectors

In APL, vectors of numeric data are represented by inserting spaces between their components. The number of spaces is not important. Thus the following are all examples of vectors.

    60   30

    1 1 0

    10   3

To define a vector variable whose name is VELOCITY with the specification given in Example 1 above, we write

    VELOCITY←60 30

For the vector variable DEDUCTION in Example 2, we write

    DEDUCTION←173.48 63.25 50.00 12.35 1.25 18.35 16.50

In Section 6.7 we will discuss a primitive function for generating vectors that is particularly useful when the desired vectors are of a certain type.

6.2.4 Naming Vector Variables

Since the rules for naming vector variables are exactly the same as for scalar variables, we have no way of telling from the name of a variable whether it is a scalar or a vector.

6.2.5 Vectors with Variable Components

A natural question at this stage is whether the components of the vector may be represented by variables. For example, suppose we have two scalar variables whose names are *SPEED* and *MAGNITUDE*. Can we define a vector called *VELOCITY* in the following way?

VELOCITY←SPEED MAGNITUDE

The answer is no. We cannot use this form as a means of specifying a vector with variable components. However, there is an easy way out of this dilemma, but it makes use of a primitive function called <u>catenate</u>, which we shall examine in Chapter 8. The function is denoted by the comma. Had we written

VELOCITY←SPEED,MAGNITUDE

then *VELOCITY* would be a vector whose components would be the values previously assigned to the variables *SPEED* and *MAGNITUDE*. In fact, the catenate function makes it possible to have vectors whose components are expressions, for example,

VELOCITY←(3×A),MAGNITUDE

From the standpoint of applications, the ability to form vectors with variable components will prove to be very important.

6.2.6 Vectors of Literals

In APL, vectors of literal characters are permitted. In fact, we dealt with vectors of literal data in Section 2.9. In a literal vector all the characters must be enclosed by the quote signs. Each component is restricted to a single character, and spaces are not inserted between characters unless the spaces are intended to be part of the vector.

EXAMPLE 1

ALPHABET←'ABCDEFGHIJKLMNOPQRSTUVWXYZ'
ALPHABET
ABCDEFGHIJKLMNOPQRSTUVWXYZ

When a literal vector is named, only what is between the quote signs is printed out.

6.3 DIMENSION AND RANK

The two properties of an array which completely reveal its structure are its dimension and rank.

By the dimension of an array we mean the number of distinct

values that each coordinate can assume. The dimension of a vector is simply the number of its components.

By the rank of an array we mean the number of coordinates required to specify any component. The term 'rank' is used so as not to confuse the dimensionality of an array with its dimensions. Since a vector component requires a single coordinate to specify its position within the vector, a vector has rank one. Since a scalar has no dimension, its rank is defined to be zero.

6.4 MATRICES

A matrix is a rectangular array of data in which each component is specified by a row number and a column number. Because two coordinates are required to specify any component, it follows that a matrix has rank two. The matrix shown in Figure 6.4.1 has dimension 12 15. By convention, the first coordinate of the dimension vector designates the row. Like vectors, matrices occur in a variety of applications, many of which will be discussed in the problems in later chapters. Our emphasis here is on illustrating the concepts of dimension and rank and on showing how matrices are specified.

EXAMPLE 1

Figure 6.4.1 shows how the National League teams performed over the course of the 1974 baseball season. Row entries represent the wins of the team designated by that row. Column entries designate the losses of the team designated by that column.

NATIONAL LEAGUE RECORDS, 1974
FINAL STANDINGS OF CLUBS
EASTERN DIVISION

	PITTSBURGH	ST. LOUIS	CHICAGO	NEW YORK	MONTREAL	PHILADELPHIA	SAN FRANCISCO	LOS ANGELES	ATLANTA	HOUSTON	CINCINNATI	SAN DIEGO	WON	LOST	PERCENTAGE
Pittsburgh Pirates	—	11	12	8	11	12	3	8	8	8	7	9	97	66	.599
St. Louis Cardinals	7	—	9	8	14	11	7	6	6	10	4	8	90	72	.586
Chicago Cubs	6	9	—	11	8	11	3	8	7	5	6	9	83	79	.512
New York Mets	10	10	7	—	9	13	4	7	5	7	4	7	83	79	.512
Montreal Expos	7	4	10	9	—	6	7	4	5	8	5	6	71	90	.441
Philadelphia Phillies	6	7	7	5	12	—	6	5	4	4	7	4	67	95	.414

WESTERN DIVISION

	PITTSBURGH	ST. LOUIS	CHICAGO	NEW YORK	MONTREAL	PHILADELPHIA	SAN FRANCISCO	LOS ANGELES	ATLANTA	HOUSTON	CINCINNATI	SAN DIEGO	WON	LOST	PERCENTAGE
San Francisco Giants	9	5	9	8	5	6	—	6	11	9	9	13	90	72	.556
Los Angeles Dodgers	4	6	4	5	8	7	12	—	9	10	11	13	89	73	.549
Atlanta Braves	4	6	5	7	7	8	7	9	—	9	9	11	82	80	.506
Houston Astros	4	2	7	5	4	8	9	8	9	—	13	10	79	83	.493
Cincinnati Reds	5	8	6	8	7	5	9	7	9	5	—	10	79	83	.489
San Diego Padres	8	4	3	5	5	8	5	5	7	8	8	—	61	100	.379

Fig. 6.4.1

EXAMPLE 2

A building contractor builds three different kinds of homes. The units
(appropriately chosen) of various raw materials which go into a house
are given by the following matrix.

	Steel	Copper	Wood	Glass	Wire	Paint
Colonial:	8	12	75	20	30	18
Cape Cod:	6	11	60	18	25	14
Ranch:	7	9	50	14	19	13

EXAMPLE 3

The system of linear equations

$$2X + 3Y + 5Z = 5$$
$$3X + 4Y + 7Z = 6$$
$$X + 3Y + 2Z = 5$$

can be represented by the matrix

$$
\begin{array}{cccc}
2 & 3 & 5 & 5 \\
3 & 4 & 7 & 6 \\
1 & 3 & 2 & 5
\end{array}
$$

The first three columns of the matrix represent the coefficients of the
variables, and the last column represents the constant terms.

6.5 SPECIFICATION OF MATRIX ELEMENTS

The elements of a matrix cannot be specified simply by separating
them by spaces. If we think of the rows of a matrix as vectors, there
is no difficulty in choosing a name for each row and specifying its
components. The problem is that we have no means for interpreting
these vectors as the rows of a matrix. In Section 6.7 we shall discuss
specification of matrices and arrays of higher rank in detail. When
named, a matrix prints out as follows:

$$
\begin{array}{cc}
1 & 2 \\
3 & 4 \\
5 & 6
\end{array}
$$

Here we see a matrix of dimension 3 2.

6.5.1 Matrices of Literal Characters

Like vectors, matrices may consist of literals. The rule is again that each component is limited to a single character. Names for matrix variables and, in fact, for all array variables obey the same rules. The name of an array variable provides no information about its dimension or rank.

6.6 ARRAYS OF HIGHER RANK

We have singled out vectors and matrices because they occur so frequently in applications that it seemed worthwhile to discuss them separately. Arrays of rank three and greater occur less frequently in applications, but there is nothing novel in their conception, and in fact, pictorially they can be displayed quite easily.

EXAMPLE 1

Figure 6.6.1 illustrates an array, M, of rank three with dimension 4 3 2. The array can be thought of as consisting of four planes, each plane being a matrix of dimension 3 2. Spaces between the matrices indicate the separation of the planes. The array has rank three because, in order to reference any component, we need to know what plane it lies in, as well as its row and column number in that plane.

M

```
1   2
3   4
5   6


7   8
9   1
2   3


4   5
6   7
8   9


1   2
3   4
5   6
```

Fig. 6.6.1

EXAMPLE 2

$$M$$

1	2	3
4	5	6

7	8	9
10	11	12

13	14	15
16	17	18

19	20	21
22	23	24

Here we see an array of rank four with dimension 2 2 2 3. The array consists of two hyperplanes of rank three. Double spaces separate the two hyperplanes. Each hyperplane consists of two planes separated by a single space. To represent an array of rank five, we would use one, two, and three spaces as separators. Most applications involve arrays of rank two or less.

6.7 GENERATING MATRICES AND ARRAYS OF HIGHER RANK

We shall now consider the general problem of generating arrays of given dimension and rank. In what follows, the variables V will denote a vector, S a scalar, and R an array of arbitrary rank. The primitive dyadic function rho, denoted by ρ and shown in Figure 6.7.1, may be used to generate an array D of specified dimension and rank. The vector V specifies the rank and dimension of D, and the components of D are chosen from the array R in cyclic fashion until the required number of elements have been chosen.

$$D \leftarrow V \rho R$$

Fig. 6.7.1

EXAMPLE 1

```
    2 3ρ6 9 1 2

6  9  1
2  6  9
```

The matrix D has dimension 2 3. Since six entries are required to fill the matrix and only four elements are available in R, we reuse the first two elements.

EXAMPLE 2

```
    2 2 2ρ5 8 6 7

5  8
6  7

5  8
6  7
```

In this case D is an array of rank three with dimension 2 2 2. Note the use of a space between the matrices to indicate separation of the planes.

EXAMPLE 3

```
    4 5ρ1

1 1 1 1 1
1 1 1 1 1
1 1 1 1 1
1 1 1 1 1
```

Here we see a matrix with identical entries. Such a matrix is called a scalar matrix.

EXAMPLE 4

```
    D←2 3ρ'THECAT'
    D

THE
CAT
```

In this case D is an array of literals.

EXAMPLE 5

$D \leftarrow 0 \rho 5$
D

This example requires some discussion. What has happened is that
D has been specified as the empty or null vector. This vector prints
as a blank line, so that in naming D, we have in fact produced a blank
line.

EXAMPLE 6

$A \leftarrow 2\ 2$
$B \leftarrow 1\ 2\ 3\ 4$
$A \rho (B+1)$

2   3
4   5

Both arguments of rho may be variables or expressions.

6.8 FINDING THE DIMENSION AND RANK OF AN ARRAY

We have seen that the dyadic rho function enables us to generate arrays. Now we shall see that the monadic rho function enables us to
obtain the dimension and rank of a given array. The monadic function
rho has the form shown in Figure 6.8.1. The function returns a vector, V, whose components are the dimensions of R.

$$V \leftarrow \rho R$$

Fig. 6.8.1

EXAMPLE 1

$M \leftarrow 3\ 2\ 1\ 5\ 7$
ρM
5
$\rho(\rho M)$
1

Since there is one component for each dimension of an array, the number of components in the vector ρM gives the rank of M. But the number of components in a vector is its dimension. Hence the rank M is given by $\rho(\rho M)$.

EXAMPLE 2

```
      N←1  7  9  11  13
      ρN
5
      ρρN
1
```

EXAMPLE 3

```
      M←9
      ρM

      ρρM
0
```

We see that the dimension of a scalar is the null vector, and its rank is 0.

EXAMPLE 4

```
      M←1ρ9
      ρM
1
      ρρM
1
```

Note the difference between Examples 3 and 4. In Example 3, the dimension of the scalar M is the null vector, which prints as a blank line. In Example 4, M is a vector of dimension 1. Repeated application of the function always produces the vector 1.

6.9 VECTORS OF CONSECUTIVE INTEGERS

There is one vector which occurs so frequently that a primitive function has been made available for generating it. It is the vector whose components are the first N consecutive integers. The monadic function <u>iota</u>, shown in Figure 6.9.1, produces such a vector. A may be any

variable or expression whose value is a nonnegative integer, I.   The
vector V consists of the integers beginning with 0 or 1 and continuing
through I. The system command $)ORIGIN$ 0, or $)ORIGIN$ 1 labels the
first element in a vector zero or one respectively.

$$V \leftarrow \iota A$$

Fig. 6.9.1

EXAMPLE 1

Assume the origin is 0.
```
      ι9
  0   1   2   3   4   5   6   7   8
```
Since the origin is 0, the integers 0 to 8 are generated.

EXAMPLE 2

An expression whose value is 2 is used as the argument of iota. Assume that the origin is set to 0.
```
        A←3
        B←7
        ι((A×B-4)<20)+1
  0   1
```

EXAMPLE 3

Assume the origin is set to 1.
```
        A←3
        ι2×A-1
  1   2   3   4
```
Since the origin is 1, the first integer in the vector is 1.

EXAMPLE 4
```
        T←7÷2
        ιT
  DOMAIN ERROR
        ιT
        ∧
```
An error results because the argument is not an integer.

In the applications which are discussed in later chapters, we shall see a good deal of the iota function. The dyadic function iota will be discussed in connection with indexing in Chapter 7.

6.10 CONFORMABLE ARRAYS

Definition: Two arrays A and B are said to be conformable relative to primitive dyadic functions if (1) they have the same dimensions or (2) one of them is a scalar. Consider the following arrays.

$A \leftarrow 2\ 3\rho 1\ 5\ 7\ 2$

$B \leftarrow 2\ 3\rho 8\ 9$

The arrays A and B are conformable because they both have dimension 2 3. On the other hand, if we define D as

$D \leftarrow 6\ 4\ 9$

then A and D are not conformable. If we specify a variable C as

$C \leftarrow 3$

then C and any of the previous arrays are conformable. Let us think of C as being extended to have the same dimension as the array with which it is said to be conformable. We shall see that the primitive functions can be extended to deal with conformable arrays in a natural way.

6.11 PRIMITIVE DYADIC FUNCTIONS WITH ARRAY ARGUMENTS

Given any two conformable arrays A and B and a primitive dyadic function d, the result R obtained by executing d with A and B as arguments

$R \leftarrow A d B$

is an array of the same dimension as its arguments. Each component of R is obtained by executing d with the corresponding components of A and B as arguments. Up till now we have been dealing with the special case in which A and B are both scalars.

EXAMPLE 1

```
        A←3 6 7 4
        B←5 8 9 6
        A+B
  8   14  16   10
```

The result of adding two vectors A and B is a vector of the same dimension, each of whose components is the sum of the corresponding components of A and B.

EXAMPLE 2

```
        C←4 1 17 3 5 2
        D←9 2 3 6 4 8
        C×D
  36   2   51   18   20   16
```

The result is a vector, each of whose components is the product of the corresponding components of C and D.

EXAMPLE 3

```
        C←2
        D←9 2 3 6 4 8
        D⋆C
  81   4   9   36   16   64
```

The result is a vector of the same dimension as D. We must remember that the scalar C has been extended to form a vector of the same dimension as D.

EXAMPLE 4

```
        A←3 1 5
        B←2 1
        A-B
  LENGTH ERROR
        A-B
        ∧
```

The error results from the fact that the arguments are not conformable.

EXAMPLE 5

```
        R←?2 2ρ54
        S←?2 2ρ45
        R

    8   41
   25   29
        S

   10    3
   31   31
        R×S

   80   123
  775   899
```

Two matrices with random integers are generated, and their product is obtained.

6.12 PRIMITIVE MONADIC FUNCTIONS WITH ARRAY ARGUMENTS

In the case of a primitive monadic function f and an array A, the result R obtained by executing f with A as the argument,

$R \leftarrow fA$

has the same dimension as A. Each component of R is obtained by executing the function f over the corresponding component of A.

EXAMPLE 1

```
        A←‾5 6 0 11 ‾12
        ×A
  ‾1  1  0  1  ‾1
```

The signum function is executed over each component of A.

EXAMPLE 2

```
        A←6.7 8.98 5.76 4.213
        ⌊A
   6   8   5   4
```

Further illustrations of the uses of the rho and iota functions are given in the exercises.

EXERCISES

1. Write APL statements to do the following.

   A. Let Z be a vector whose components are the first 50 odd integers (origin is 1).

   B. Let M be a matrix of dimension 3 5 whose elements are chosen randomly from the integers 1 to 73.

   C. Let M and N be two arrays of the same dimension. Let Z be defined as an array such than an element of Z is the maximum of the corresponding elements of M and N.

   D. Repeat C, changing the specification from maximum to minimum.

   E. Let Z consist of the first 30 powers of 2.

   F. Evaluate the expression $z = e^X \sqrt{1+X+X^2}$ for $X = 1.1, 1.2,$ ..., 5.

   G. Vandermonde's matrix is given by

   $$A_{ij} = X_j^i$$

   $$A = \begin{pmatrix} X_1 \ldots \ldots X_n \\ X_1^2 \qquad X_n^2 \\ \ldots \ldots \ldots \\ \ldots \ldots \ldots \\ X_1^n \ldots \ldots X_n^n \end{pmatrix}$$

   Write an APL expression for this matrix, assuming that the X's are given as a vector. Let n = 7.

   H. Repeat G, except that $A_{ij} = Y + \delta_{ij}X$. This is the combinatorial matrix. Let n = 11.

   $$A = \begin{pmatrix} X+Y & Y & Y & \ldots \ldots & Y \\ Y & X+Y & \ldots \ldots \\ \ldots \ldots \ldots \ldots \\ Y & & & X+Y \end{pmatrix}$$

   $\delta_{ij} = 1$ if $i = j$

   $\delta_{ij} = 0$ if $i \neq j$

2. Write an APL expression for the array C, defined as follows:
Let A and B be two arrays of the same dimension and rank. If corresponding elements of A and B are identical, the same element appears in C. Otherwise a zero is entered in C.

3. Let $A \leftarrow 2\ 3\ 5\ 7$, $B \leftarrow \iota 4$, $C \leftarrow 2\ 2\rho\iota\ 3\ 5$. Evaluate

A. $A+B$ B. $A*B$ C. $2 \times A - B$ D. $5\rho C$ E. $A+7$

F. $3\ 2\rho C$ G. ρC H. $\rho 5$ I. $8 - \iota 8$ J. $3 \times \iota 0$

K. $A \lceil B$ L. $A \lfloor B$ M. $200 \lceil B$ N. $A \leq B$

4. Define Z as the 10×10 unit matrix.

5. Given Ohm's law for alternating current

$$I = E/R$$

find the current in a circuit for the following combinations of voltage
and resistance using a single APL statement.

E(volts)	R(ohms)
12	3.6
19	5.2
110	20.3
220	18.6

6. A prime number (integer) is a number which is divisible only by
itself and 1. A Swiss mathematician, Leonard Euler (1707 – 1783),
proposed the following formula to produce prime numbers:

$$p = x^2 + x + 41$$

where x is a positive integer and p is a prime.
    Write an APL expression to evaluate Euler's formula for the integers
from 1 to 41. Are they all prime? Does the formula work for all integers?
Use the iota function to generate the "alleged primes."

7. Write a single APL expression using four different vector variables
for the squares, square roots, cubes, and cube roots of the integers
from 1 to 100. Print the cube roots of the numbers.

8. Write an APL expression to produce a vector V consisting of the
numbers 6.000, 6.025, 6.050,...,7.0. Assign the number of elements

in V to a scalar variable D in the same expression.

9. Execute the following statements for $X \leftarrow 3\ 2\ 1\ ^-8\ 4$ and

$Y \leftarrow 2\ 3\ ^-1\ 7\ 6$

A. $Z \leftarrow X \geq Y$

B. $Z \leftarrow (3 = Y) > X$

C. $Z \leftarrow (X + Y) * Z$

D. $Z \leftarrow X \times Y + 1$

10. Hamming's Law of Logarithms states

$$\log_2 y \approx \ln y + \log_{10} y$$

with no more than 1% error. Test the law for the integers from 1 to 100 by calculating the percentage error.

7.1 INTRODUCTION

In this chapter we shall learn how to reference, modify, and work with individual components and subsets of a given array. We begin with a discussion of how vectors and matrices are indexed and extend the results developed to arrays of higher rank. We show that indices are not limited to scalar constants but may themselves be arrays of any dimension and rank. This permits the construction of complex structures whose components are selected from the array being referenced. We examine the dimension and rank of these new structures and then go on to discuss the inverse problem, namely, to determine the indices of a given element belonging to an array. This leads to a discussion of the primitive dyadic function iota.

7.2 INDEXING A VECTOR

The simplest kind of array we can reference is a vector, and so we begin by defining a vector.

$A \leftarrow 2\ 3\ 5\ 1\ 6$

To reference a component or components of A, we place a pair of brackets immediately to the right of A. The numbers inserted in the brackets are the index numbers which determine what components of A are selected. The index numbers must be non-negative integers.

7.2.1 Scalar Indices

EXAMPLE 1

An integer scalar designates the corresponding component of the array.

$$A[3]$$
5

To modify this component, we could write

$$A[3] \leftarrow 6$$

The component may appear in an expression.

$$R \leftarrow 2 \times A[3] + 5$$

There is one thing that we must remember. We are assuming the origin is 1. If the origin were 0, then A[3] would be the fourth component of the vector.

EXAMPLE 2

The index may take the form of a scalar variable,

$$E \leftarrow 4$$
$$A[E]$$
1

or even an expression.

$$A[(2 \times E) - 3]$$

EXAMPLE 3

An invalid index results in an error.

$$A[6]$$
INDEX ERROR
$$A[6]$$
$\wedge$

EXAMPLE 4

An expression whose value is an array may be referenced, but it must be inserted in parentheses.

$$(2 \times A + 5)[2]$$
16

EXAMPLE 5

A constant vector, whether numeric or literal, can be referenced.

```
        'WHO'[1]
  W
        1  5  9  [3]
  9
```

EXAMPLE 6

It is not possible to index an array until it has been defined.

```
        ARRAY[2]←1
  RANK ERROR
        ARRAY[2]←1
        ∧
```

7.2.2 Vectors as Indices

If a vector is used as an index, the result is a vector of the components being referenced.

EXAMPLE 1

Any sequence of valid index numbers may be used as the components of the index vector.

```
        A[2 1 2 3 5 4]
  3  2  3  5  6  1
```

The results of Examples 1–6 of the previous section apply to vectors as well. In particular, a vector variable or an expression whose value is a vector may be used as an index.

EXAMPLE 2

```
        A←2  3  5  1  6
        E←2  1  3  4
        A[E+1]
  5  3  1  6
```

7.2.3 Arrays of Higher Rank as Indices

All of the results developed for scalars and vectors hold for arrays of rank two or greater when these arrays are construed as indices. For example, if A is a vector and R is an array such that *

$$S \leftarrow A[R]$$

then ρS is equal to ρR.

7.3 INDEXING A MATRIX

To index a matrix, we need two numbers, namely, a row index and a column index. These indices are inserted in brackets and separated by a semicolon. The left index specifies the row, and the right index specifies the column. Among other things, we should like to see what happens when the indices are also specified as arrays.

7.3.1 Scalar Indices

Let M be a matrix.

```
      M←3 4ρι12
      M

  1    2    3    4
  5    6    7    8
  9   10   11   12
```

EXAMPLE 1

A pair of scalar indices selects an element of the matrix.

```
          M[3;4]
    12
```

To modify this component we can write

```
    M[3;4]←1
```

The component can appear in an expression.

```
          2×M[3;4]
     2
```

EXAMPLE 2

Both row and column indices may be specified as variables or expressions.

```
      E←2
      M[2×E-1;E]
  6
```

EXAMPLE 3

A matrix expression may be indexed, provided that the expression is
placed in parentheses.

```
      (M*3)[2;1]
  125
```

EXAMPLE 4

A matrix of literals may be indexed.

```
      L←3 3ρ'HOWAREYOU'
      L

HOW
ARE
YOU
      L[1;1]
  H
```

7.3.2 Vector Indices

EXAMPLE 1

Selecting the first two rows of M and the second column of M results
in a vector of two elements.

```
      M[1 2;2]
  2   6
```

EXAMPLE 2

Using vectors for both indices results in a matrix.

```
      M←3 4ρι12
      M[1 3;2 4]

   2    4
  10   12
```

EXAMPLE 3

If no index appears for one of the dimensions, it is assumed that all
of the dimension is wanted.   The semicolon must still appear.

```
        M[;1]
   1   5   9
```

7.3.3 Matrix Indices

Let us define two matrices as follows:

```
        A←2 2ρ1 2 2 1
        B←2 2ρ2 1 1 2
        A

   1   2
   2   1
        B

   2   1
   1   2
```

EXAMPLE 1

```
        T←M[A;B]
        T

   2   1
   1   2

   6   5
   5   6


   6   5
   5   6

   2   1
   1   2
```

T is an array of rank four.   To understand why this is so, consider the
following: It requires two indices, for example I and J, to index A and
two more indices, for example, K and L, to index B.   Therefore four
indices are required to index T.

7.4 FINDING THE INDICES OF AN ARRAY OF ELEMENTS

In the previous sections we were concerned with the problem of referencing the elements of a given array by an array of indices. Now we wish to consider the inverse problem, namely, given a vector V and an arbitrary array R, to determine the indices of the components of R in V. The mechanism for doing this is the primitive dyadic function, iota, shown in Figure 7.4.1, where V is a vector and R an array. The function returns an array S whose components are the indices in V of the corresponding components of R. It follows that S has the same dimension as R and, consequently, the same rank.

Fig. 7.4.1

EXAMPLE 1

We find the index of a scalar.

$$A \leftarrow 3.2\ 6.9\ 7.5\ 8.4\ 9.625$$
$$A \iota 7.5$$
3

EXAMPLE 2

If R is a vector, then S is a vector.

$$V \leftarrow 6.9\ 9.625\ 3\ 7$$
$$R \leftarrow 6.9\ 9.625$$
$$S \leftarrow V \iota R$$
$$S$$
1   2

EXAMPLE 3

Both arguments of iota may be variables or expressions.

$$B \leftarrow 16.8$$
$$(2 \times A) \iota B$$
4

EXAMPLE 4

Literals may be indexed.

```
        C←'THE NAME OF THE GAME'
        Cι'GAME'
  17  6  7  3
```

EXAMPLE 5

If there is more than one occurrence of an element in V, then the index of the first occurrence is always given.

```
        Cι'T'
   1
        Cι'TGT'
   1  17  1
```

EXAMPLE 6

If an index is requested for an element which does not appear in V, then the index number returned is equal to $1 + \rho V$.

```
        A←2  6  8
        Aι3
   4
        A←'NAME'
        Aι'F'
   5
```

EXAMPLE 7

For a matrix argument a matrix of indices is returned.

```
        A←ι4
        B←2 2ρ4 2 1 5
        B
   4  2
   1  5
        Aι2×B

   5  4
   2  5
```

7.5 THE CODING PROBLEM

Given two distinct vectors V and U of the same dimension, we define
a correspondence between U[R] and V[R] in which each element of U is
replaced by the corresponding element of V. Let us assume that R is
an array of allowable indices for U.

This correspondence, which can be construed as a coding of the
set of elements of U by the elements of V, is very easy to carry out
using the dyadic iota function. If we write

$S \leftarrow V[U \iota R]$

then S is the array with the desired property.

EXAMPLE 1

```
U←1 2 3 4 5 6 7 8 9 10 11 12 13 14 15
V←'ABCDEFGHIJKLMNO'
R←13 1 7 9 3 9 1 14
S←V[UιR]
S
MAGICIAN
```

EXERCISES

1. Given the following variables:

$A \leftarrow 2\ 3\ 5\ 7$

$B \leftarrow \iota 4$

$P \leftarrow 2\ 2\rho 1\ 3\ 5$

$G \leftarrow 'AEFHWO'$

$H \leftarrow 3\ 5\ 7\rho \iota 30$

Evaluate the following:

A. $A[B[3]]$ B. $G[A[B[3]]]$ C. $P[;1]$

D. $G[5\ 4\ 6]$ E. $A[\iota 2]$ F. $H[1;\ ;2]$

G. $G[P]$ H. $H[;1\ 2;\ ]$

2.   Find the dimension and rank of each of the arrays in Exercise 1.

3.   Let M be the matrix $M \leftarrow 3 \quad 3\rho 5 \quad 2 \quad 1 \quad 7 \quad 7 \quad 9 \quad 4 \quad 5 \quad 8$.
Write an expression for each of the following:

   A.   The first row of M

   B.   The second column of M

   C.   The first two rows of M

   D.   The submatrix $N \leftarrow 2 \quad 2\rho 5 \quad 2 \quad 7 \quad 7$

   E.   The four corner elements

   5   1

   4   8

4.   Evaluate

   A. $B \iota A$ B. $G \iota (P-1)$ C. $A \iota B[3]$ D. $B \iota H$

5.   Write APL expressions for the following. Assume $)ORIGIN$ 1 indexing and (ρX) equal to 25. Let Y be the vector formed from X by the following operations:

   A.   five consecutive elements starting at element six,

   B.   every fifth element starting with element five,

THE RAVEL, CATENATE, AND LAMINATE FUNCTIONS

8.1 INTRODUCTION

In Chapter 6 we saw that the primitive dyadic functions rho and iota required vectors as their left arguments. We shall see later that there are certain other primitive functions which also require one of their arguments to be a vector. In certain applications it is also convenient to operate on an array as though it were a vector. It seems that it would be useful to have a primitive function for transforming any array into a vector. Such a function exists, and its monadic form is called 'ravel'. The ravel function is discussed in this chapter, and a number of examples of its use are given.

The dyadic form of the function, called 'catenate', is used to chain two vectors to form a single vector. The catenate function makes it possible to form arrays with variable elements, and because of this property, it is extremely important in applications. Some of the applications will be illustrated in the examples.

8.2 TRANSFORMING AN ARRAY INTO A VECTOR

The primitive monadic function <u>ravel</u>, shown in Figure 8.2.1, is used to convert an array R into a vector V. The array is linearized, or stretched out, from most to least significant element. For example, a matrix is transformed row by row, an array of rank three is transformed first by plane and then by row, etc.

Fig. 8.2.1

EXAMPLE 1

A scalar is converted to a vector with a single component.

```
A←3
B←,3
ρA

ρB
```
1

From Example 1 we see something that was pointed out in Chapter 6, namely, that there is a difference between a scalar and a vector with a single element. The ravel function is perhaps the easiest way to convert a scalar into a single-element vector. There are applications in which it is convenient to do so. Consider a numeric variable A which may be specified as either a scalar or a vector. To obtain the mean value of A, we have to sum the components of A and divide by the dimension of A, which is ρA. If A is specified as a scalar, then (ρA) is the empty vector and the division results in an error. We avoid this difficulty by writing ,A to guarantee that no error will result from the division since (ρA) will be equal to 1.

EXAMPLE 2

If the variable being operated on is a vector, it is not changed.

```
A←3 6 8 4
B←,A
B
3   6   8   4
```

EXAMPLE 3

A matrix is transformed, row by row.

```
A←2 3ρ1 2 5
A

1   2   5
1   2   5
,A
1   2   5   1   2   5
,A*2
1   4   25  1   4   25
```

Again, the data may consist of literals.

```
        B←2 3ρ'THECAT'
        B

THE
CAT
          ,B
THE CAT
```

EXAMPLE 4

```
        A←3 2 4ρ?ι12
        A

  1   1   2   4
  1   1   4   6

  1   4   1   6
  1   1   2   4

  1   1   4   6
  1   4   1   6
        ,A
1  1  2  4  1  1  4  6  1  4  1  6  1  1  2  4
         1  1  4  6  1  4  1  6
```

For an array of rank three the transformation takes place first by plane, then by row, and finally by column.

8.3 CHAINING VECTORS

The dyadic form of the function denoted by the comma is called catenate and has the form shown in Figure 8.3.1, where $V1$ and $V2$ may be either scalars or vectors and C is the vector obtained by chaining $V2$ to $V1$.

```
┌─────────────┐
│  C←V1,V2    │
└─────────────┘
```

Fig. 8.3.1

EXAMPLE 1

Two vectors of constants may be catenated.

```
        A←2 3 6 8
        B←9 1
        A,B
  2   3   6   8   9   1
```

Literals may be catenated.

```
        A←'WHO'
        B←'KNOWS'
        A,B
  WHOKNOWS
```

But literals cannot be catenated with numerics.

```
        A←'WHO'
        B←9 1
        A,B
  DOMAIN ERROR
        A,B
        ∧
```

EXAMPLE 2

Expressions which result in vectors may be catenated.

```
        A←2 3 6 8
        (A*2),(A+2)
  4   9   36   64   4   5   8   10
```

EXAMPLE 3

An array of rank greater than one cannot be catenated with a vector.

```
        B←2 3ρι6
       ˙B

  1   2   3
  4   5   6
        A←5 8 1
        B,A
  RANK ERROR
        B,A
        ∧
```

If one ravels B first, it is possible to catenate it.

```
        ( ,B ),A
  1  2  3  4  5  6  5  8  1
```

8.3.1 Catenation and Lamination of Arrays *

In general, conformable arrays of any rank may be catenated along
an existing coordinate.

EXAMPLE 1

```
      □←A←2 5ρ10?10

  1   5   9  10   6
  2   7   4   8   3
```

```
      □←B←2 5ρ10?10

  4   2   3   9   7
  1   5   8   6  10
      A ,B
```

```
  1   5   9  10   6   4   2   3   9   7
  2   7   4   8   3   1   5   8   6  10
```

```
      A ,[1]B

  1   5   9  10   6
  2   7   4   8   3
  4   2   3   9   7
  1   5   8   6  10
```

* The function symbol □ is discussed in Section 16.2. It enables us to
  print out the arrays A and B.

EXAMPLE 2

Rows and columns may also be added to matrices.

A

```
1   5   9   10   6
2   7   4    8   3
    V
```

```
1   2
    A,V
```

```
1   5   9   10   6   1
2   7   4    8   3   2
```

EXAMPLE 3

Lamination joins two arrays along a new coordinate.

$A,[.7]B$

```
1  5  9  10  6
2  7  4   8  3
```

```
4  2  3  9   7
1  5  8  6  10
```

$A,[1.7]B$

```
1  5  9  10  6
4  2  3   9  7
```

```
2  7  4   8  3
1  5  8   6  10
```

The .7 in the examples above has no special significance; the same result would follow for any digit between 1 and 9.

8.4 VECTORS WITH VARIABLE COMPONENTS

Consider a vector V with two components. Think of the vector as representing the velocity of a body. Let the components of the vector be X and Y, respectively. If the components of a vector can themselves be variables, then the specification of the vector will be changed when the specification of the variable components is changed.   The dyadic catenate function makes if permissible to write expressions such as:

$V \leftarrow X , Y$

If the specification of X and Y is changed, V will assume a new value when the statement specifying V is executed.

8.5 ARRAYS WITH VARIABLE COMPONENTS

It is now easy to see that once we have vectors with variable components, we can have arrays of any rank with variable components. We know from Section 6.7 that when an array is formed by use of the rho function, the right argument of rho must be a scalar or vector from which the elements of the array being generated are chosen. Since we can have a vector with variable components, it follows immediately that we can have an array of any rank with variable components.

To form the matrix R, we write

$R \leftarrow 2 \quad 2\rho((2\circ ALPHA),(-1\circ ALPHA),(1\circ ALPHA),(2\circ ALPHA))$

where $ALPHA$ is assumed to have been specified previously.

EXAMPLE 1

Not only can we have arrays with variable components, but the dimension of an array may also be a variable. Consider, e.g., the unit matrix of dimension N. Such a matrix consists of N ones on the main diagonal and zeros elsewhere. If we call this matrix U, we can write it as follows:

$U \leftarrow (N,N)\rho(1,N\rho 0)$

The dimension of the matrix U depends on the current value of N when the expression defining U is executed.

```
N←7
U←(N,N)ρ(1,Nρ0)
U
```

```
1 0 0 0 0 0 0
0 1 0 0 0 0 0
0 0 1 0 0 0 0
0 0 0 1 0 0 0
0 0 0 0 1 0 0
0 0 0 0 0 1 0
0 0 0 0 0 0 1
```

EXERCISES

1. Given $V←3\ 5\ 9\ 1; M←4\ 4ρ\iota16; A←3\ 2\ 5ρ\iota30$. Evaluate the following:

A. $,M$ B. $,A$ C. $V*2$ D. $V,2*V$

2. Write an APL expression for the vector whose elements are:

A.   ⁻50 ⁻49 ⁻48 ... ⁻1 1 2 3 ... 50

3. A department store wishes to issue the following sales-analysis report.

Item Number	Cost Price	Selling Price	Number of Items Sold
1	19.60	31.12	1612
2	21.30	26.80	811
3	34.80	41.70	616
4	39.70	52.10	512
5	65.20	85.99	432

The body of the report may be thought of as a matrix M. Think of each row of the matrix as a vector. Using appropriate names, show how the matrix M may be produced by catenating the vectors.

4. Consider the partitioned matrix shown below. Show how the matrix may be formed form its partition by catenation. Choose an appropriate name for each submatrix.

```
1 0 0 | 0 0 1
0 1 0 | 0 1 0
0 0 1 | 1 0 0
-------+-------
0 0 1 | 1 0 0
0 1 0 | 0 1 0
1 0 0 | 0 0 1
```

5. Let:

$$X \leftarrow {}^-5, 3, 1, {}^-2, 4$$

$$Y \leftarrow 7, {}^-8, {}^-5, 1$$

Evaluate the following expressions:

A. X, Y

B. Y, X

C. $Y, (\iota 3), X$

6. Let V be a vector (make one up) such that $(\rho V) > 75$ and let A be a vector (make one up). Write an APL expression to insert A between the 63rd and 64th elements of V.

7. Given a vector V and two scalars J and K such that $(\rho V) > J + K$ write an APL expression which deletes the $(J+1)$ st through the $(J+K)$ st elements of V. Make up a vector and appropriate scalars.

9.1 INTRODUCTION

In Section 3.2 we noted that there are two modes of computation, but so far we have concentrated exclusively on one, the execution mode. For the most part, our primary concern has been with illustrating how the different primitive functions work and in using the computer as a kind of super desk calculator. This is all right, as far as it goes, but it does not go far enough.

Most of the applications that occur in science and engineering call for certain capabilities which we have so far not discussed. To understand what these capabilities are, consider any computation which is iterative, e.g., the numerical solution of a differential equation by the Runge-Kutta method or Newton's method for determining the roots of an equation. Algorithms for solving these problems require the same computation to be performed again and again until some specified set of conditions is met. It would be impractical and intolerable if each iteration required us to retype a sequence of statements. The manual intervention required would cancel out the speed with which the computer operates and limit its use as a tool.

Even if the computation were not iterative, it would be terribly inefficient to have to reenter the sequence of statements which defines some application every time we wanted that application executed. What we really would like to have is the capability of imposing some kind of structure or organization on a sequence of statements, numbering them, giving the sequence a name, and treating the name as a function symbol whose invocation causes the sequence of statements to be executed. What we also require is a means of executing any subsequence of statements as often as we like without the necessity of further intervention on our part.

In APL the kind of structure we are talking about is called a user-defined function. The anatomy and physiology of user-defined functions bear a strong resemblance to those of primitive functions. Taking the primitive functions as building blocks, each user can make

up functions he needs. In essence, each user has an infinite number
of functions available to him. This chapter is devoted to the mechanics of user-defined functions. We shall see how these functions are
constructed and how they can be modified, edited, and displayed.

9.2 FUNCTION HEADERS

Every user-defined function begins with a header line that describes
the syntax of the function. Each header line has one of the six forms
shown in Figure 9.2.1.

(1) ∇ *NAME*

(2) ∇ *NAME X*

(3) ∇Y *NAME X*

(4) $\nabla Z \leftarrow NAME$

(5) $\nabla Z \leftarrow NAME X$

(6) $\nabla Z \leftarrow Y$ *NAME X*

Fig. 9.2.1

Just as each primitive function is denoted by a function symbol,
so each user-defined function has a name. As with all variables, the
name must begin with an alphabetic character and may contain numerics and the underscore character but none of the other special
characters. The name chosen for the function must be one that is
not being used for some other variable in the workspace.

Every function header must begin with the inverted triangle ∇,
called delta, and must contain a name. The character ∇ causes the
computer to switch from the execution mode to the definition mode.
In the latter mode the sequence of commands that will follow the
header line is stored but not executed when the RETURN key is
pressed.

When we are through defining the function, we again type the
character delta. This closes the definition and causes the computer to

revert to the execution mode. Now that we have established what is common to every function header, let us proceed to examine some of the differences.

9.2.1 Monadic, Dyadic and Niladic Functions

The primitive functions have either one or two explicit arguments; a user-defined function may have zero, one, or two explicit arguments. Forms (2) and (5) in Figure 9.2.1 tell us that the function has one explicit argument. As with primitive monadic functions, the argument must appear to the right of the name. The letter X designates a dummy variable. When the function is invoked, the name of a variable to which a value has been assigned is substituted for X. In the body of the function there will be references to the variable denoted by X. Whatever is substituted for X when the function is invoked will be substituted uniformly for X in the body of the function.

In the case of a dyadic function, for example, (3) and (6), the two dummy variables X and Y straddle the function name. In the statement which invokes the function, variables to which a value has been assigned will be substituted for X and Y.

When no explicit arguments appear in the function header, e.g., (1) and (4), the arguments of the function may be thought of as constants. All the variables appearing in the body of the function will have to be assigned values prior to the time when the function is invoked.

The remaining differences in the function headers, i.e., between (1) and (3) and (2) and (4), will now be explained.

9.2.2 Explicit Results

Just as a primitive function may appear as part of a statement, so one user-defined function may appear in the body of another user-defined function.

For example, suppose we wish to define a function called DIFF for solving a differential equation. As part of this function we may wish to define another function, called INT, which performs numerical integration. The result produced by INT will be operated on by DIFF to produce the desired solution.

In order for the result produced by a user-defined function to be used as an argument within a statement, the header line must have one of the forms (4) through (6). The variable Z is a dummy variable, and the specification of Z in the body of the function makes the result produced by the function available to other functions. Somewhere in the body of the function, Z must be specified.

Functions of the form (1) through (3) must appear either by themselves in a statement or, if the statement is compound, as the last function to be executed.

The fact that a function may have 0, 1, or 2 arguments (three possibilities) and either 0 or 1 explicit result (two possibilities) accounts for the six different forms of the function header.

9.3 THE BODY OF THE FUNCTION

Once the header of the function has been typed and the RETURN key struck, the computer will repond with the character 1 enclosed in brackets, [1]. You must now type in the first statement in the function. When you press the RETURN key, this statement will be stored but not executed. The computer will now respond with [2], and you will then type in the next statement, if any. Because of the vast array of primitive functions available, many user functions will consist of a single statement. If the function has an explicit result, then Z will be specified in the very first statement. When you have typed your last statement and the computer responds, for example [6], you signal completion of the function by typing the character ∇, (Fig. 9.3.1). The second occurrence of this character causes the computer to revert to execution mode. The last statement of the function is the one numbered [5].

Let us look at some examples of functions.

In Figure 9.3.1, we see a function called RECT which transforms a given set of spherical coordinates (R, THETA, PHI) presented as a vector into the equivalent set of rectangular coordinates (X, Y, Z). The function RECT is an explicit monadic function. The dummy variable A is a vector variable whose components are the three spherical coordinates with the two angles THETA and PHI given in radians. The corresponding rectangular coordinates produced by the function are catenated in statement [5] to form a vector which is the explicit result produced by the function.

In Figure 9.3.2 we see another function, called DIST. This function computes the distance between two points whose coordinates are given in a spherical coordinate system. The function DIST makes use

```
     ∇  T←RECT A
[1]     X←A[1]×(1○A[2])×2○A[3]
[2]     TEMP←TEMP*2
[3]     Y←A[1]×(1○A[2])×1○A[3]
[4]     Z←A[1]×(2○A[2])
[5]     T←X,Y,Z
     ∇
[6]    ∇
```

Fig. 9.3.1

of the function RECT to convert the spherical coordinates to rectangular coordinates. The function DIST is a dyadic function whose dummy arguments, C and D, are vector variables representing the spherical coordinates of the two points. The distance between the points is printed out.

```
     ∇  C DIST D
[1]     TEMP←((RECT C)-(RECT D))*2
[2]     DISTANCE←(TEMP[1]+TEMP[2]+TEMP[3])*0.5
[3]     DISTANCE
     ∇
[4]    ∇
```

Fig. 9.3.2

9.4 EXECUTING A FUNCTION

A function is executed by a calling statement containing the name of the function. The syntax of the function in the calling statement must be identical with the syntax given in the function header. The delta character is omitted, and in the case of an explicit function, the dummy variable to which the result is assigned is also omitted. In particular, the dummy arguments must be replaced by constants or variables to which a value has been assigned.

For example, if we define variables S and T as

```
S←1,(○0.25),0.25
T←1,(○1.25),0.25
```

where S and T represent two points in a spherical coordinate system, we can compute the distance between these points by writing

```
      S DIST T
  2
```

Note that the syntax of the function DIST and that of the function RECT are identical with the syntax appearing in their respective function headers. When the function DIST is executed, the variables S and T are substituted for C and D uniformly.

If we write

```
      C←(2×RECT S)+1 1 2
      C
  2   2   3.414213562
```

we see that the result an explicit function produces can be used as the argument of another function in the same way as the result produced by a primitive function.

9.5 LOCAL AND GLOBAL VARIABLES

Let us take another look at the function RECT shown in Figure 9.3.1. The result produced by the function is assigned to the variable T in statement [5]. The values assigned to the variables X, Y, and Z may be thought of as intermediate results for which we no longer have any use once the function has been executed. As things stand, we have now introduced them into our workspace, reducing the amount of available space. Furthermore, if we had previously introduced variables X, Y, and Z, then in executing the function RECT, we would have unintentionally reassigned values to these variables. This is a rather unhappy state of affairs. It would certainly make things difficult if the name of a variable appearing in one function could not be used for a variable appearing in another.

Fortunately, there is an easy way out. The variables which are defined in the body of the function and which represent intermediate results can be declared to be local. When a variable is local, it exists only when the function is executed. A variable that is not local is said to be global. A global variable is accessible to everything in the workspace.

Since a local variable appearing in a function has no existence outside function execution, the same name can be used for local variables in different functions or for a local variable and a global variable.

Variables are made local to a function by naming them in the header of the function. Each local variable appears on the extreme right. The first such variable is separated from the rest of the header by a semicolon, and other local variables named in the header must also be separated by semicolons. The statement that calls for a function to be executed does not contain any references to local variables.

Suppose, e.g., we would like to make the variables X, Y, and Z in the function RECT local. We would then write the header

$T \leftarrow RECT\ A; X; Y; Z$

Suppose that, prior to executing this function, we have defined global variables X and Y in our workspace,

```
X←7
Y←3
```

We then issue the commands

```
        S←1 ,(0.25),(0.25)
        C← (2×RECT S)+1 1 2
        C
 2   2   3.414213562
```

The local variables X and Y defined in the body of RECT are dominant during function execution, but the global variables X and Y defined previously retain their value.

```
        X
7
        Y
3
```

If such global variables have not been defined, then any attempt to display X and Y will result in a value error because the local variables of the same name do not exist when the function is not being executed.

If a function called FUN with local variables A and B invokes
another function, FUN1, then the local variables of FUN are accessible to FUN1, provided that FUN1 has no local variables called A or
B. The statement also holds for any function called on by FUN1. If
either FUN or FUN1 has local variables A or B, then those local variables will be dominant when that function is being executed.

Local variables play an important role in making the same names
available to different functions and in helping to keep each user's workspace free of unwanted variables.

Apart from the fact that dummy variables may have their values
assigned at the time a function is to be executed, there is no distinc-
tion between dummy variables and local variables.

9.6 EDITING FUNCTIONS

In the process of constructing a user-defined function, it is normal to
make changes in the body of the function and often in the header as
well. In the natural sequence of events, certain lines will be modified,
others added, and some deleted from the function. It will be both necessary and desirable to display individual statements, as well as the
entire function.

All these operations come under the category of editing, and
every time we define a function we are sure to become involved with
editing operations. In this section we are going to learn how to carry
out the different editing operations available in APL.

Editing operations can take place only in the definition mode.
You will recall that the computer, at any instant, is either in the execution mode or in the definition mode awaiting a command at a particular statement number. In describing the various editing operations, we will have to take into account where the computer is at the
time we decide to carry out the operation. For purposes of illustra-
tion, we will use the function RECT shown in Figure 9.3.1.

9.6.1 Displaying Part or All of the Function

Before any changes are made in a function, it is good practice to look
at the line or lines that require change. Therefore we shall learn how
to display part or all of the function.

Suppose that we are in execution mode and we would like to display the function RECT. We write

∇ RECT[□]

The delta character puts us in definition mode, and since RECT has already been defined, the presence of the quad character, □ , enclosed in brackets means that the function is to be displayed. The sequence of events is shown in Figure 9.6.1.

```
        ∇RECT[□]
    ∇   T←RECT A  ;X ;Y ;Z
[1]     X←A[1]×(1○A[2])×2○A[3]
[2]     TEMP←TEMP*2
[3]     Y←A[1]×(1○A[2])×1○A[3]
[4]     Z←A[1]×(2○A[2])
[5]     T←X,Y,Z
    ∇
[6]     ∇   (typed in after the function is displayed)
```

Fig. 9.6.1

When the display is completed, the computer awaits input at the statement number after the last statement of the function, [6]. If we have no other changes to maek, we type the delta character, thus closing the function and putting us back in execution mode. The single command

∇RECT[□]∇

would have caused the computer to display the function and revert to execution mode.

If we are in definition mode, e.g., on line number 2, then we write

[2]   [□]

causing the function to be displayed and the computer to await input at statement 2. If there is nothing more to do, we type the delta character, closing the function and reverting to executing mode.

To display statement number N, we write

∇RECT [N□] or [N□]

depending on what mode we are in, and only that statement number will be displayed. The computer then awaits input at that statement number. Substituting 0 for N enables us to display the function header.

To display the function beginning with statement number N and continuing to the end, we write

$\nabla RECT[\Box N]$ or $[\Box N]$

When that part of the function has been displayed, the computer will await input at the statement after the last statement of the function, [6].

9.6.2 Adding, Inserting, Changing, or Deleting a Command

ADDING A COMMAND

If we are in execution mode, then writing ∇RECT will elicit the response [6]. The computer is now awaiting input at statement 6. You can now add as many statements as you like in the normal way.

If we happen to be at statement number 2 when we make the decision to add one or more commands, we override the current statement number, 2, by writing [6] followed by the statement we want to add. For example, suppose we decide to print the rectangular coordinates one at a time. If we are at statement number [2], we write [2] [6] X. The computer will respond with [7]. We can then write [7] Y. The computer will respond with [8], and we can then write [8] Z∇.

To make sure that all these changes have taken place properly, we can then display the function beginning with statement 6.

INSERTING A COMMAND

To insert a command, e.g., between statements 3 and 4, we override the current statement number by typing [3.1] followed by the command. Statement numbers up to four decimals [3.XXXX] are acceptable.

If we write [3.1] G←X+Y+Z, the computer will respond with [3.2]. Had we written [3.11] G← X+Y+Z, the computer would have responded with [3.12].

When in the execution mode, it is of course necessary to shift to the definition mode. Thus a statement is inserted between statement numbers 3 and 4 by writing

$\nabla RECT[3.1]$ $G{\leftarrow}X{+}Y{+}Z$

When we close the function by typing the delta character, all state-ments will be renumbered as integers. Had we added statements 6, 7, and 8 and inserted the statement indicated between statements 3 and 4 before closing the function, this is what we would have seen when it was next displayed.

```
        ∇ RECT[□]
    ∇    T←RECT A ;X ;Y ;Z
[1]     X←A[1]×(1○A[2])×2○A[3]
[2]     TEMP←TEMP*2
[3]     Y←A[1]×(1○A[2])×1○A[3]
[4]     G←X+Y+Z
[5]     Z←A[1]×(2○A[2])
[6]     T←X,Y,Z
[7]     X
[8]     Y
[9]     Z
    ∇
```

When the function is closed, integer statement numbers are reassigned beginning with 1 and continuing to the last statement.

CHANGING A COMMAND

To change an existing command, e.g., statement number 4, from the execution mode and return to the execution mode, we write

```
∇ RECT[4] T←Z,Y,X  ∇
```

If we are in the definition mode at statement 2 and we want to re-main in that mode, we write

```
[2] [4] T←Z,Y,X
```

DELETING A COMMAND

To delete a command, we proceed as though we are going to change it. Instead of introducing the new command, we hit the ATTN key, followed as usual by the RETURN. For example, if we want to delete statement 2 of RECT and we are in execution mode, we write ∇ RECT[2] ATTN. In definition mode we override the current state-ment with [2] ATTN. In either case, the computer responds by await-ing input at the next highest statement number, [3]. When the function is closed, the deleted lines no longer exist, and the statements in the body of the function will be renumbered in sequence.

9.7 LINE EDITING

In addition to the editing operations we have described, there are editing features which are particularly useful when we want to change some part of a statement or add to it.

Suppose that in defining the function RECT, we had originally typed statement 1 as follows:

[1] $X \leftarrow A[1] \div (10A[2]) \times 20B[3]$

By looking at statement [1] of the current version of RECT, we can see that there are three errors present. Looking from right to left, we see that the expression 2oB[3] should really be 2oA[3]. The character B should be A. The expression (10A[2]) should be (1oA[2]). We inadvertently typed a 0 for o. Finally, the division symbol, ÷, should have been the multiplication symbol, ×.

The replacement of o by 0 and A by B would be detected when we tried to execute the function since both lead to errors. The other mistake would be discovered sooner or later when we realized that the results produced by the function were incorrect. If we are fortunate, we may notice these mistakes before we proceed too far. In any case, we must take some kind of corrective action. If we attempt to retype the statement, we run the risk of making additional errors, as well as doing a lot of unnecessary work. This would be all the more true if statement 2 were a long line, say, 120 characters. Line editing makes it easy to change those things and only those things that are wrong.

To initiate line editing we type

[N☐K]

where N is the number of the statement to be edited, and K is the number of the first character in error, counting from the left margin. Suppose that we are attempting to correct line 1 of RECT and we type

[1☐6]

This is what happens. First, statement 1 is displayed.

[1] $X \leftarrow A[1] \div (10A[2]) \times 20B[3]$

The carriage moves up one line and is positioned under the character 6 spaces from the left. The integer K should correspond to the first character, counting from the left, that requires changing. Since it is often inconvenient to count and determine what the position of that character is, we make a guess at what K should be. By using the SPACE or BACKSPACE bar, we reposition the carriage so that it is under the proper character. In our example we would move the carriage seven spaces to the right. The carriage is now positioned as follows:

[1] $X \leftarrow A[1] \div (10\ A[2]) \times 2 \circ B[3]$

DELETING A CHARACTER

To delete a character, we key in a slash, /, below it—one slash for every character that requires deletion. When a character is deleted, the space occupied by it disappears. Since we want to get rid of the ÷ symbol, we put a slash below it.

[1] $X \leftarrow A[1] \div (10\ A[2]) \times 2 \circ B[3]$
           /

INSERTING A CHARACTER

In order to replace the character ÷ by ×, we must provide a space for it. Therefore we type a 1 under the character (immediately to the right). The digits 1 to 9 specify how many blank spaces are to be added to the left. The alphabetic character A denotes 5 spaces, B denotes 10 spaces, etc. The number of characters that can be typed depends on the space remaining on the line, i.e., the width of the line less the number of columns used. Since we have only 1 character to insert, we type a 1.

[1] $X \leftarrow A[1] \div (10 A[2]) \times 2 \circ B[3]$
            /1

When we have deleted all the characters that require deletion and left spaces for those that need to be inserted, we will have

```
[1]     X←A[1]÷(10A[2])×20B[3]
          /1 /1          /1
```

We then press the RETURN key. The line is again displayed, now without those characters that have been deleted and with the number of spaces between characters that have been requested. The computer will position the carriage to the first blank space counting from the left.

```
[1]     X←A[1]   (1 A[2])×20 [3]
              ___↑
```

We now type the character × in the first blank space and fill in the rest of the blanks with the appropriate characters. If we wish, we can also add to the line. The actual order in which the blank spaces are filled does not matter. Furthermore, if we make typing mistakes when inserting characters, they can be corrected in the usual way, but we will have to retype everything to the right of the character corrected. When we have filled in all the blank spaces, the line will be

```
[1]     X←A[1]×(10A[2])×20A[3]
```

When the RETURN key is pressed, the line as it now appears will be the new statement 1.

The function header can be edited in the same way. It is referred to as line 0.

The statement number itself may be modified. Suppose, for example, we want to add to RECT a statement numbered 6 that is identical with statement 1. We write

```
[1□1]
```

causing line 1 to be displayed, the paper moved up a line, and the carriage positioned under the character [.

We then delete the character 1 and key in a 1 underneath the character], so that the line appears as follows:

```
[2]     [1□1]
[1]     X←A[1]×(10A[2])×20A[3]      (displayed)
 /1                                 (type in)
[ ]     X←A[1]×(10A[2])×20A[3]      (displayed)
```

Now we type in a 6 and press the RETURN key. Statement 1 remains as it is, and a new statement is added to the function definition.

ERRORS

If you fail to insert the proper number of spaces and overstrike a character, a character error will result. For example,

```
[7]    [1□12]
[1]    X←A[1]×(10A[2])×20A[3]
                                 /
[1]    X←A[1]×(10A[2])×20Aβ]
CHARACTER ERROR
[1]    X←A[1]×(10A[2])×20A
                              ∧
```

When the error occurs, editing is inhibited and it is necessary to begin all over again.

An error report will also be given if you attempt to edit a function header so that it is syntactically incorrect or assign a name to the function which is already in use in the workspace.

ADDING TO A LINE

If you are editing a line solely for the purpose of adding to it, wait until the line is displayed and position the carriage at the end of the line for an addition. For example,

```
[7]   [1□12]
[1]  X←A[1]×(10A[2])×20A[3]
     ─────────────↑
```

TERMINATING EDITING

Apart from the normal way of terminating, editing can be halted by striking the ATTN key while the line is being printed out or, as mentioned previously, by causing a character error.

9.8 BRANCHING

In the introduction we noted that many algorithms involve iteration, i.e., going through a well-defined sequence of computations many times until some condition is met. For example, to solve the equation

$$f(x) = 0$$

by the Newton–Raphson method, we make an initial guess x_0, and use it to make a new estimate, x_1, defined by

$$x_1 = x_0 - \frac{f(x_0)}{f'(x_0)}$$

In general, we have

$$x_n = x_{n-1} - \frac{f(x_{n-1})}{f'(x_{n-1})}$$

We might decide to terminate the process when two successive estimates differ in absolute value by some specified amount. Clearly it seems natural to regard the algorithm as one in which a well-defined set of computations is performed over and over again with a different set of numbers.

In the user–defined function RECT, statements are executed sequentially and the function terminates after statement 4 is executed. By branching we mean specifying what statement is going to be executed next. There are really two kinds of branching, unconditional and conditional. Unconditional branching specifies the number of the next statement to be executed. Conditional branching specifies the next statement to be executed if some logical relationship holds. In APL, branching is carried out by a primitive function.

9.8.1 The Primitive Branching Function

Branching is carried out by means of the monadic primitive function denoted by the character →. If the user function H contains a statement of the form →S, where S is any APL expression, an action will result which depends on the value of S. The rules are as follows:

1. If the value of the expression is a scalar integer that lies within the range of the statement numbers of the function, then statement number S will be executed next.

2. If S lies outside the range of the function, the execution of the function terminates, that is, →0. Since 0 is the number assigned to the function header, and since the function header is not an executable statement, branching to statement number 0 always terminates execution of the function.

3.   In the event there is no argument after the branching function,
→, then the function H will terminate, and furthermore, if there are
functions F, G, etc., such that F invokes G, which invokes H, then
F and G will also be terminated.

4.   If the evaluation of S produces a vector, then the first component
of the vector determines what action is to be taken. When the vector
is empty, the statement executed is the one immediately following the
branching instruction.

   Conditional branching requires the introduction of an additional
primitive function, which is dealt with in greater detail in Section 14.3.
The primitive function we need is called compression and denoted by
the symbol /. When we write

   $→L/G$

L must be a logical expression, i.e., an expression consisting of a
scalar 1 or 0 or a vector of ones and zeros; G is an expression whose
value is interpreted as a statement number. In the event that either
L or G is a vector, the other is extended to the same length.

   The components of L where a 1 appears select the corresponding
components of G. For example, suppose that we have

   [7] $→((X+Y)>7)/START+2×M$

This is how such a statement is interpreted. The value of the expression START+2×M is computed. If the value of ((X+Y)>7) is 1, then
the branch will be to the statement whose number is the value of
START+2×M. Otherwise, the branch is vacuous, and statement number 8 will be executed next.

   The usual way in which we use the conditional branching statement is to set up a logical relationship such that when the logical relationship holds, we branch and perform some sequence of computations. When the relationship fails, we continue in sequence with a different series of computations. For example, in Newton's method,
which we discussed earlier, we could define two variables XNEW and
XOLD which represent the last two estimates of the solution of the
equation. Suppose that we also define a variable EPSILON, to which
some number is assigned. We shall terminate Newton's algorithm
whenever the relationship

$(|XNEW-XOLD)<EPSILON$

holds.

In our user-defined function which implements the algorithm, we might have a statement of the form

$\rightarrow((|XOLD-XNEW)<EPSILON)/0$

and this would accomplish our objective.

Conditional branching gives us flexibility in planning the logic of our problem. For example, let L be a logical expression. Suppose that we want to branch to the statement defined by the variable S when L has a value of 1 and to the statement defined by the variable T when L has a value of 0. We can accomplish this goal by the statement

$\rightarrow(L,\sim L)/S,T$

Or suppose that L1 and L2 and L3 are mutually exclusive logical expressions which determine branches to statements S1 and S2 and S3, respectively. We can accomplish this by writing

$\rightarrow(L1, L2, L3)/S1, S2, S3$

The possibilities are limitless, and as we master some of the more sophisticated primitive functions, which will be introduced in subsequent chapters, we will be in an even better position to take advantage of the flexibility this kind of branching affords us.

9.8.2 Statement Labels

When you branch to a statement, whether conditionally or unconditionally, i.e.,

$[5]\rightarrow START+2$

or

$\rightarrow((J\neq 7)\vee(K=9))/21$

you must remember that if the function is redefined so that the statement you want to branch to has a different statement number, then your branch command will have to be revised. For example, if by deleting a statement we cause the statement numbered 21 to become

20, then the second branch command above will no longer be correct. The insertion of a statement between statements 20 and 21 would also force us to revise our branch command.

To avoid this kind of problem, each APL statement may be given a line label. In essence, a line label is a name, given in the same way a name is given to any variable. However, a line label precedes the command and is separated from it by a colon. Suppose, for example, we give statement number 21 the line label NEXT. This is how statement 21 might appear.

[21] $NEXT : J \leftarrow J * K + L \times {}^{-}1 + U$

Instead of writing

$\rightarrow ((J \neq 7) \vee (K = 9)) / 21$

we would write

[7] $\rightarrow ((J \neq 7) \vee (K = 9)) / NEXT$

Redefining the function so that statement 21 becomes statement 26 will not affect the branch command in statement 7 because the value of the line label NEXT becomes the value of the line it is associated with when the function is closed. Line labels act as local constants and have no value when the function is not being executed. Line labels also serve another purpose. The use of mnemonics for names makes it easier to understand what different parts of the function are doing and how the parts fit together. Therefore they offer a means for providing a certain amount of self-documentation.

9.9 RECURSIVE FUNCTIONS

By a recursive function we mean one which is defined so that its name appears in the body of the function definition. To illustrate this concept consider a simple function, the factorial function. Let k be an integer greater than or equal to zero. Then the expression k! means

$$k \times (k - 1) \times (k - 2) \times (k - 3) \ldots$$

that is, the product of the first k integers. Now suppose

$$k! = f(k) = k \times f(k - 1) \tag{1}$$

$$f(k - 1) = (k - 1) \times f(k - 2) \tag{2}$$

$$f(k - 2) = (k - 2) \times f(k - 3) \tag{3}$$

$$\vdots \qquad \vdots \qquad \vdots$$

$$f(0) = 1$$

Many functions are defined recursively because it is a natural way to
look at them and is often advantageous from a computing standpoint.
APL permits a function to be defined recursively. For example, consider the following APL definition of the factorial function given by (1).

```
        ∇FACTORIAL[☐]
      ∇ Z←FACTORIAL N
[1]     →(N≠0)/NEXT
[2]     →0,Z←1
[3]     NEXT:Z←N×FACTORIAL(N-1)
      ∇
[4]     ∇
```

When the function is invoked the multiplication specified in statement
number   does not take place until all of the arguments have been obtained. At this point, the results of the above equations are utilized
in reverse order, i.e., the last equation is substituted into the next to
last equation, etc. From a computational standpoint, this can be a
very powerful technique. As with most things, however, there is a
tradeoff. In this case, we gain efficiency at the price of storage because all of the arguments necessary to compute the function must be
retained. Each call to the function may be thought of as initiating a
new level of prodedure to which an argument is passed. When the
final argument is passed, results are returned in reverse order. This
list reference process is referred to as a last-in/first-out list (LIFO).

9.10 ERASING FUNCTIONS

Suppose that you have no further use for a function and that it is clut-
tering up the workspace. What can be done to remove it? The systems command

```
    )ERASE F
```

will remove the function F from your workspace. Any attempt to invoke F once it has been erased will result in a value error.

9.11 LOCKING FUNCTIONS

If the del character in the function header is overstruck with the tilde,
⍫, the function is locked. This means it can no longer be displayed
or edited in any way. Any attempt to edit it will result in an error.
However, it may continue to be used in the normal way. Locking is
an irreversible process; once locked, a function cannot be opened.
The reason for locking a function is to allow its use while keeping the
body of the function proprietary. In an examination, e.g., a teacher

might permit a student to use it, but at the same time the proprietary information it contains would be protected.

9.12 FUNCTION COMMENTS

When the first character of a statement is ⍝, formed by overstriking the character above the C on the APL keyboard with the small circle above the J, the statement is interpreted as a comment, and no attempt is made to execute it. Comments make a function easier to understand and use, especially for someone who is not totally familiar with it. They can be used to document the function or to provide reference material or any other information that the user cares to impart.

All lines containing comments must begin with the character ⍝. For example, Figure 9.9.3 shows the function RECT. Statements 1 to 3 are comments and provide information about the function.

```
      ∇ RECT[□]
      ∇ T←RECT A ;X ;Y ;Z
[1□] ⍝THE FUNCTION RECT CONVERTS A GIVEN SET OF SPHERICAL COORDINAT
      S
[2]  ⍝ IN THE FORM (R,α,ω) TO THE EQUIVALENT CARTESIAN COORDINATES
     (X,Y,Z)
[3]  ⍝THE ANGLES α AND ω MUST BE GIVEN IN RADIANS.
[4]  X←A[1]×(1○A[2])×2○A[3]
[5]  TEMP←TEMP*2
[6]  Y←A[1]×(1○A[2])×1○A[3]
[7]  Z←A[1]×(2○A[2])
[8]  T←X,Y,Z
      ∇
[9]  ∇
```

Fig. 9.9.3

9.13 COMPLEX ARITHMETIC

The implementation of complex arithmetic in APL is easily handled by means of user-defined functions. Arrays of complex data can be represented in a variety of ways, but here we shall illustrate a relatively straightforward method.

Given an array A of complex data of rank n, we shall represent the data by means of an array B of rank n+1. The array B, looked at from the first coordinate, will consist of two arrays of rank n, representing the real and complex coefficients, respectively. For example, given the vector of complex data,

(1+2i, 3–6i, 8+4i)

we will represent it by the matrix

$$\begin{pmatrix} 1 & 3 & 8 \\ 2 & -6 & 4 \end{pmatrix}$$

Calling this matrix A, we specify it by

$A \leftarrow 2\ 3\ \rho\ 1\ 3\ 8\ 2\ {}^-6\ 4$

The matrix B of complex numbers,

$$\begin{pmatrix} 3+5i & 1+2i & 3-5i \\ 9-2i & 3+0i & 8+i \\ 6+4i & 2+8i & 9+7i \end{pmatrix}$$

would be specified as

$B \leftarrow 2\ 3\ 3\rho 3\ 1\ 3\ 9\ 3\ 8\ 6\ 2\ 9\ 5\ 2\ {}^-5\ {}^-2\ 0\ 1\ 4\ 8\ 7$

With this representation scheme it is an easy matter to construct functions which carry out arithmetic operations on arrays of complex data (see Exercise 11).

EXERCISES

1. Find the errors, if any, in the following function headers.

    A. $\Delta Z \leftarrow ARC\ A$ B. $\nabla XANGLE$ C. $B\ SIDE\ A$

    D. $\nabla Z \leftarrow 1ANGLE\ B$ E. $Z \leftarrow TRIG\ A$ F. $\nabla QUAD$

2. Write a function to do the following:
Given a triangle ABC,

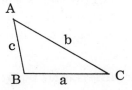

assume that you are given the length of the sides a,b,c. Compute the sine, cosine, and tangent of each angle, and print it. Find the angles A,B,C in degrees and the area of the triangle, and print both. Make use of the following formulas.

3. Define an explicit monodic function called $\nabla Z \leftarrow D\ PRIMES\ N$ which produces as a result all primes between the integers $M\ AND\ N$ exclusively where $1 \leq N$.

4. Write a function to determine whether two numbers are relatively prime, i.e., have no common factors except 1. Print any common factors other than 1.

5. A married person with a monthly payroll period has Federal withholding tax according to the Percentage Withholding Table.

PERCENTAGE WITHHOLDING TABLES

MONTHLY Payroll Period

(b) MARRIED Person —

If the amount of wages is:		The amount of income tax to be withheld shall be:	
Not over $88		0	
Over—	*But not over —*		*of excess over—*
$88	—$183	14%	—$88
$183	—$333	$13.30 plus 17%	—$183
$333	—$708	$38.80 plus 16%	—$333
$708	—$1,167....	$98.80 plus 19%	—$708
$1,167	—$1,667....	$186.01 plus 21%	—$1,167
$1,667	....	$291.01 plus 25%	—$1,667

Write an APL function to compute his or her tax.

6. Write a function which simulates tossing a coin N times where N is a number specified by the user. Let the explicit result of the function be a two-element vector containing the number of heads and tails respectively produced in the N tosses.

7. The method of Runge–Kutta for solving the differential equation

$y = f'(x,y)$ with initial value (x_0, y_0)

with $x_n = x_{n-1} + h$ is as follows: Let y_n be the solution corresponding to x_n. The point (x_{n+1}, y_{n+1}) is obtained by the following steps.

$$k_1 = hf(x_n, y_n)$$

$$k_2 = hf(x_n + h/2, y_n + k_1/2)$$

$$k_3 = hf(x_n + h/2, y_n + k_2/2)$$

$$k_4 = hf(x_n + h, y_n + k_3)$$

$$y_{n+1} = y_n + 1/6(k_1 + 2k_2 + 2k_3 + k_4)$$

Write a function which implements the Runge-Kutta method and calculate the solutions of the following differential equations.

A. $y' = xy$
   $x = 0.5$; $y = .8825$; $h = .01$
   Find solutions for $x = .6$ to $x = 1.0$ inclusive.

B. $y' = 2y/x$
   $x = 1$; $y = 1$; $h = .1$
   Find solutions for $x = 1.1$ to $x = 2.0$ inclusive.

8. The Chebyshev polynomials of the first kind are given by

$$T_n(x) = \cos(n\cos^{-1} x)$$

Write a function which evaluates these polynomials using the recursion formula

$$T_{n+1}(x) - 2xT_n(x) + T_{n-1}(x) = 0$$

9. A step function $F(x)$ is defined in the following way.

$F(x)$	x
0	$x \le -10$
0.25	$-10 < x \le 25$
0.50	$25 < x \le 41$
0.75	$41 < x \le 92$
1.0	$92 < x$

Define a function called FUN having one argument x which gives $F(x)$ as an explicit result.

10. Using the scheme for representing complex numbers (Section 9.13), write functions to implement the following.

    A. Complex addition
    B. Complex subtraction
    C. Complex multiplication
    D. Extraction of the modulus of a complex number

10.1 INTRODUCTION

In Chapter 6 we saw how the primitive dyadic functions were extended to handle arrays of data. It turned out that when the arguments of these functions were conformable arrays, execution of the functions took place over corresponding components of the arrays. In many applications this is exactly the kind of thing we want to do. Nevertheless, so simple a problem as summing the elements of a vector does not involve addition of corresponding components of different arrays but rather addition of the components within an array. What we really want is a means of extending the primitive dyadic functions to operate internally over the elements of an array using the array name as a variable. In APL this operation is called reduction. The reason for its name will become apparent later.

In this chapter we are going to take a close look at the reduction operator, denoted by d/, where d is one of the functions in Figure 10.2.1. We shall see how it is applied first to vectors, and then to matrices and arrays of higher rank. Finally, some special cases will be considered. To illustrate the utility of the reduction operator, we shall consider various applications.

10.2 PERMISSIBLE FUNCTIONS FOR THE REDUCTION OPERATOR

The only functions which can be used in connection with the reduction operator are those shown in Figure 10.2.1.

10.3 REDUCTION OF VECTORS

Let d denote a permissible function for reduction, and let V be a vector of dimension N. If we write

$S \leftarrow \text{d}/V$

Function symbol	Name	Function symbol	Name
+	plus	∧	and
-	minus	∨	or
×	times	⩟	nand
÷	divide	⩒	nor
⌈	maximum	<	less
⌊	minimum	≤	not greater
*	power	=	equal
⊕	logarithm	≥	not less
|	residue	>	greater
!	binomial coefficient	≠	not equal
o	circular		

Fig. 10.2.1 Primitive dyadic functions

what we are in fact saying is

$S \leftarrow V[1]dV[2]dV[3]d.....dV[N]$

where S is a scalar whose value depends on V and d.

EXAMPLE 1

Sum the components of a vector A.

$A \leftarrow 2\ 3\ 9\ 11$
+/A
25

We see that +/A is equivalent to ΣA.

EXAMPLE 2

Obtain the product of the components of A.

```
        ×/A
594
```

We see that ×/A is equivalent to ΠA.

The components of A must lie in the domain of the function chosen. Observe that the reduction of a vector results in a scalar.

EXAMPLE 3

```
        ∧/A
DOMAIN ERROR
        ∧/A
        ∧
```

The logical 'and' function requires a vector of ones and zeros as its argument. Since A contains components which are not ones and zeros, an error results.

10.4 THE REDUCTION OF MATRICES

If the reduction operator is applied to a matrix M,

```
    T←d/M
```

then reduction takes place over each row of M and the result is a vector T.

EXAMPLE 1

```
        M←3 3ρ?ι9
        M

    1   2   1
    1   3   5
    1   4   1
        T← +/M
        T
    4   9   6
```

EXAMPLE 2

To get the maximum element in each row, we write

```
      ⌈/M
  2   5  4
```

To reduce the columns of M, we write [1] M instead of M

```
      +/[1]M
  3   9  7
      ×/[1]M
  1  24  5
```

When no index appears, reduction takes place over the last dimension of M, which for a matrix means over the columns (row reduction).

10.5 REDUCTION OVER ARRAYS OF HIGHER RANK

In general, the reduction operator takes the form shown in Figure 10.5.1.

$$T\leftarrow d/[I]R$$

Fig. 10.5.1

Let R be a given array of rank two or greater, and let I denote a co-ordinate of R. The rank of array T is one less than that of R and is obtained by reducing the function d over the coordinate I. The first coordinate is labeled zero or one, depending on the setting of the origin. When no coordinate appears in the reduction statement, the last coordinate is implied.

EXAMPLE 1

```
      R←2 2 3ρ(12?100)
      R

  59  32  41
   7  15  45

  86  33  54
  28   9  22
      T←⌊/[2]R
      T

   7  15  41
  28   9  22
```

Since R is an array of rank three, the result of reducing it is an array
of rank two, or a matrix. It is not difficult to see what happens in
higher dimensions.

10.6 SOME SPECIAL CASES

The observant student will be wondering what happens if we attempt to
apply reduction to a scalar or to a vector with a single component or
perhaps to the null vector. In the first two cases the result is a
scalar.

10.6.1 Reduction of a Scalar or a Single-Element Vector

EXAMPLE 1

The reduction of a scalar results in the same scalar.

$$A \leftarrow 3$$
$$+/A$$
3

EXAMPLE 2

The reduction of a single-element vector results in a scalar of the
same magnitude.

$$A \leftarrow ,3$$
$$\rho A$$
1

$$T \leftarrow +/A$$
$$T$$
3

$$\rho T$$

10.6.2 The Identity Element

With the empty vector the result returned is the identity element of
the primitive function being reduced if the function has an identity
element.

By an identity element for a primitive function d, we mean a
scalar I which satisfies one of the following:

1. IdN is equal to N for every N in the domain of d; or
2. NdI is equal to N for every N in the domain of d.

If (1) is satisfied, we say that I is a left identity. If (2) is satisfied, we say that I is a right identity. For example, the number one is the identity element for multiplication since for any number N,

$1 \times N$ is equal to N
$N \times 1$ is equal to N

For subtraction, zero is the identity element since for every real N,

$N - 0$ is equal to N

In this case zero is a right identity only. Not every function has an identity element. Furthermore, some functions have one but not both identity elements. Figure 10.6.1 shows the identity elements for the primitive dyadic functions.

Dyadic function		Identity element	Left-right
Times	×	1	L R
Plus	+	0	L R
Divide	÷	1	R
Minus	−	0	R
Power	*	1	R
Logarithm	●		None
Maximum	⌈	‾7.237...E75	L R
Minimum	⌊	7.237...E75	L R
Residue	|	0	L
Circle	○		None
Out of	!	1	L
Or	∨	0	L R
And	∧	1	L R
Nor	⩑		None
Nand	⩒		None
Equal	=	1	L R
Not equal	≠	0	L R
Greater	>	0	R
Not less	≥	1	R
Less	<	0	L
Not greater	≤	1	L

(For Equal through Not greater: Apply for logical arguments only)

Fig. 10.6.1 (Reprinted by permission from APL\360 Users Manual, copyright 1968, 1969 by International Business Machines Corporation)

EXERCISES

1. Fourier analysis. Consider the classical problem of representing a function which is known at a discrete number of equally spaced points by a finite Fourier series.

Assume that an arbitrary function f(x) can be written in the form

$$f(x) = \frac{a_0}{2} + \sum_{k=1}^{N-1} \left(a_k \cos \frac{\pi}{N}kx + b_k \sin \frac{\pi}{N}kx \right) + \frac{a_n}{2} \cos \pi x \qquad (1)$$

It turns out that[1]

$$a_k = \frac{1}{N} \sum_{x=0}^{2N-1} f(x) \cos \frac{\pi}{N}kx \qquad (k = 0, 1, 2, \ldots, N)$$

$$\qquad (2)$$

$$b_k = \frac{1}{N} \sum_{x=0}^{2N-1} f(x) \sin \frac{\pi}{N}kx \qquad (k = 1, 2, \ldots, N - 1)$$

With the reduction operator it is an easy matter to construct a user–defined function which calculates the Fourier coefficients of a given function. Assume the values of the function are given as vector V. Write a function which calculates the Fourier coefficients and prints them out. Assume that b_0 and b_k are zero.

2. The function shown in the figure is a square wave of amplitude h and period 2T.

The Fourier series coefficients may be obtained analytically and are given by

$$g(x) = \frac{4h}{\pi} \sum_{n=1,3,\ldots}^{\infty} \frac{1}{n} \sin \left(\frac{n\pi x}{T} \right)$$

---

[1]   Numerical Methods for Scientists and Engineers, R. Hamming, McGraw–Hill, 1962, pp. 67–71.

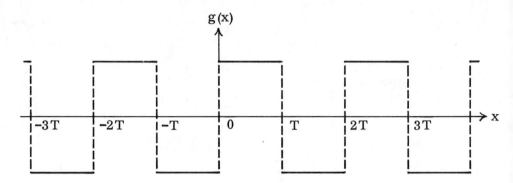

Figure for Exercise 10.2 The square wave of amplitude h and period 2T

Let $g(x) =$ 0 at $y = 0, 20$

$g(x) =$ 1 at $y = 1, 2, 3, \ldots, 19$

$g(x) = -1$ at $y = 21, 22, \ldots, 39$

Use your program to obtain the Fourier series coefficients.

3. The Lagrange interpolating polynomial[2] is a polynomial of the form

$$I(x) = y_0 L_0^{(n)}(x) + y_1 L_1^{(n)}(x) + \cdots + y_n L_n^{(n)}(x)$$

where

$$L_j^{(n)}(x) = \frac{(x - x_0)(x - x_1)(x - x_2) \cdots (x - x_n)}{(x_j - x_0)(x_j - x_{j-1})(x_j - x_{j+1})(x_j - x_n)}$$

It is a polynomial of degree n which takes on the values $y_0, y_1, \ldots, y_n$ at $x_0, x_1, \ldots, x_n$. It has the advantage that the coefficients do not depend on the y's and also that the coefficients are invariant under the linear transformation x=hz+c, where z is a new variable. Construct a function called INTERPOLY which implements the Lagrange interpolating polynomial. Make use of the reduction operator.

[2]   Numerical Calculus, W. E. Milne, Princeton University Press, 1949, pp. 83–88.

4. Let X and Y be two points represented in coordinate form as $(x_1, x_2, \ldots, x_n)$ and $(y_1, y_2, \ldots, y_n)$. The distance between X and Y, $d(X, Y)$, may be defined in different ways. Write an APL expression for each of the following definitions of distance, assigning the value to a variable called DIST.

    A. $d(X, Y) = \sqrt{\Sigma (x_i - y_i)^2}$

    B. $d(X, Y) = (\Sigma |x_i - y_i|^p)^{1/p} \quad p > 1$

    C. $d(X, Y) = \max_{1 \leqslant i \leqslant n} |x_i - y_i|$

5. Let M be a matrix defined as

$$M = \begin{pmatrix} 2 & 7 & 5 \\ 5 & 2 & 1 \\ 7 & 7 & 9 \end{pmatrix}$$

Compute

    A. +/M   B. ×/M   C. |/M   D. ⌈/M   E. ⌊/M

6. A department store buys and sells five items at the prices shown in the following table.

Item	Cost Prices	Selling Price	Number Items Sold
1	12.40	14.25	212
2	18.21	21.74	611
3	62.50	78.61	74
4	112.30	145.82	12
5	1060.00	1200.00	86

Write APL expressions to do the following:

A. compute the percent of profit on each item;

B. compute the average profit in percent;

7. Let $r_1, r_2, \ldots, r_n$ be a series of n real numbers. The arithmetic, geometric, and harmonic mean of these numbers is given by

A. $A = \dfrac{r_1 + r_2 + \cdots + r_n}{n}$

B. $G = \sqrt[n]{r_1 r_2 \ldots r_n}$

C. $H = \dfrac{n}{\dfrac{1}{r_1} + \dfrac{1}{r_2} + \cdots + \dfrac{1}{r_n}}$

Write an APL expression for each of these means, assigning the values to variables A, G, and H, respectively. Assume the real numbers are the components of a vector R.

8. Given two vectors of real numbers, R equal $(r_1, r_2, \ldots, r_n)$ and S equal $(s_1, s_2, \ldots, s_n)$, write APL expressions for the following well-known inequalities.

A. The triangle inequality

$$|r_1 + r_2 + \cdots + r_n| \leq |r_1| + |r_2| + \cdots + |r_n|$$

B. The Cauchy–Schwarz inequality

$$|r_1 s_1 + r_2 s_2 + \cdots + r_n s_n|^2 \leq (|r_1|^2 + \cdots + |r_n|^2)(|s_1|^2 + \cdots + |s_n|^2)$$

C. Holder's inequality

$$|r_1 s_1 + \cdots + r_n s_n| \leq (|r_1|^p + |r_2|^p + \cdots + |r_n|^p)^{1/p} \, (|s_1|^p + \cdots + |s_n|^p)^{1/p}$$

D. Chebyshev's inequality

if $r_1 \geq r_2 \geq \cdots \geq r_n$ and $s_1 \geq s_2 \geq \cdots \geq s_n$

$$(r_1 + r_2 + \cdots + r_n)(s_1 + s_2 + \cdots + s_n) \leq n(r_1 s_1 + r_2 s_2 + \cdots + r_n s_n)$$

E. Minkowski's inequality

if $r_1, r_2, \ldots, r_n, s_1, s_2, \ldots, s_n$ are > 0 and $p > 1$

$$((r_1 + s_1)^p + (r_2 + s_2)^p + \cdots + (r_n + s_n)^p)^{1/p} \leq (r_1{}^p + \cdots + r_n{}^p)^{1/p}$$
$$+ (s_1 + \cdots + s_n{}^p)^{1/p}$$

9. Let A and B be vectors. Write APL expressions which yield the value 1 when the following statements are true and 0 when they are

false.

    A. Every component of A is greater than the corresponding component of B.

    B. At least one component of A is greater than the corresponding component of B.

    C. At least one component of A and one of B are identical.

10. Let A and B be matrices of the same dimension. Determine the number of corresponding components of A and B which are identical.

11. Let M be a matrix. Write an APL expression for each of the following.

    A. The sum of the row components of M

    B. The maximum element in the second column

    C. The minimum element in the first two rows of M

12. If a function $F(x)$ is evaluated at equally spaced intervals h, then Simpson's rule says that the integral $\int_a^b F(x)dx$ may be approximated by

$$S = \frac{h}{3} (y_0 + 4y_1 + 2y_2 + 4y_3 + 2y_4 + \cdots + y_{n-1})$$

where $y_i = F(x_i)$, $(x_i = a + ih)$, $h = (b - a)/h$, and the number of ordinates is odd; the weight of the first and the last ordinate is 1, and the weights of the others are alternately 4 and 2. Write a function which implements Simpson's method. Assume that the function values y_1, y_2 are given in the form of a vector and that h is also given. Evaluate.

    A. $\int_0^1 (1 + x^4) \, dx$, $h = 0.1$

    B. $\int_0^{2.8} \sqrt{1 + x^3} \, dx$, $h = 0.2$

13. Given n numbers x_1, x_2, ..., x_n, the mean m and variance v of these numbers are defined as:

$$m = \frac{1}{n} \sum_{i=1}^{n} x_i$$

$$v = \frac{1}{n-1} \sum_{i=1}^{n} (x_i - m)^2$$

Assuming the numbers x_1, x_2, ..., x_n are given as a vector v, write an APL expression which computes both the mean and the variance.

14. A class of students earned the following grades for five examinations taken in a history course.

Name	Examination Scores				
Atwood	60	75	84	71	64
Barker	50	70	62	55	63
Clancy	75	80	73	62	40
Darrow	20	50	30	40	60
Fisher	30	55	65	75	65
Jones	90	95	92	89	97
Klein	80	70	65	82	75
Martin	69	75	73	81	80
Osgood	75	78	80	76	74
Richards	60	65	72	74	76
Stark	63	78	72	64	76
Taylor	94	92	88	97	100

Assuming that the grade table is given as a matrix M such that the grades appear in columns 1 to 5 write an APL expression to determine each student's average grade. Do the same thing assuming that the grades are weighted by the following percentages 15, 15, 20, 30, 30.

INNER AND OUTER PRODUCTS

11.1 INTRODUCTION

We have already discussed two classes of operators which facilitate the handling of arrays of data: (1) component by component operation; and (2) reduction. In this chapter we introduce two more classes of operators, the inner and outer product. The inner product, as we shall see, is a generalization of the concept of matrix multiplication, which is itself a combination of component by component operations and reduction.

We shall see that the inner product operator, like the reduction operator, is confined to primitive dyadic functions. In addition to this restriction, arrays used as arguments in inner product operations must satisfy certain other requirements. Since matrix multiplication plays a crucial role in applied mathematics, the inner product operation affords a compact and powerful method for performing matrix multiplication and extending it in various directions.

The outer product of two arrays is obtained by executing one of the primitive dyadic functions, using each element of one array and every element of the other as arguments. The result of an outer product operation is always an array of higher rank, whose dimension vector is obtained by catenating the dimension vectors of the arrays which appear as arguments. Like its counterpart, the outer product operator offers a convenient and powerful method for constructing arrays with special properties.

11.2 THE DOMINO FUNCTION

The primitive monadic function domino[1], formed by overstriking the quad character with the division sign, has the form shown in Figure

---

[1]   For an excellent discussion of the domino function, see "Domino: An APL Primitive Function for Matrix Inversion—Its Implementation and Applications," M. A. Jenkins, APL Quote Quad, Vol. 3, No. 4, February 1972. This informal publication, an excellent source of current information about APL, is issued by the Association for Computing Machinery (ACM).

11.2.1, where M is a matrix and R is the inverse of M if M is not essentially singular.   If it is, the function produces a domain error.

Fig. 11.2.1

EXAMPLE 1

```
        M←3 3ρ1 3 3 1 4 3 1 3 4
        M
  1   3   3
  1   4   3
  1   3   4
        R←⌹M
        R
 7.000000000E0     ¯3.000000000E0    ¯3.000000000E0
¯1.000000000E0      1.000000000E0     1.523213423E¯16
¯1.000000000E0     ¯1.977207712E¯17   1.000000000E0
```

Verification

```
        R+.×M
 1.000000000E0     ¯7.105427358E¯15  ¯7.105427358E¯15
 2.220446049E¯16    1.000000000E0     6.661338148E¯16
 6.106226635E¯16    1.554312234E¯15   1.000000000E0
```

EXAMPLE 2

A singular matrix produces a domain error.

```
        M←5 5ρι25
        M
  1    2    3    4    5
  6    7    8    9   10
 11   12   13   14   15
 16   17   18   19   20
 21   22   23   24   25

        R←⌹M
DOMAIN ERROR
        R←⌹M
        ∧
```

The dyadic function (Figure 19.3.2) results in the inner product of the inverse of M (provided M has an inverse) and V.   The resulting vec–

tor R is seen to be the solution of the system of equations whose coefficient matrix is M and whose constant terms are V.

Fig. 11.2.2

Consider, e.g., the system

3X + 2Y + 3Z = 16

2X – Y + 5Z = 15

X + Y+ 2Z = 9

Then

```
        M←3  3ρ3  2  3  2  ¯1  5  1  1  2
        V←16  15  9
        R←V⊟M
        R
1   2   3

        M+.×R
16   15   9
```

11.3 INNER PRODUCTS WITH MATRICES

EXAMPLE 1 (given on next page)

We see that C is the matrix product of the matrices A and B. C [I;J]
is obtained by multiplying the components of the Ith row of A by the
Jth column of B and summing. This imposes the requirement that the
number of columns of A be equal to the number of rows of B. The
character . denotes an inner product operation. The function to the
right, denoted in this case by multiplication, is executed on a component by component basis using the components of the Ith row of A and
the Jth column of B. The resulting array, in this case a vector, is

reduced by the function to the left of the inner product operation.

EXAMPLE 1

```
A←3 2ρ1 3 5 6 4 1
B←2 4ρ1 5 7 6 2 1 8 5
A
```

```
1   3
5   6
4   1
    B
```

```
1   5   7   6
2   1   8   5
    C←A+.×B
    C
```

```
 7    8   31   21
17   31   83   60
 6   21   36   29
```

EXAMPLE 2

```
B←2 3ρι3
C←A+.*B
C
```

4	10	28
11	61	341
5	17	65

In this case $C[I;J]$ is equal to the sum of the Jth powers of the elements of the Ith row of A.

The functions appearing in inner product operations are restricted to the primitive scalar dyadic functions.

11.4 EXTENSION TO ARRAYS OF HIGHER RANK

Let R be an array of rank M with dimension vector V, and let S be an array of rank N with dimension vector U. We assume that M and N

are greater than or equal to two. Furthermore, let V[M] equal U[1] .
Let d and e denote any two primitive scalar dyadic functions. If we
write

   $C \leftarrow Rd.eS$

the array C has dimension

   $V[1],V[2],..,V[M-1],S[2],S[3],..,S[N]$

C is obtained by executing the function e over dimension V[M] of R
and U[1] of S on a component by component basis and reducing the result by d. This is the reason for saying earlier that the inner product
operation is a combination of reduction and component by component
operation.

EXAMPLE 1

```
     R←3 2ρι4
     S←2 3 3ρι18
     R

 1   2
 3   4
 1   2
     S

  1    2    3
  4    5    6
  7    8    9

 10   11   12
 13   14   15
 16   17   18
     C←R+.×S
     C

 21   24   27
 30   33   36
 39   42   45
```

(continued)

```
43   50   57
64   71   78
85   92   99

21   24   27
30   33   36
39   42   45
```

11.5 SOME SPECIAL CASES

The inner product function is not restricted to arrays of rank two and greater but is applicable to scalars and vectors as well. What happens in these cases is shown in Figure 11.5.1.

Let d and e be any two primitive dyadic functions, and let A and B be arrays whose dimension and rank are shown in Figure 11.5.1. Then the inner product C of A and B under d and e is given by

$C \leftarrow A$ d.e B

The dimension and rank of C corresponding to the arrays A and B are shown in the figure.

11.6 THE OUTER PRODUCT OF VECTORS

As we remarked earlier, the outer product function (denoted by the pair of characters ∘.) employs the primitive dyadic functions using all pairs of elements from two different arrays as arguments.

EXAMPLE 1

```
A←ι2
B←ι10
A∘.×B
```

```
1   2   3   4   5    6    7    8    9    10
2   4   6   8   10   12   14   16   18   20
```

C is an array obtained by multiplying each component of the vector B by each component of A. ρC is equal to (ρA), ρB.

ρA	ρ B	ρ(ρA)	ρ(ρB)	ρ C	ρ(ρC)		EXAMPLE
E[1]	E	0	0	E	0	12	3+.×4
E[2]	V	0	1	E	0	30	3+.×ι4
V	E[3]	1	0	E	0	30	(ι4)+.×3
V[4]	U	1	1	E	0	4	(ι4)+.=ι4
							M←2 2ρι4
							3+.×M
E[5]	V[1],...,V[N]	0	N	V[2],...,V[N]	N−1	12 18	M+.×3
V[1],...,V[N]	E[6]	N	0	V[1],...,V[N−1]	N−1	9 21	M+.×ι2
V[1],...,V[N]	U[7]	N	1	V[1],...,V[N−1]	N−1	5 11	(ι2)+.×M
U[8]	V[1],...,V[N]	1	N	V[2],...,V[N−1]	N−1	7 10	

[1] E is the empty or null vector.

[2] The scalar A is extended to be a vector of length V.

[3] The scalar B is extended to be a vector of length U.

[4] V must equal U.

[5] The scalar is extended to be a vector of length V[1].

[6] The scalar is extended to be a vector of length V[N].

[7] V[N] must equal U.

[8] V[1] must equal U.

Fig. 11.5.1

EXAMPLE 2

```
        A←ι3
        B←ι3
        A∘.≥B

1 0 0
1 1 0
1 1 1
```

We obtain a lower triangular matrix with

$$C[I ; J] = 1 \quad \text{if } I \leq J$$

$$C[I ; J] = 0 \quad \text{if } I > J$$

By choosing appropriate vectors, we can generate matrices which
have useful properties.

11.6 EXTENDING THE OUTER PRODUCT
TO ARRAYS OF HIGHER RANK

Let R be an array of rank M with dimension vector V[1], V[2], ...,
V[M], and let S be an array of rank N with dimension vector S[1],
S[2], ..., S[N]. The array C defined by

$$C \leftarrow R \circ . dS$$

where d is a primitive dyadic function, has dimension

$$V[1], V[2], .. V[M], S[1], S[2], .., S[N]$$

EXAMPLE 1

```
A←ι10
B←2 3
C←A∘.*B
C
```

1	1
4	8
9	27
16	64
25	125
36	216
49	343
64	512
81	729
100	1000

C[I;J] is equal to I*(J+1) for I = 1, 10; J = 1, 2

EXERCISES

1. Let $S \leftarrow 5\ 5\rho 2\ 3\ 4$ and let $R \leftarrow 5\ 5\rho 3\ 1\ 8$ and let $G \leftarrow 5\ 2\ 2\rho\iota 20$. Compute the following.

A. $S+.\times R$ B. $S\lceil .*R$ C. $R+.\times S$

D. $R+.\neq S$ E. $S\times .\div R$ F. $S+.\times G$

2. Use the Domino function to compute the inverse of the following matrix. Test your result by multiplying the matrix by its inverse to see how close you come to producing the identity matrix.

$K \leftarrow 3\ 3\rho 3\ 7\ 3\ 7\ 8\ 4\ 3\ 2\ 1$

3. Let V be a vector with N components. Let Y be a vector whose components are $V[1], (V[1]+V[2]), \ldots, (V[1]+\ldots+V[N])$. Write an expression for Y.

The following examples show how the inner and outer product may be used to implement the classical functions of mathematical physics.[1]

4. Least square polynomial fitting. Consider the problem of minimizing the residuals

$$\sum_{i=1}^{M} E_i^2$$

where $E_i = Y_i - Y(X_i)$ and $Y = A_0 + A_1 X + \cdots A_n X^n$, for $n < M + 1$, as illustrated.

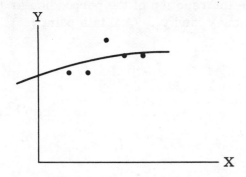

Differentiating with respect to each A_i, $i=1, 2, \ldots, n$, we obtain the following system of equations.

$$G_0A_0 + G_1A_1 + \cdots + G_nA_n = H_0$$

$$G_1A_0 + G_2A_1 + \cdots + G_{n+1}A_n = H_1$$

$$\vdots$$

$$G_nA_0 + G_{n+1} + \cdots + G_{2n}A_n = H_n$$

where

$$\Sigma \ X_i^k = G_k \qquad (k = 0, 1, \ldots, 2n)$$

$$\Sigma \ X_i^k Y_i = H_k \qquad (k = 0, \ldots, n)$$

Construct a function to carry out a least square polynomial fit. Fit a polynomial of degree 2 to the following data.

X	Y
.78	2.50
1.56	1.20
2.34	1.12
3.12	2.25
3.81	4.28

5. In linear interpolation we are given a pair of points (x_1, y_1) and (x_2, y_2), and we wish to determine a value of y corresponding to a point x satisfying $x_1 \leq x \leq x_2$. Geometrically speaking, the function $y = f(x)$ is approximated by a straight line connecting y_1 and y_2 (see following figure).

The value of $f(x)$ at x is the intersection of the perpendicular to the X axis at x and the line joining y_1 and y_2. Call this point y.

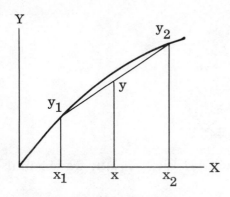

Algebraically

$$y = \frac{x - x_1}{x_2 - x_1} (y_2 - y_1) + y_1$$

Construct a user–defined function which performs linear interpolation.

6. Consider N points numbered 1, 2, ..., N and suppose that line segments join some pairs of points while for other pairs there is no direct connection. The $N \times N$ matrix $M(i,j)$ has a 1 in the ith row and column if there is a direct link between i and j, and 0 otherwise. Construct a function to accept a matrix M and a pair of points i and j, and determine whether there is a path from i to j and if so the length of the shortest path, i.e., the fewest number of lines which must be traversed.

The following exercises are highly specialized and require a mathematical background.[1]

7. The Bessel function of the first kind of order n is given by

$$J_n(x) = \sum_{k=0}^{\infty} \frac{(-1)^k (x/2)^{n+2k}}{k! \, (n+k+1)!}$$

The function can also be given in integral form as

$$J_n(x) = \frac{1}{\pi} \int_0^\pi \cos(n\Theta - x\sin\Theta) d\Theta$$

By use of the gamma function, it is possible to define the Bessel function for nonintegral n.

Descriptions of six different functions for evaluating various kinds of Bessel functions follow.

1) Z←N BESX X calculates the nth–order Bessel function for a scalar integer N and a vector X of arguments.

2) Z←N BESN X calculates the nth–order Bessel functions for a vector of integers N and a scalar X argument.

(1) R. B. Roden and E. A. Bucheit, Research Report CSRR 2029, November 1970, Department of Applied Analysis and Computer Science, Faculty of Mathematics, University of Waterloo, Waterloo, Ontario, Canada.

The spherical Bessel function of the first kind is defined by

$$J'_j (z) = \sqrt{\frac{\pi}{2z}} \ J_{j+1/2}(z)$$

For integral values of j, the spherical Bessel functions are elementary transcendental functions,

$$J'_0(z) = \frac{\sin z}{z}$$

$$J'_1(z) = \frac{\cos z}{z}$$

(Either BESN or BESX will work if N and X are both scalars.)

3) Z←N FRACBES X calculates the nth-order Bessel functions for a vector of arguments X and a scalar order N, which may be any value except a negative integer. If N is not an integer, then X must not be negative.

4) Z←N FRACBESL X produces the same result as FRACBES. It is slower than FRACBES but will work on large values of X (X>15) and N (N>25), where FRACBES produces a domain error.

5) BESN and BESX use the integral form of the integer-order Bessel function. FRACBES sums the first 20 (or 30 if 10≤⌈/X) terms in the power series of the Bessel function. FRACBESL sums terms until a term less than .000000000001 × current sum is encountered.

6) Z←N SPHRBES X and Z←N SPHRBESL X use FRACBES and FRACBESL to compute the spherical Bessel function of integer order N for a vector of positive arguments X.

Tests indicate that accuracy is at least 8 significant digits (except in the neighborhood of zeros) if 50>|X and 40>|N.

```
        ∇BESX[⎕]∇
     ∇   Z←N BESX X;T
[1]      Z←0.025×(2|N+1)++/20(X∘.×10T)-((ρX),39)ρN×T←(00.025)×ι
     ∇
```

```
        ∇BESN[⎕]∇
     ∇   Z←N BESN X;T
[1]      Z←0.025×(2|N+1)++/20(((ρN),39)ρX×10T)-N∘.×T←(00.025)×ι
     ∇
```

```
        ∇FRACBES[☐]∇
     ∇   Z←N FRACBES X;K
[1]      Z←((0.5×X)∘.*N+2×K)+.÷(!K)×!N÷K←0,ι20+10×V/,10≤X
     ∇
```

```
        ∇FRACBESL[☐]∇
     ∇   Z←N FRACBESL X;T;K
[1]      Z←T←((0.5×X)*N)÷!N+K←0
[2]      →2×ιV/,(|T)>|1E¯12×Z←Z+T←-T×X×X÷4×K×N+K←K+1
     ∇
```

Use these functions to evaluate the following.

A. $J_0(2)$ B. $J_8(1.75)$ C. $J_{3.2}(6.2)$ D. $J_{4.1}(5)$

E. $J_{.75}(8.25)$ F. $J'_{.5}(6.34)$ G. $J'_1(2)$

8. The error function is given by

$$\text{erf}(x) = \frac{2}{\sqrt{\pi}} \int_0^x e^{-u^2} \, du$$

Here is a description of an APL function which evaluates the error function.

DERF

The function Z←ERF X evaluates the error function for a set of X values. Accuracy is at least 10 significant figures for $0 \leq X \leq 3$.

```
        ∇ERF[☐]∇
     ∇   Z←ERF X;K
[1]      Z←1.128379167095513×(X∘.*K)-.÷(K←1+2×K)×!K←0,ι40
     ∇
```

Evaluate the following.

A. erf(o)   B. erf(3.5)   C. erf(.6)

9. The Hermite polynomials are given by

$$H_n(x) = (-1)^n e^{x^2} \frac{d}{dx^n}(e^{-x^2})$$

DHERMITE

Z←N HERMITE X evaluates the Hermite polynomial of order N (a non-negative integer) for a set of arguments X.

```
        ∇HERMITE[□]∇
    ∇   Z←N HERMITE X;K;S
[1]     Z←((2×X)∘.*K)-.×(!N)÷(!K←N-2×S)×!S←0,⍳⌊N÷2
    ∇
```

Evaluate the following.

    A. $H_1(5)$ B. $H_7(-3.2)$ C. $H_5(1.2)$

10. The Laguerre polynomial of order n is given by

$$L_n(x) = e^x \frac{d^n}{dx^n}(x^n e^{-x})$$

Z←N LAGUERRE X evaluates the Laguerre polynomial of order N (a non-negative integer) for a set of arguments X.

```
        ∇LAGUERRE[□]∇
    ∇   Z←N LAGUERRE X;K
[1]     Z←(X∘.*K)-.×((¯1*N)×!N)÷((!K←N-K)*2)×!K←0,⍳N
    ∇
```

Evaluate the following.

    A. $L_0(1)$ B. $L_5(-2.1)$ C. $L_6(3.25)$

11. The Legendre polynomial of order n is given by

$$P_n(x) = \frac{1}{2^n n!} \frac{d^n(x^2-1)}{dx^n}$$

Z←N LEGENDRE X evaluates the Legendre polynomial of order N (a non-negative integer) for a set of arguments X.

```
        ∇LEGENDRE[□]∇
    ∇   Z←N LEGENDRE X;K;P
[1]     Z←(X∘.*P)-.×(!N+P)÷(2*N)×(!K)×(!N-K)×!P←N-2×K←0,⍳⌊N÷2
    ∇
```

Evaluate the following.

    A. $L_0(3)$ B. $L_5(-2.1)$ C. $L_6(3.25)$

12. An eigenvalue problem. Given a square matrix A of order n and the identity matrix I of the same order, the equation

determinant $(A - \lambda I) = 0$ (1)

leads to an nth-degree polynomial in λ . The solutions λ_i of (1) are called eigenvalues and play an important role in many applications. For each eigenvalue λ_i there is a corresponding nonzero eigenvector x_i which satisfies

$$AX_i = \lambda_i X_i$$ (2)

If λ_i is not a multiple root of (1), the components of the eigenvector can be determined to within a constant multiplier. What we should like to discuss here is a method for approximating the largest eigenvalue and the associated eigenvector of a matrix with distinct eigenvalues.

Let A be a square matrix of order n with real eigenvalues λ_i satisfying $|\lambda_i| > |\lambda_{i+1}|$ i=1, 2, ..., n. The power method is based on making an initial guess at the eigenvector $X^{(1)}$ and systematically iterating the equation

$$\lambda^{(k)} X^{(k)} = A X^{(k-1)}$$

The value for $\lambda^{(k)}$ is a constant chosen to make one of the elements of $X^{(k)}$ equal to 1. When $\lambda^{(k)}$ and $X^{(k)}$ change by some sufficiently small amount, we terminate the process and take $X^{(k)}$ as our eigenvector and $\lambda^{(k)}$ as our eigenvalue. It can be shown that the iteration will converge to the eigenvector. Construct a function called MAXEIGEN which implements the power method.

13. The Gauss–Seidel method is an iterative scheme for solving a system of linear equations. One criterion which guarantees convergence to the solution vector is that the absolute value of terms on the main diagonal must be greater than the sum of the absolute values of all the other terms in the row.

Let the system of n equations be given by

$$\sum_{i=1}^{n} \sum_{j=1}^{n} A_{ij} X_j = b_i$$

We make an initial guess $X_j^{(0)}$, j=1, 2, ..., n, at the solution. A set of improved values is obtained from the formula

$$X_i^{(p+1)} = \frac{b_i - \sum_{j=1}^{i-1} A_{ij}X_j^{(p+1)} - \sum_{j=i+1}^{n} A_{ij}X_j^{(k)}}{A_{ii}} \qquad i=1, 2, \ldots, n$$

The process continues until such time as two successive iterations do not improve the solution. Construct a function which implements the Gauss–Seidel algorithm.

Use your function to solve the following system of equations.

$10X + 2Y + 6Z = 28$

$X + 10Y + 9Z = 7$

$2X - 7Y - 10Z = -17$

Stop when two successive iterations produce a difference of less than .02 in all the variables.

12.1 INTRODUCTION

The interpretation and understanding of many phenomena are often
facilitated by measuring and quantitatively ranking some property of
those phenomena. For example, a chemist may wish to rank the
atomic elements according to atomic weight or atomic number, while
an economist might rank years by their rate of inflation. It is important therefore to have some means of conveniently and efficiently
sorting different sets of data that may be associated with a given
variable.

In APL there exist two primitive functions which permit us to
sort or rank data. These functions, called grade up and grade down,
are concerned with the sorting of data in either ascending or descending order. Applied to vectors, these functions produce the permutation of the indices which orders the components of the vector. In arrays of higher rank it is necessary to specify the dimension over
which the sorting is to take place.

In addition to the sorting functions, we shall examine two related
functions called take and drop. These functions permit us to form
new vectors from old ones by selecting the first or last K elements,
and they can be extended to arrays of higher rank.

12.2 RANKING THE COMPONENTS OF A VECTOR

Figure 12.2.1 gives the critical temperatures and pressures of some
common gases. Let us represent the temperatures in the form of a
vector.

$TEMP \leftarrow 405.5 \ 304.1 \ 417 \ 5.1 \ 33.2 \ 126.0 \ 154.3 \ 430.3 \ 647.3$

Gas	$T_c(°K)$	$P_c(atm)$
Ammonia, NH_3	405.5	111.5
Carbon dioxide, CO_2	304.1	72.9
Chlorine, Cl_2	417	76
Helium, He	5.1	2.26
Hydrogen, H_2	33.2	12.8
Nitrogen, N_2	126.0	33.5
Oxygen, O_2	154.3	49.7
Sulfur dioxide, SO_2	430.3	77.7
Water, H_2O	647.3	218.2

Fig. 12.2.1

If we wish to sort the temperatures in ascending order, we write

$$\text{\AA} T$$
$$4 \quad 5 \quad 6 \quad 7 \quad 2 \quad 1 \quad 3 \quad 8 \quad 9$$

What we obtain is the vector of indices which orders the elements of T. The lowest numbered index is 0 or 1, depending on the setting of the origin. We shall assume it is set at 1. The character $\text{\AA}$ is formed by overstriking the characters Δ and $|$. Having the indices of the sorted temperatures, we can easily reorder the associated pressures to correspond to the ordering of the temperatures. Assume that the pressures are also represented in vector form as

$$P \leftarrow 111.5 \quad 72.9 \quad 76 \quad 2.26 \quad 12.8 \quad 33.5 \quad 49.7 \quad 77.7 \quad 218.2$$

Then

$$P[\text{\AA} P]$$
$$2.26 \quad 12.8 \quad 33.5 \quad 49.7 \quad 72.9 \quad 111.5 \quad 76 \quad 77.7 \quad 218.1$$

is the order of the corresponding pressures. The function denoted by Ψ works exactly the same way and corresponds to sorting in descending order.

12.3 GRADING ARRAYS OF HIGHER RANK

In general, the grading functions have the form shown in Figure
12.3.1, where R is an array of rank 1 or greater and [I] indicates
that the operation is to be carried out over the vectors lying on the
Ith coordinate of R. If the dimension is not explicitly mentioned, the
last dimension is understood to be implied.

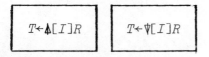

Fig. 12.3.1

EXAMPLE 1

Let us suppose that M is a matrix whose first two rows consist of the
temperatures and pressures of Figure 12.2.1.

```
    G←T,P
    M←2 9ρG
    M
```

405.5		304.1		417	
	5.1		33.2		126
	154.3		430.3		647.3
111.5		72.9		76	
	2.26		12.8		33.5
	49.7		77.7		218.2

Then writing

```
    M[1;]←M[1;ΔT]
    M[2;]←M[2;ΔP]
    M
```

5.1		33.2		126	
	154.3		304.1		405.5
	417		430.3		647.3
2.26		12.8		33.5	
	49.7		72.9		76
	77.7		111.5		218.2

we obtain a matrix in which temperature and pressure have been
ranked independently in ascending order. If we wanted the pressures
to correspond to the ranked temperatures, as in the previous example,
we would write

```
    M←2 9 ρG
    M[2;]←M[2;⍋T]
    M[2;]
2.26  12.8  33.5  49.7  72.9  111.5  76  77.7
    218.2
```

12.4 DUPLICATE ELEMENTS

If the vector being graded contains duplicate elements, the index corresponding to the lowest ordered element comes first.

```
    V←2 7 6 9 6 7 5
    ⍋V
1  7  3  5  2  6  4
```

We shall see when we come to the primitive function rotate in the next
chapter that this treatment of duplicate elements provides a means of
determining when the components of a vector are distinct elements.

12.5 THE PRIMITIVE TAKE FUNCTION

The primitive function take applied to vectors permits us to select
either the first K or last K elements of the vector. The function has
the form shown in Figure 12.5.1, where V is a vector and K is an
integer such that | K is less than or equal to ρV. T consists of the
first K or last K elements of V, depending on whether K is positive
or negative.

Fig. 12.5.1

EXAMPLE 1

```
V←3 9 4 1 5 7
T←¯2↑V
T
5   7
```

The last two elements of V are selected. In certain applications we wish to select the K smallest or K largest elements of a set. The take function permits us to do this rather easily. If S is a vector and K is a positive integer, then

```
T←K↑S[⍋S]
```

is a vector of the K smallest elements. By substituting ⍒ for ⍋ we get the K largest elements.

EXAMPLE 2

Form the vector consisting of the four smallest elements of V.

```
V←9 1 8 2 6 11 13 7
T←4↑V[⍋V]
T
1   2   6   7
```

EXAMPLE 3

If K is chosen to be zero, the result is the null vector.

```
0↑V
```

EXAMPLE 4

Choosing a scalar greater than $|\rho V$ yields an error.

```
9↑V
DOMAIN ERROR
  ·9↑V
    ∧
```

12.6 EXTENSION TO ARRAYS OF HIGHER RANK

For arrays of rank two and greater the take function has the form
shown in Figure 12.6.1, where R is an array of rank greater than or
equal to 2, and K is a vector of integers whose dimension is equal to the
rank of R. The component K[J] selects what is to be taken along the
Jth coordinate.

$$T \leftarrow K \uparrow R$$

Fig. 12.6.1

EXAMPLE 1

```
      R←3  4ρι12
      K←2  ¯1
      R

  1   2   3    4
  5   6   7    8
  9  10  11   12
      T←K↑R
      T

4
8
```

EXAMPLE 2

```
      R←4  3  2ρι24
      R
  1   2
  3   4
  5   6

  7   8
  9  10
 11  12
```

```
13  14
15  16
17  18

19  20
21  22
23  24
    K←2 ¯1 1
    K↑R

  5

 11
```

12.7 THE PRIMITIVE DROP FUNCTION

The primitive function <u>drop</u> works like <u>take</u>, except that elements are
dropped rather than taken. The function is denoted by ↓.

EXAMPLE 1

The first element is dropped.

```
      V←2 3 6 9
      1↓V
  3  6  9
```

EXAMPLE 2

```
      R←3 4ρι12
      K← ¯2 1
      R
  1    2    3    4
  5    6    7    8
  9   10   11   12
      T←K↓R
      T
  2  3  4
```

Together the functions take and drop provide the capability for dealing with ordered vectors where the first or last K elements are removed and subjected to some kind of processing that is repeated until the original set of elements is exhausted.

EXAMPLE 3

Let T be a vector and suppose that each element of T is chosen in order and subjected to some kind of processing. The processing is complete when the last element of T has been processed. The following sequence of instructions tests to see of a given vector H is empty. If H is empty, processing is terminated. If not, the first element of H is assigned to the variable G and the vector H is redefined with the first element dropped:

```
→(H=ι0)/0
G←H[1]
H←1↓H
```

EXERCISES

1. Let V be a vector of numeric data. Define a new vector variable V1 in which the components of V appear in

  A. ascending order
  B. descending order
  C. ascending order of absolute value

2. The median of a set of data is defined as the midpoint when the data are ordered, e.g., in ascending order. When the number of data elements is even, the median is defined as the mean of the two midpoints. Write a function called MEDIAN whose single argument is V and whose explicit output is the median of V.

3. The amplitude of a complex number a+bi is defined as $+\sqrt{a^2+b^2}$. Let the real and imaginary coefficients of a set of N complex numbers be given in the form of a 2×N matrix, M. Construct an explicit function called AMP whose argument is the matrix and which produces the amplitudes in ascending order.

4. Let $V \leftarrow 1\ 9\ 8\ 2\ 6\ 5$ and let $M \leftarrow 5\ 5\rho\iota 25$. Evaluate the variable W in each of the following expressions.

$$W \leftarrow \texttt{\textDelta}\ ^-3\uparrow V$$

$$W \leftarrow \texttt{\textnabla}\ ^-1\downarrow V$$

$$W \leftarrow ,1\ ^-2\uparrow M$$

5. Given a matrix M such that each row is a character item, define a function to sort and print these items.

6. A queue is a data structure where an element is removed from the top of the list and added to the end of the list. It is sometimes called a first-in/first-out (FIFO). Define two APL functions which add an element to a queue and remove it from the queue respectively.

7. Given a vector D of numeric elements, we define the difference vector DIFF as the vector obtained from D by taking differences of consecutive elements, that is, D[n] – D[n – 1] . Define an APL function, i.e., an explicit dyadic function with arguments D and N where N indicates that N successive differences are to be taken $(N \leq (\rho D) - 1)$.

8. A very commonly used type of data structure is called a stack. It is also known as a push-down list and a last-in/first-out list (LIFO). Objects can be either taken off the top of the stack or put on top of the stack. At any point in time, only the top object is accessible. Construct two APL functions to simulate the addition and removal of objects from a LIFO list.

13 PERMUTING THE ELEMENTS OF AN ARRAY

13.1 INTRODUCTION

In this chapter we shall be concerned with some primitive functions which permute or in some way rearrange the elements of an array. The three functions we shall study are called *transpose*, *rotate*, and *reverse*. The monadic transpose function permits us to interchange the last two coordinates of an array, e.g., the rows and columns of a matrix. The dyadic function allows a more general kind of permutation and provides a convenient means of obtaining certain subsets of the array, e.g., the main diagonal. The rotate function provides a way of executing cyclic rotation of the elements of a vector and extends in a general way to the vectors along the Ith coordinate in arrays of higher rank. The reversal function reorders the elements of a vector so that they appear in reverse order. In arrays of higher rank the reversal takes place along the Ith coordinate.

13.2 THE MONADIC TRANSPOSE FUNCTION

The *transpose* function is denoted by the character ⍉, formed by overstriking the circle o with the backslash \. The monadic transpose function has the form shown in Figure 13.2.1, where R is an array of rank 1 or greater, and T is the array formed from R by interchanging the last two coordinates of R.

```
T←⍉R
```

Fig. 13.2.1

EXAMPLE 1

The transpose function leaves a vector unchanged.

```
        V←2 6 8 4
        ⍉V
  2   6   8   4
```

EXAMPLE 2

The rows and columns of a matrix are interchanged.

```
        M←3 3⍴?(⍳9)
        M

  1   2   2
  3   2   1
  5   6   9
        ⍉M

  1   3   5
  2   2   6
  2   1   9
```

EXAMPLE 3

With arrays of rank 3 or greater, the last two coordinates are interchanged.

```
        R←2 2 3⍴⍳12
        R

  1   2   3
  4   5   6

  7   8   9
 10  11  12
        ⍉R

  1   4
  2   5
  3   6

  7  10
  8  11
  9  12
```

13.3 PERMUTATION VECTORS

Before we discuss the dyadic transpose function, it is necessary to say something about permutation vectors. A permutation vector P is a vector whose components are a dense set of positive integers. By a dense set we mean a set consisting of integers between 1 and $\lceil/P$ and containing every such integer at least once. For example, the vector P specified by

$P\leftarrow$1 3 4 2 5

is a permutation vector, and Q specified by

$Q\leftarrow$1 2 2 1

is also a permutation vector. But S specified by

$S\leftarrow$1 3 4

is not a permutation vector, since the integer 2 is not a component of S.

    We may think of a permutation vector as a transformation of one set of numbers into another, e.g., the components of the vector into the indices of the vector. For vector P the correspondence is

```
1   2   3   4   5
↓   ↓   ↓   ↓   ↓
1   4   2   3   5
```

For vector Q, the correspondence is

```
 1     2    3   4
↙↘   ↙↘
1 4 2 3
```

The correspondence in P is one to one and represents a permutation of the indices. In Q, the transformation is one to many. If we think of the permutation vector P as an operation applied to an array R of rank 5, then the array R is transformed into an array T such that

$T[I;K;L;J;M] \leftarrow R[I;J;K;L;M]$

In vector Q, we have

$T[I;J] \leftarrow R[I;J;J;I]$

Bearing these concepts in mind, we can now examine the dyadic transpose function.

13.4 THE DYADIC TRANSPOSE FUNCTION

The dyadic transpose function has the form shown in Figure 13.4.1, where R is an array of rank 1 or greater, V is a permutation vector such that ρV is equal to $\rho\rho R$, and T is the array into which R is transformed by V under $\lozenge$. Some examples will clarify the situation.

$T \leftarrow V \lozenge R$

Fig. 13.4.1

EXAMPLE 1

```
        M←3  5ρ?(ι10)
        M
1   1   1   4   4
5   5   1   6   9
1   1   1   4   4
        T←2 1⍉M
        T
1   5   1
1   5   1
1   1   1
4   6   4
4   9   4
```

T is the transpose of M defined by

$T[J;I] \leftarrow M[I;J]$

The dimension of T is

$(\rho M)[2\ 1]$

EXAMPLE 2

```
        T←1 1⍉M
        T
1   5   3
```

In this case T is a diagonal section defined by

$$T[I] ← M[I;I]$$

The dimension of T is given by

$$⌊/\rho M$$

EXAMPLE 3

```
        R←3 2 3ρ?(⍳18)
        R
1    1    3
2    2    2

3    2    5
9   11    1

12    8    8
 6   17    9

        T←2 1 2⍉R
        T
1    2    8
2   11    9
```

T is a diagonal section defined by

$$T[J;I] ← R[I;J;I]$$

The dimension of T is given by

$$(\rho R[2],(⌊/(\rho R)[1\ 3]))$$

13.5 THE DIMENSION AND RANK OF A TRANSPOSED ARRAY

In general, the rank of T is given by $⌈/V$. Furthermore, if the index I is a component of $⍳\rho\rho T$, then $(\rho T)[I]$ is equal to $⌊/(V=I)/R$.

13.6 THE REVERSE FUNCTION APPLIED TO VECTORS

The primitive reverse function may be thought of as a permutation which rearranges the elements of a vector so that the last element is first, the next to the last second, etc. Let

$V \leftarrow 9\ 3\ 1\ 6$

If we write

$T \leftarrow \phi V$
T
6   1   3   9

we see that the components of T are the components of V in reverse order. The character ϕ, which denotes the reverse function, is formed by overstriking the circle o with the stroke |.

EXAMPLE 1

The reverse function gives us a convenient way of generating a set of indices in descending order.

$\phi\iota 5$
5   4   3   2   1

13.7 EXTENSION TO ARRAYS OF HIGHER RANK

If R is an array of rank 2 or greater, then reversal takes place along some specified coordinate of R.

EXAMPLE 1

$R \leftarrow 2\ 3\rho(\iota 6)$
R

1   2   3
4   5   6
ϕR

3   2   1
6   5   4

When no coordinate is specified, reversal takes place along the last coordinate.

EXAMPLE 2

$\phi[1]R$

```
4  5  6
1  2  3
```

In this case reversal takes place over the first coordinate.

13.8 THE PRIMITIVE ROTATE FUNCTION

The dyadic function denoted by ϕ is called rotate and enables us to
execute a cyclic rotation of the elements of a vector. For example,
if we write

$V\leftarrow 9\ 4\ 6\ 3\ 1\ 7$

then

$3\phi V$
```
3  1  7  9  4  6
```

denotes a cyclic rotation of 3 places in the counterclockwise direction.
If we write

$\bar{\ }3\phi V$
```
3  1  7  9  4  6
```

the rotation is still 3 places, but this time it takes place in the clock-
wise direction. If I is a scalar, or one-element vector, then $I\phi V$ is
equivalent to

$V[1+(\rho V)\ |\ \bar{\ }1+I+\iota\rho V]$

in a system where the origin is 1 and to

$V[(\rho V)\ |\ I+\iota\rho V]$

in a system where the origin is 0.

13.9 EXTENSION TO ARRAYS OF HIGHER RANK

The rotate function is extended to arrays of rank 2 or greater by
specifying the coordinate I along which rotation takes place and by

specifying the nature of the rotation for each vector along the Ith co-ordinate.

EXAMPLE 1

```
      M←3 4ρι12
      M
  1     2     3     4
  5     6     7     8
  9    10    11    12
      1  ‾2  1φM
  2     3     4     1
  7     8     5     6
 10    11    12     9
```

When no coordinate is specified explicitly, rotation takes place along the last coordinate—in this case, over the rows. Since there are three rows, the left argument of φ has three components, each of which specifies the nature of the rotation for its respective row.

EXAMPLE 2

If we write

```
      1 2 ‾1 2φ[1]M

  5    10    11    12
  9     2     3     4
  1     6     7     8
```

then rotation takes place over each column, and since there are four columns, the left argument of φ contains four components. In general, if

```
      T←Qφ[I]R
```

where R is an array of rank 2 or greater, then the dimension of Q must be equal to the dimension of R with the Ith coordinate removed. Each component of Q specifies the nature of the rotation for the corresponding vector along the Ith coordinate.

EXAMPLE 3

$R{\leftarrow}2\ 3\ 2\rho(\iota30)$
$Q{\leftarrow}2\ 2\rho1\ 2\ ^-1\ ^-2$
R

```
 1    2
 3    4
 5    6

 7    8
 9   10
11   12
```

If we write

$Q\phi[2]R$

```
 3    6
 5    2
 1    4

11   10
 7   12
 9    8
```

then rotation takes place over the columns of each plane of R.

EXERCISES
_____

1. Let V be a vector of numerical data. The data can be smoothed by replacing V[I] by (V[I] + V [I + 1])/2 for I less than N, where N is the dimension of the vector. Write an expression for U1, the vector of the smoothed data.

2. A. Define a function called SYMMETRIC whose single argument is a matrix M and which yields the result 1 if M is symmetric and 0 otherwise.

    B. Let M be any square matrix. What can you say about the matrix Z, defined as Z←M+⍉M ?

3. The trace of a square matrix M is the sum of the elements on the principal diagonal. Write an APL expression for the trace T.

4. Which of the following are permutation vectors?

    A. 1 3 4 1

    B. 2 1 4 3

    C. 5 6 3 4 2 2

    D. 6 3 5 1 2

SET OPERATIONS

14.1 INTRODUCTION

The primitive functions grouped together in this chapter provide the means for describing and implementing standard operations on sets. Unfortunately, the term 'set' and the operations associated with sets, i.e., union, intersection, difference, etc., are ambiguous and subject to varying interpretations. Perhaps, therefore, we will use the term 'set' and define the various functions in ways that are different from what the student understands. This is in itself not too important. What is important from the student's point of view is to gain understanding and mastery of these functions so that he can use them as building blocks for implementing those definitions which are most useful to him. The examples and exercises given at the end of this chapter are designed to illustrate some applications which are likely to be encountered in probability theory and statistics.

14.2 SETS AND VECTORS

Definition: A set S is a collection of distinct elements represented as a vector. By this definition the vector S1, defined as

$S1\leftarrow1$ 2 7 3 8

is a set, but S2, defined by

$S2\leftarrow1$ 2 3 3 5

is not a set.

Recognizing that many people might consider S2 a set, we shall continue to use the term 'vector' to refer to either S1 or S2 but only S1 will be called a set. All set operations described in Section 14.8 will be

defined on vectors. We shall now examine some new primitive functions
which will provide the mechanisms for implementing set operations.

14.3 THE PRIMITIVE COMPRESS FUNCTION

Let X be a vector. If we write

$T \leftarrow L/X$

where L is a scalar or a logical vector of the same dimension as X,
then T is a vector consisting of the components of X corresponding to
the components of L which are equal to 1.

EXAMPLE 1

The first, third, and fourth components of X are selected.

$X \leftarrow 5\ 6\ 2\ 9$

$T \leftarrow 1\ 0\ 1\ 1/X$

T

5   2   9

If L is a scalar, it is extended in the usual way so that 1/X selects all
the components of X, and 0/X produces the null vector. From the
point of view of applications, the importance of the vector L is that it
may come about from various logical operations defined on X.

EXAMPLE 2

A physicist has measured temperature at fixed intervals of time and
wishes to eliminate from her data any temperature greater than or
equal to 120°C. Let T be the vector of observed temperatures,

$T \leftarrow 100.0\ 109.9\ 109.9\ 109.2\ 111.0\ 121.2$

Then

$V \leftarrow (T<120)/T$

is the vector of valid temperature data.

EXAMPLE 3

In Example 2 suppose a particular temperature value, 109.9, is to be eliminated from the data. The vector V of valid temperature data is given by

$$V \leftarrow (T \neq 109.9)/T$$

$$V$$

100   109.2   111   121.2

EXAMPLE 4

We want all temperatures which are not divisible by 10.

$$V \leftarrow (0 \neq 10 | T)/T$$

$$V$$

109.9   109.9   109.2   111   121.2

EXAMPLE 5

Literals can also be dealt with.

$$T \leftarrow 'ABCDE'$$

$$V \leftarrow (T \neq 'E')/T$$

$$V$$

ABCD

14.4 EXTENSION TO ARRAYS OF HIGHER RANK

In general, the primitive compress function has the form shown in Figure 14.4.1, where R is an array of rank 2 or greater, and L is a logical vector whose dimension is equal to the dimension of the vectors lying on the Ith coordinate. When no mention is made of a coordinate, compression takes place along the last coordinate.

$$T \leftarrow L/[I]R$$

Fig. 14.4.1

EXAMPLE 1

Compression of the second and fourth columns of a matrix:

```
M←5 4ρ(ι20)
M
```

```
 1    2    3    4
 5    6    7    8
 9   10   11   12
13   14   15   16
17   18   19   20
      T←1 0 1 0/M
      T
```

```
 1    3
 5    7
 9   11
13   15
17   19
```

EXAMPLE 2

For an array of rank 3, the second plane would be compressed as follows:

```
M←3 4 2ρ(ι24)
M
```

```
1   2
3   4
5   6
7   8
```

(continued)

```
 9   10
11   12
13   14
15   16

17   18
19   20
21   22
23   24
      T←1 0 1/[1]M
      T

 1    2
 3    4
 5    6
 7    8

17   18
19   20
21   22
23   24
```

14.5 THE PRIMITIVE EXPAND FUNCTION

The inverse of compression is expansion. The expand function expands a vector by filling in a numeric vector with zeros and a literal vector with blanks. The function has the form shown in Figure 14.5.1, where X is a vector and U is a logical vector such that

ρX is equal to +/U

and Y is a vector defined as follows:

1. If X is a numeric vector, then

    Y[I] is equal to X[I] when U[I] is equal to 1
    Y[I] is equal to 0   when U[I] is equal to 0

2. If X is a literal vector, then

    Y[I] is equal to X[I] when U[I] is equal to 1
    Y[I] is equal to b   when U[I] is equal to 0
    (b = blank character)

Fig. 14.5.1

EXAMPLE 1

```
      X←1 9  7  6
      U←1 0  0  1  0  1  1
      Y←U\X
      Y
 1   0   0   9   0   7   6
```

EXAMPLE 2

```
      X←'VOLTSANDOHMS'
      U←1 1 1 1 1 0 1 1 1 0 1 1 1 1
      Y←U\X
      Y
VOLTS AND OHMS
```

Because X is a literal vector, spaces rather than zeros are inserted.

14.6 EXTENSION TO ARRAYS OF HIGHER RANK

The expand function is applicable to arrays of rank 2 or greater in the usual way. If we write the function as shown in Figure 14.6.1, then expansion takes place over the vectors lying on the Ith coordinate of R. When no coordinate is mentioned, the last coordinate is implied.

```
      Y←U\[I]R
```

Fig. 14.6.1

EXAMPLE 1

```
      M←3 3ρ2?9
      U←1 0 1 0 1
      M

  3   9   3
  9   3   9
  3   9   3
      U\M

  3   0   9   0   3
  9   0   3   0   9
  3   0   9   0   3
```

14.7 THE MEMBERSHIP FUNCTION

The membership function, denoted by ϵ, has the form shown in Figure 14.7.1.

```
┌─────────────┐
│             │
│   Y←R∈U     │
│             │
└─────────────┘
```

Fig. 14.7.1

Let R and U be arrays of arbitrary rank. Then Y is a logical array of the same dimension as R, such that a component of Y is one of the corresponding components of R belongs to U and zero otherwise.

EXAMPLE 1

The components of Y whose indices are given by U are equal to 1; all other components of Y are equal to 0.

```
      R←ι9
      U←2 9 7 5
      Y←R∈U
      Y
  0   1   0   0   1   0   1   0   1
```

EXAMPLE 2

```
        R←4 4ρ?ι30
        U←3 2ρι6
        R

    1    1    2    4
    1    1    4    6
    1    4    1    6
    9    9   14   14
        U

  1   2
  3   4
  5   6
        Y←RεU
        Y

1 1 1 1
1 1 1 1
1 1 1 1
0 0 0 0
```

EXAMPLE 3

Literals may be used as arguments of the membership function.

```
        ALPHA←'ABCDEFGHIJKLMNOPQRSTUVWXYZ'
        VOWEL←'AEIOU'
        ALPHAεVOWEL
1 0 0 0 1 0 0 0 1 0 0 0 0 0 1 0 0 0 0 0
1 0 0 0 0 0
```

14.8 SET OPERATIONS

The compress and membership functions provide the necessary building blocks for implementing set operations. Among the set operations to be discussed are:

1. set inclusion
2. set intersection
3. set difference
4. set union

All these concepts will be defined for vectors. When the vectors are sets, the definitions will have their usual meaning.

14.8.1 Characteristic Vector

<u>Definition</u>: Given vectors S and T, the characteristic vector of S on T is defined as the vector $T\epsilon S$. Many of the definitions introduced will make use of the characteristic vector of one set on another.

14.8.2 Set Inclusion

A vector S is said to be included or contained in a vector T, written $S \subseteq T$, if each element of S belongs to T. This is equivalent to saying that the function $\wedge/S\epsilon T$ is equal to 1. If T is also contained in S so that $\wedge/T\epsilon S$ is equal to 1, we say that S and T are similar. This is written as $S \equiv T$. We can now define similarity as follows:

<u>Definition</u>: S and T are similar if and only if $(\wedge/T\epsilon S)\wedge(\wedge/S\epsilon T)$ is equal to 1.

EXAMPLE 1

S and T are similar vectors.

```
S←ι6
T←2 3 1 4 6 5 4
(∧/TϵS)∧(∧/SϵT)
1
```

EXAMPLE 2

Two similar sets are identical if they are considered unordered.

```
S←3 5 4 7 2

T←2 5 7 4 3
(∧/TϵS)∧(∧/SϵT)
1
```

If $S \subseteq T$ but $S \not\equiv T$, then we say that the inclusion is strict. This is written $S \subset T$. The symbols $\subset$ and $\subseteq$ have not been defined in APL\360.

EXAMPLE 3

> S←3 5 9 6 2
> T←ι9

S⊂T, since

>   ∧/SεT
>   1

But T⊄S, since

>   ∧/TεS
>   0

14.8.3 **Set Intersection**

Definition: The intersection of the two vectors S and T is written S∩T and defined as the vector (S ε T)/S. The symbol ∩ has not been defined in APL\360.

EXAMPLE 1

> S←3 5 3 1 4
> T←2 6 3 1 8
>
>   (SεT)/S
>   3   3   1
>   (TεS)/T
>   3   1

In general, S∩T is not equal to T∩S although it is true that

>   (S∩T) ≡ (T∩S)

Definition: We say that the vector S∩T is ordered on S.

Definition: Two vectors S and T are said to be disjoint if

>   (SεT)/S

is the null vector.

EXAMPLE 2

We must remember that the null vector prints as a blank line.

$$S \leftarrow 2 \ 4 \ 6 \ 8$$
$$T \leftarrow 1 \ 3 \ 5 \ 7 \ 9$$
$$(S \epsilon T)/S$$

14.8.4 Set Difference

<u>Definition</u>: The vector difference of S and T is defined as the vector consisting of those elements of S which do not belong to T. The vector can be written

$$(\sim(S \epsilon T))/S$$

EXAMPLE 1

$$S \leftarrow 3 \ 4 \ 5 \ 3 \ 9$$
$$T \leftarrow 1 \ 4 \ 5 \ 9 \ 8 \ 10$$

$$(\sim(S \epsilon T))/S$$
$$3 \quad 3$$

EXAMPLE 2

$$S \leftarrow \epsilon 3$$
$$T \leftarrow \epsilon 6$$
$$(\sim(S \epsilon T))/S$$

14.8.5 Set Union

<u>Definition</u>: The union of two vectors S and T is written S$\cup$T and defined as the vector

$$S,(\sim(T \epsilon S))/T$$

It is a vector consisting of the elements of S followed by the elements of T which do not belong to S. In general S$\cup$T is not equal to T$\cup$S but (S$\cup$T) $\equiv$ (T$\cup$S). The symbol $\cup$ has not been defined in APL\360.

EXAMPLE 1

$$S \leftarrow 1\ 3\ 3\ 5\ 5\ 7$$
$$T \leftarrow\ 3\ 1\ 5\ 8$$
$$S,(\sim(T \epsilon S))/T$$
$$1\quad 3\quad 3\quad 5\quad 5\quad 7\quad 8$$

EXAMPLE 2

For disjoint sets the vector S∪T is equal to S, T.

$$S \leftarrow 2\ 4\ 7\ 9$$
$$T \leftarrow 1\ 3\ 5$$
$$S,(\sim(T \epsilon S))/T$$
$$2\quad 4\quad 7\quad 9\quad 1\quad 3\quad 5$$
$$S,T$$
$$2\quad 4\quad 7\quad 9\quad 1\quad 3\quad 5$$

14.9 THE PRIMITIVE DEAL FUNCTION

The primitive deal function enables us to select a set of distinct integers at random from a given set of integers. The function has the form shown in Figure 14.9.1.

$$T \leftarrow S?P$$

Fig. 14.9.1

Let P and S be integers with S less than or equal to P. T is a vector consisting of S distinct integers chosen at random from the integers 0 or 1 through P, depending on the origin.

EXAMPLE 1

Let the cards in a deck of ordinary playing cards be denoted by the integers 1 to 52. In a deal of bridge the hand held by a particular player, NORTH, is simulated by

```
    NORTH←13?52
    NORTH
34   39   1   14   12   17   43   47   6   32   24   10   21
```

EXAMPLE 2

A manufacturer supplies transistors in lots of 1000. In order to determine whether the lot should be accepted, 10 items are selected at random for testing. The particular items chosen are those whose numbers are given by

```
        T←10?1000
        T
238   275   360   167   487   898   910   61   905   505
```

The set operations described, together with the primitive function deal, provide the basis for handling applications in probability theory.

EXERCISES

1. Let V←3 9.2 14.8 ¯1.6 18 76.3 ¯36.1. Write APL expressions for the following.

    A. The positive components of V

    B. The negative components of V

    C. The components of V greater than 11

    D. The first and third components of V

2. Let A be a literal vector whose components are the letters of the alphabet. Define B as the vector whose components are the letters of the alphabet separated by spaces. Write an expression for B.

3. Let M and N be matrices, and let U be the number of elements of M which also appear in N. Write an expression for U.

4. Let V←ι30; let U←7↓ι30. Write APL statements for the following.

A. V∩U

B. V∪U

C. U∩V

D. V△U

5. Assume that 52 playing cards are numbered from 1 to 52 with 1 to 13 representing spades, 14 to 26 hearts, 27 to 39 diamonds, and 40 to 52 clubs. Construct a niladic function which simulates the dealing of a bridge hand.

6. Given a literal vector D, define an APL function to generate a sequence of N randomly chosen characters on D.

THE DECODE AND ENCODE FUNCTIONS

15.1 INTRODUCTION

The two primitive functions to be examined in this chapter are called
decode and encode. The decode function is useful in conversion problems, such as going from degrees, minutes, and seconds to seconds
or from one number system to another, e.g., from binary to decimal.
It also provides a simple means for evaluating polynomials. The
function is often called the base value function because its two arguments consist of a weighted vector called the base and another vector
which is evaluated by the base.

The encode function, which is the inverse function to decode, is
often called the representation function. The encode function provides
a convenient mechanism for representing a scalar within a particular
number system or in converting from one system of units to another

15.2 THE PRIMITIVE DECODE FUNCTION

The decode function is denoted by the character $\perp$ and has the form
shown in Figure 15.2.1, where V and T are vectors of the same
dimension or scalars. A scalar is extended if necessary to match the
dimension of the other variable. The result S is a scalar. The vector V determines a weighting vector U, defined as follows:

$U[\rho V]$ is equal to 1   (1)

$U[I]$ is equal to $V[I] \times U[I]$ for I equal 1 to T equal $(\rho V)-1$.   (2)

The scalar S is defined as $S \leftarrow +/U \times T$

$S \leftarrow V \perp T$

Fig. 15.2.1

EXAMPLE 1

We wish to convert 75° 28' 47'' to seconds. We define a vector V

   $V \leftarrow 360\ 60\ 60$

The vector T is defined as

   $T \leftarrow 75\ 28\ 47$

Then, by (2)

   $U \leftarrow 3600\ 60\ 1$

so that

         $S \leftarrow +/T \times U$
         S
   271727

All of this is carried out by writing

         $S \leftarrow V \perp T$
         S
   271727

EXAMPLE 2

Consider the problem of converting from the octal system (base 8) to the decimal system. We use the subscript $_8$ to denote the octal representation of a number. What, then, is the decimal equivalent of 3257_8? Let

   $T \leftarrow 3\ 2\ 5\ 7$
   $V \leftarrow 8$

Although V is a scalar, it is extended to match the dimension of T, so that

   $V \leftarrow 8\ 8\ 8$

We therefore define U as

   $U \leftarrow 512\ 64\ 8\ 1$

so that

$S \leftarrow +/U \times V$

Again, all of this takes place when we write

$V \perp T$
1711

15.3 EVALUATION OF POLYNOMIALS

Let a polynomial of nth degree be written

$$A_n X^n + A_{n-1} X^{n-1} + \cdots + A_0$$

where the A's are real numbers, and X is the polynomial variable. To evaluate the polynomial for some constant C means to substitute C for X and carry out the indicated operations. The decode function makes it very easy to do this. Let the coefficients of the polynomial be represented by a vector A, and let the variable V take on the value C for which the polynomial is to be evaluated. The weighting vector U becomes

$U \leftarrow C \star N, C \star (N-1), \ldots, 1$

so that

$V \perp A$

gives us the value of the polynomial for C.

EXAMPLE 1

Find the value of

$$X^5 + 3.2 X^4 + 1.72 X^3 + X^2 + 6.81 X + .5$$

at X=2

```
A←1 3.2 1.72 1 6.81 .5
V←2
V⊥A
```
115.08

15.4 MAPPING THE INDICES OF AN ARRAY OF HIGHER RANK

As we have already seen, it is often convenient to transform an array
A of rank two or greater into a vector V. In this transformation an
element of an array of rank N whose indices are I[1],I[2],...,I[N] is
mapped into V[K]. We wish to determine K, given I[1],...,I[N].
This is easily accomplished by the decode function. Let A be an array of rank N and let

   $D \leftarrow \rho A$

Let I be the vector of indices of some element of A. Then

   $K \leftarrow D \perp (I[1]-1),(I[2]-1),...I[\rho V]$

EXAMPLE 1

Let A be the array defined by

   $A \leftarrow 3\ 5\ 2 \rho (\iota 30)$

What will the index K be of the element whose indices are 2 4 1 in A
when A is raveled?

        3 5 2⊥1 3 1
   17

15.5 THE PRIMITIVE ENCODE FUNCTION

The encode function is denoted by T and has the form shown in Figure
15.5.1, where S is a scalar, or one-element vector, V is a vector,
and Z is a vector such that ρZ is equal to ρV. The vector V determines a weighting vector U according to equations (1) and (2) of Section 15.2. Z is the vector such that

   $S \leftarrow +/Z \times U$

In other words, Z is the representation or encoding of S in the base
U determined by V.

$$\boxed{Z \leftarrow V \top S}$$

Fig. 15.5.1

EXAMPLE 1

In Example 1 of Section 15.2 we converted degrees, minutes, and seconds to seconds. Suppose now that we wish to convert seconds to degrees and minutes. Then the quantity 14230 seconds is converted as follows:

```
      Z←60 60 60⊤14230
      Z
3  57  10
```

EXAMPLE 2

Suppose that we wish to represent 1367 as an octal number. Let

```
      S←1367
      V←8 8 8 8
      V⊤S
2   5   2   7
```

EXAMPLE 3

If A is an array of rank N and if the element with indices I[1], I[2], ..., I[N] is mapped onto the same element with index K, when A is raveled, then for a given K the indices of the corresponding element of A are determined as follows:

```
      A←3 5 2ρ1
      K←17

      Z←((((ρA)-1)ρ1),0)+(ρA)⊤K
2   4   1
```

The decode and encode functions have also been extended to arrays of higher rank.

EXERCISES

1. Evaluate the following polynomials at the points indicated.

   A. $X^2-16x+9$ at X=3.1

   B. $2X^6+5x^3-13X^2+11X+2$ at X=6.2

   C. $X^4+3X^2-6X+11$ at X=.07

2. Convert the following angles from degrees, minutes, and seconds to decimal degrees and to radians.

   A. 26° 10' 13"

   B. 105° 38' 15"

3. Convert the following decimal numbers to the indicated base.

   A. 15911 to binary (base 2)

   B. 3716 to octal (base 8)

   C. 1612 to base 5

4. Construct a monadic function whose argument X is a decimal integer and which converts X to a hexadecimal (base 16). Use the letters A through F in addition to the integers 0 through 9 as the elements of the hexadecimal system.

5. Let D be an arbitrary array. Construct two monadic functions with argument D which compute the indices of

   A. the maximum element of D;
   B. the minimum element of D.

PART THREE
I/O AND SYSTEM COMMANDS

16.1 INTRODUCTION

In this chapter we discuss certain topics which come under the heading of input-output. On the input side we introduce a new primitive function called quad, denoted by the character □. With the aid of this function, any user-defined function can be designed to request input from the terminal, during execution, rather than in the statement which invokes it. The quad function makes it possible to relieve the user of the burden of having to memorize the nature and order of the inputs. It also provides a mechanism for using functions as arguments of other functions.

On the output side we are going to talk in much more detail about displaying information. In almost every application that uses the computer as something more than a desk calculator, it will be necessary to present the results of computations in the form of a report. Depending on the nature of the problem and the requirements of the person or persons for whom the results are intended, the format of the report may be quite simple or relatively complex. We shall examine the facilities available for producing titles, subtitles, column headings, proper column widths, etc. In addition, we shall look at some functions that will enable us to display information in the form of a graph. This capability is extremely useful in that a graph often conveys information not readily apparent in a table.

16.2 NUMERICAL AND LITERAL INPUT AND THE QUAD FUNCTION

The primitive function quad, denoted by the character □, which appears on the APL keyboard to the right of the specification function, for example,

$$X \leftarrow 2 \times \square + C \times 3$$

is interpreted to mean that an APL expression will be substituted for the quad symbol and entered from the terminal. When the computer scans the statement and detects the quad symbol, it moves the carriage up one line and prints

$\square$:

The keyboard is then unlocked, waiting for an entry from the user. When the entry is made, the input is substituted for the quad and execution of the statement resumes. In order to tell the user the significance of the information being requested, a function statement containing a quad will normally be preceded by a statement describing the nature of the input, for example,

[2] *'ENTER COEFFICIENT OF EXPANSION'*

When the function is invoked, this is what the user will see.

ENTER COEFFICIENT OF EXPANSION
$\square$:

Now it is clear to him what kind of information is being requested. A function may have many such inputs, and each one will normally be preceded by an appropriate description. For example, in Figure 16.2.1 we see a portion of the APL function RUNGEKUTTA, which implements the method of Runge-Kutta for solving a differential equation of the form

$y'=f(x,y)$

with initial value y_0 at x_0 at the equally spaced points $x_0, x_0+h, x_0+2h, \ldots$. The APL function requests the points x_0 and y_0, followed by the step width h, and a bound for the largest value of x for which a solution is to be computed. If we were using RUNGEKUTTA to solve the equation

$y'=x^2-y^2$

with y = 1 at x = 0, h = 0.01 from x = 0 to x = 2, the printout in Figure 16.2.1 is what would appear on paper when we reached statement 18.

For functions which are used only occasionally, for which the order or nature of the input is not readily grasped, or which must be

```
        RUNGEKUTTA
SPECIFY AN INITIAL VALUE FOR X[0].
□:
        0
SPECIFY AN INITIAL VALUE FOR Y[0].
□:
        1
SPECIFY A VALUE FOR THE INTERVAL H
□:
        .01
SPECIFY THE UPPER LIMIT FOR X
□:
        2.0
```

Fig. 16.2.1

given to other users, the quad function preceded by an appropriate
description makes use easier.

16.2.1 Functions as Arguments

Another important use of the quad function occurs in certain applications where the argument of a function is also a function. For example, suppose we have a function called SIMPSON which implements
Simpson's method of numerical integration. Obviously, we must supply SIMPSON with the function which is to be integrated, but how?
The natural way would be to have a dummy variable in the header of
SIMPSON. But when SIMPSON is invoked, the variable would have to
be replaced with something for which a definite value has been specified. What we would like to do is to replace this variable by a function and have the function substituted uniformly throughout the body of
SIMPSON for the dummy variable. Unfortunately, this is not permitted because, as we have pointed out, functions cannot be passed
as arguments. However, there is a good way out. One solution consists in using the quad as a means of entering the function. In
Figure 16.2.2 we see how this is done. The function to be integrated
is expressed in terms of the variable X and entered from the terminal.

```
      ∇SIMPSON[▯]
    ∇ Z←N SIMPSON A;X
[1]   Z←(| -/A÷N×3)×+/▯×1,((N-1)ρ 4 2),1,0ρX←A[1],A[1]+(ιN)×| -/A÷N
[2]   ⍝FUNCTION MAY BE ANY APL FUNCTION EXPRESSED IN X
[3]   ⍝N IS THE NUMBER OF INTERVALS FOR EVALUATION
[4]   ⍝A IS A VECTOR CONTAINING THE LOWER AND UPPER LIMIT
[5]   ⍝OF THE INTEGRAL
    ∇
[6]  ∇
```

Fig. 16.2.2

16.2.2 Non-Normal Input to the Quad Function

When input other than what is normally expected is entered, any one
of a number of different things may happen. For example, entering
the character → will terminate the request for input, and pressing
the RETURN key will cause the request for input to be repeated.
Some kinds of input will result in an error condition.

Certain system commands also terminate the request for input,
but others have no effect on it. We shall describe the system commands in Chapter 18.

16.2.3 Using Quad with Literal Input

If the quad symbol is overstruck with the quote symbol, that is, ▯,
what is entered is interpreted as literal data. This obviates the need
to surround literal input with quote signs. When the character ▯ is
detected, the carriage is moved up a line, but the symbol ▯ is not
printed and input begins at the left margin.

EXAMPLE 1

```
      X←▯
PERKIN-ELMER CORP
      X
PERKIN-ELMER CORP
```

EXAMPLE 2

```
        A←5
        X←⎕
  2×A+3
        X
  2×A+3
```

Note that when X is displayed the result is 2×A+3, not 16, because the variable X is specified as a literal.

In certain applications, titles or other literal data may be variable. For example, we might want to attach to the nodes of a network labels that depend on the elements constituting the network. The quad function makes it easy to do so. For example, in Figure 16.2.3 we see a portion of a function called NETWORK.

```
        ∇NETWORK[⎕15]
  [15]   BEGIN:→(DIM[1]<I←I+1)/NEXT
  [16]   'NAME OF NODE ';I
  [17]   NAME[I;]←((15-ρTEMP)ρ' '),TEMP←⎕
  [18]   →BEGIN
```

Fig. 16.2.3

Statements 15 to 17 create a matrix of names called NAME. They are the names of the nodes of a network. When the function is invoked, it tells the user that it wants a name for each node and requests input. If the name of a node is less than 15 characters, spaces are inserted to give a total of 15 characters. Each of the names is a row entry of the matrix.

16.2.4 Terminating Literal Input

To terminate a request for literal input, you must overstrike the three alphabetic characters O, U, and T by using the BACKSPACE key. Any other sequence of characters will be accepted as input. If the function which requests the input tests to see whether it is permissible, you may continue to receive a request for input if you do not know the correct format.

16.2.5 Using the Quad to Display Information

When the quad function appears to the left of the specification function ←,

```
     □←X
12
```

the value of the expression is displayed.

Inserting the quad function at strategic points in a long and complicated expression makes it possible to see how the expression is built up. If the result at any point is incorrect, it is easier to see what corrections should be made.

16.3 DISPLAYING INFORMATION

We learned at the outset that a variable or expression, whether numeric or literal, can be displayed by naming it. In many cases the easiest way to create a title will be to define a literal vector and display it, for example,

```
'FOURIER SERIES COEFFICIENTS'
```

Since we know what the width of our page is and where the tabs are set, it is not difficult to center the title. On the other hand, it is also relatively easy to design a function that accepts literal input and does these things for us (see Figure 16.3.1).

```
    ∇ W CENTER L
[1]     ⍝THIS FUNCTION CENTERS THE TITLE GIVEN BY THE
[2]     ⍝LITERAL VARIABLE L. W IS THE WIDTH OF THE LINE.
[3]     ⍝IF THE NUMBER OF CHARACTERS IN THE TITLE EXCEEDS W, AN ERR
[4]     ⍝MESSAGE IS PRINTED.
[5]     →((ρL)>W)/PRINT
[6]     G←W-ρL
[7]     (⌊0.5×G)ρ' ';L
[8]     →0
[9]     PRINT:'TOO MANY CHARACTERS IN TITLE'
[10]    →0
    ∇
```

Fig. 16.3.1

16.4 HETEROGENEOUS OUTPUT

In certain kinds of applications it is convenient to have literal information and numeric information on the same line. For example, given a function that produces the roots of a quadratic equation, we might want to display the roots as follows:

ROOT 1 = 120.365

ROOT 2 = 94.812

Output consisting of both literal and numeric data on the same line is referred to as mixed.

Mixed output is obtained by separating literal and numeric output by a semicolon. Let two variables X1 and X2 denote the roots of the quadratic equation and suppose that statements 10 and 11 of a function called QUADRATIC request that the roots be printed. This is what statements 10 and 11 will look like.

[10] '*ROOT*1=   ';*X*1

[11] '*ROOT*2=   ';*X*2

No spaces are inserted by the computer between the numeric and literal portions of the data. Therefore the spaces are included as part of the literal data. If one of the outputs is a matrix or an array of higher rank, it will be displayed on the next line.

'*THE INVERSE OF THE MATRIX IS*' ;3 3ρ9?9

You may put as much literal or numeric information on a line as you wish, but literal and numeric information must always be separated by the semicolon.

16.5 FORMATTING NUMERIC OUTPUT

We have seen that when numeric data is displayed, the computer has its own set of rules for determining what the format will be. To have to be at the mercy of the computer is very undesirable, and so there are user-defined functions that give us considerable control in determining the format of the output. These functions are part of a workspace called PLOTFORMAT, which is itself contained in one of the public libraries that come with APL\360. They will therefore be available at the installation where you are working. In fact, the workspace which contains them also contains a description of how they work. Intelligent use of the functions demands only that we know what inputs are required and what outputs will be produced. It is not really necessary to be familiar with the contents of the functions although we shall display them later. The one great deficiency of these functions is that they are very time consuming.

16.5.1 Functions DFT and EFT

The function DFT (decimal form tabular) and EFT (exponential form tabular) make it easy to present an array of numbers in either decimal or exponential form, respectively.

The function headers have the form

   A DFT B

   A EFT B

where B, which is to be displayed, must be an array of rank less than or equal to 3. For an array of rank 3, only the first plane is significant.

The left argument, A, may consist of a single integer, a pair of integers, or as many pairs of integers as there are columns of B. This is how A is interpreted.

A (single integer):
DFT: Specifies the number of digits to the right of the decimal point in decimal format.
EFT: Specifies the number of significant digits in exponential format. One digit always appears to the left of the decimal point. Columns will be spaced uniformly and there will be two spaces between the closest numbers.

A (pair of integers):
The first integer specifies the total number of spaces to be allocated to each column, and the second is used as above.
DFT: The first number must be at least two larger than the second.

EFT: The first number must be at least six larger than the second.
      If the first number is too small, a domain problem will be
      signaled.
More than one pair of integers:
There must be one pair for each column of output (or each element of
a vector). Each pair will be interpreted as above and will apply to the
layout of the corresponding column. If the number of pairs does not
match the number of columns, a length problem will be signaled.

Figures 16.5.1 and 16.5.2 show how the functions DFT and EFT
are composed.[1]

```
∇DFT[□]
     ∇ Z←W DFT X;D;E;F;G;H;I;J;K;L;Y
[1]     D←' 0123456789.¯'
[2]     →(∨/W≠⌊W←,W+(H←0)×L←1<ρρX)/DFTERR+0×F←2
[3]     →(3 2 1 <ρρX)/(DFTERR+F←0), 2 3 +I26
[4]     →(ρρρX←((∨/ 1 2 =ρW)⌽ 1 2)⍉(1,ρ,X)ρX)/2+I26
[5]     X←(0 1 1 /ρX)ρX
[6]     →((∧/(ρW)≠ 1 2 ,2×E←1ρφρX),1≠ρW)/(DFTERR×F←1),3+I26
[7]     I←1+⌈/0,,⌊10⍟|X+1> |X
[8]     W←(2+I+W+(W≠0)+∨/,X<0),W
[9]     →(∨/2>-/[1]W←⍉(E,2)ρW)/DFTERR+0×F←2
[10]    Z←((K←1ρρX),+/W[1;])ρ' '
[11]    X←⌊0.5+X×10*(ρX)ρW[2;]
[12]    DFTLP:→(E<H←H+1)/DFTEND
[13]    J←1+⌊10 |( |Y←X[;H])∘.÷10*¯1+φιI←W[1;H]
[14]    J←(,J)×G←,⍉(⍒ρJ)ρ(,⍉(J≠1)∨.∧(ιI)∘.≤ιI-F+1),(K×1+F←W[2;H])ρ1
[15]    →(∧/0≤Y)/2+I26
[16]    J[1+(ρJ)|¯1+(I-+/(K,I)ρG)+I×¯1+ιK]←12×Y<0
[17]    J←(K,I)ρJ
[18]    →(0=F)/3+I26
[19]    J←J[;(1φιG),(G←-/W[;H ])+ιF]
[20]    J[;G]←11
[21]    →DFTLP×ρρρZ[;(+/W[1;ιH-1])+ιI]←D[1+J ]
[22]    DFTEND:→L/0
[23]    →0×ρZ←,Y
[24]    DFTERR:'DFT ',(3 6 ρ' RANK LENGTHDOM IN')[F+1;],' PROBLEM.'
     ∇
[25]    ∇
```

Fig. 16.5.1 The Function DFT

_____

[1]   The four functions presented in this section are reprinted by
permission from APL 360 Users Manual, copyright 1968, 1969 by
International Business Machines Corporation.

```
      ∇EFT[□]
    ∇ Z←W EFT X;D;E;H;J;K;L;Q;S;T;U;Y
[1]    D←'0123456789.E ¯'
[2]    →(∨/W≠⌊W←,W+(H←0)×L←1<ρρX)/EFTERR+0×K←2
[3]    →(3 2 1 <ρρX)/(EFTERR+K←0), 2 3 +⍳26
[4]    X←((∨/ 1 2 =ρW)⌽ 1 2)⍉(1,ρ,X)ρX
[5]    X←(⌽2ρ⌽ρX)ρX
[6]    →((∧/(ρW)≠ 1 2 ,2×E←1ρ⌽ρX),1≠ρW)/(EFTERR×K←1),2+⍳26
[7]    W←(W+6+(∨/,X<0)+∨/,1> |X),W
[8]    →(∨/6>-/[1]W←⍉(E,2)ρW)/EFTERR+0×K←2
[9]    Z←((K+1ρρX),+/W[1;])ρ' '
[10]   EFTLP:→(E<H←H+1)/EFTEND
[11]   S←1+⌊10⍟|Y+0=Y←X[;H]
[12]   U←1+⌊10⍟|Y+0=Y←⌊0.5+(10*Q-15)+Y×10*(Q+W[2;H])-S
[13]   J←(((T-4)ρ1),4ρ0)\1+⌊10 |(|Y÷10*U>Q)∘.÷10*¯1+⌽⍳¯4+T←W[1;H]
[14]   J[;T- 2 1]←1+⌊10 |(|S-U≤Q)∘.÷ 10 1
[15]   J[;(⍳U←T-4+Q),T]←13
[16]   J[;1,U,T,T-3]←⍉(4,K)ρ(Kρ11),(13+0>Y,S-1),Kρ12
[17]   J[;⍳T-3]←J[;(1⌽⍳U+1),(U+1+⍳Q)]
[18]   J[;T- 2 1 0]←(-S≤0)⌽J[;T- 2 1 0]
[19]   →EFTLP×ρρρZ[;(+/W[1;⍳H-1])+⍳T]←D[J]
[20]   EFTEND:→L/0
[21]   →0×ρZ←↓ ⍝
[22]   EFTERR:'EFT ',(3 6 ρ' RANK LENGTHDOMAIN')[K+1;],' PROBLEM.
     ∇
[23]   ∇
```

Fig. 16.5.2 The Function EFT

EXAMPLE 1

The array is displayed in decimal form with two digits after the
decimal point. Each column is 8 spaces wide.

```
      A←5 5ρ25?25
      B←5 5ρ25?25
      8 2DFT (A÷B)
```

7.00	.95	.79	1.44	3.00
.57	1.29	3.50	2.18	.10
2.50	.58	.11	.20	2.60
17.00	2.00	.15	1.14	.67
.65	.86	.52	.77	1.07

EXAMPLE 2

```
      A←6 6ρ36?36
      B←A⋆2
      8 2 EFT (A÷B)
```

```
2.5E‾01 3.7E‾02 2.0E‾01 5.6E‾02 6.3E‾02 7.7E‾02
1.7E‾01 1.3E‾01 3.1E‾02 5.0E‾01 1.0E‾01 6.7E‾02
2.9E‾02 3.4E‾02 1.4E‾01 1.0E00  4.8E‾02 3.3E‾01
3.2E‾02 4.3E‾02 5.9E‾02 7.1E‾02 1.1E‾01 3.3E‾02
2.9E‾02 4.5E‾02 5.3E‾02 8.3E‾02 3.8E‾02 4.0E‾02
9.1E‾02 3.0E‾02 2.8E‾02 5.3E‾02 3.6E‾02 4.2E‾02
```

EXAMPLE 3

```
      A←1.23 300.1 6000 0.235
      B←4 4ρ(4?9042)÷612
      7 1 EFT C
```

```
9.E00  8.E00  1.E01  7.E00  9.E00  1.E01
5.E00  1.E00  1.E01  1.E00  8.E00  4.E00
6.E00  7.E00  2.E00  1.E01  6.E00  1.E01
```

16.5.2 The Auxiliary Function AND

There is in the same workspace a function called AND which will be
especially useful if you are working with a version of APL\360 which
does not permit catenation of arrays other than vectors.

   The function AND is essentially a column catenator, which permits two matrices or a matrix and a vector to be joined. It is thus a
way of providing input to DFT and EFT. Figure 16.5.3 shows the body
of the function and an example of its use is shown in Fig. 16.5.4.

16.5.3 The Auxiliary Function VS

Essentially a column catenator, similar to AND except that the right-
hand argument must be of rank ≤ 1, VS is designed primarily to provide convenient formation of input for plotting. Whether used by itself
or with AND, VS will cause its right argument to appear as the leftmost
column of the resultant array. (The resultant will be an array of rank
three, consisting of a single plane.) Figure 16.5.4 shows the body of
the function.

```
      ∇AND[⎕]
    ∇ L←A  AND  B;C;D
[1]    →(((2<ρρA)∨3<ρρB),0≠ρρB)/ 17 3
[2]    B←,B
[3]    →(((3=ρρB)∧1≠1ρρB),2=ρρA)/ 17 7
[4]    A←,A
[5]    →(∧/((ρA)≠1,D),1≠D←1ρ¯2⌽ρB)/16
[6]    A←(((D×ρA)⌊D⌈ρA),1)ρA
[7]    →(1≠ρρB)/9
[8]    B←(((ρB)⌈(1=ρB)×1ρρA),1)ρB
[9]    →((∧/D≠1,1ρρA),1≠D←1ρ¯2⌽ρB)/ 16 11
[10]   B←(((3=ρρB)ρ1),(1ρρA),1ρ⌽ρB)ρB
[11]   →(3=ρρB)/14
[12]   L←(((C←1ρ⌽ρA)ρ0),(1ρ⌽ρB)ρ1)\B
[13]   →0×ρρL[;⍳C]←A
[14]   L←(1,((C←1ρ⌽ρA)ρ0),(¯1+1ρ⌽ρB)ρ1)\B
[15]   →0×ρρL[;;1+⍳C]←A
[16]   →0=ρ⍞←'ARGUMENTS OF  AND  ARE NOT CONFORMABL.
[17]   'AN ARGUMENT OF  AND  IS OF IMPROP R RANK.'
    ∇
[18]   ∇
```

Fig. 16.5.3 The Function AND

```
         ∇ VS[▯]
       ∇ M←A VS B;C;D
[1]      →(((ρρB←,B)<ρρB), 2 1 0 <ρρA)/ 8 8 4 3
[2]      A←((ρB),1)ρA
[3]      A←((×/ρA),1)ρA
[4]      →(∧/(ρB)≠1,1ρρA)/9
[5]      M←(0,(1ρϕρA)ρ1)\A
[6]      M[;ι1]←B
[7]      →0×ρρM←(1,ρM)ρM
[8]      →0=ρ▯←'AN ARGUMENT OF  VS  IS OF IMPROPER RANK.'
[9]      'ARGUMENTS OF  VS  ARE NOT CONFORMABLE.'
       ∇
[10]   ∇
```

Fig. 16.5.4 The Function VS

EXAMPLE

```
       A←3 3ρ12?12
       B←3 3ρ12?12
       A
  6  10   4
 12   3   1
  2  11   5
       B
  3   1   7
 10  11   2
  9   6   4
       C←A AND B
       C
  6  10   4   3   1   7
 12   3   1  10  11   2
  2  11   5   9   6   4
       6 0 DFT C
      6      10      4      3      1      7
     12       3      1     10     11      2
      2      11      5      9      6      4
```

16.5.4 Some More Printing Functions

Because the functions DFT and EFT are both time consuming and space consuming, many users have constructed their own functions to overcome these deficiencies. The following functions[2] ΔFT and ΔET are so

(2) These functions are due to Robert A. Stephan of the Department of Operations, Research and Administrative Sciences, Naval Postgraduate School, Monterey, California. They appeared in APL Quote-quad, Vol. 5, Issue 4, Winter 1974, and are reproduced here.

designed. The functions ΔFT and ΔET exhibited herewith may be of interest to many readers because they are much smaller and faster than DFT and EFT respectively but do the same job when the left-hand argument is either one or two integers. Part of the gain in efficiency comes from eliminating all looping and hence the provision for different format specifications for each column; however, even for vectors, execution time is usually reduced to half of that of DFT and EFT. This increase efficiency often makes it profitable to use ΔFT or ΔET several times for portions of the same array in preference to once for the slower DFT or EFT. Except for the multiple format capability, the use of these functions is the same as DFT and EFT, and the result is always a matrix.

ΔFT also has provisions for left justification and deletion of trailing zeros. If the first (field width) entry of the left argument is negative, the interpretation is to left-justify the result. This is done in line (8). If the second or only left argument entry (decimal positions) is negative trailing zeros will not be deleted. Otherwise lines (5) and (6) will take out the unwanted zeros. If either of these provisions is not needed the appropriate lines can be deleted along with their associated branching statements in lines (4) and (7), thereby making the function even more compact. In any event, whenever a result is too large for the specified field width, that field will be filled with asterisks.

```
      ∇ΔFT[□]
    ∇ L←W ΔFT R;D;T;O;I;J;N;M;Δ;S;Q
[1]    S←(Q,Δ←∨/S)ρ(S←0>R←(⌊0.5+N×(Q←×/M←
1⌈‾2↑ρR)ρR)÷N←10*J←|D←1↓W←⌈‾2↑,W)\' '
[2]    →E×10=I←O⌈ .×~T←(|W←W+(0=W←1↑W)×T+2
+⌈/O)<(T←Δ+J+×J)+O←1+⌊10⊛1⌈R←|R
[3]    S←(ρO)ρ(,O←ΔφO)\(,O←(O⌈I-O)∘.<φΔφφ
ιI+Δ)/,S,(L←'0123456789')[1+⍉(Iρ10)T⌊R]
[4]    →(D≤1)/Z,R←ρL←((Q,×J)ρ'.'),L[1+⍉(J
ρ10)T⌈N×1|R]
[5]    D←,(-R)↑(('0'≠0 2↓L)⌈.×D)∘.<D←ιD-1
[6]    L←Rρ L,L[D/ιρL←,L]←' '
[7]    Z:→(W≥0)/E-ρ,L[T/ι1↑S←ρL←S,L;]←'*'
[8]    L←Sρ(,φO)\(,O←O,Rρ1)/,L
[9]    →0,ρL←(M×1,|W)ρ(Q,-W)↑L
[10] E:'ΔFT FIELD WIDTH PROBLEM'
        ∇
[11]    ∇
```

```
        ∇ΔET[□]
      ∇ NO←W ΔET MI;L;D;G;T;O;WI;J;N;Δ
[1]   MI←MI÷10*O←⌊10⊛|MI+0=MI←(N←×/L←1⌈‾
2↑ρMI)ρMI
[2]   G←(N,J←∨/G)ρ(G←0>MI←⌊0.5+MI×Δ←10*D
←‾1+|1↓W←⌈‾2↑,W)\'‾'
[3]   →E×ι(|W←W+(0=W←1↑W)×2+J)<J←D+(N←O∨
.<0)+3+J+WI←1+10⌈.≤|O←O+T←(Δ×10)≤MI←|MI
[4]   J←1↑ρMI←(NO←'0123456789.+‾')[1+MI[
1;],10,⌽(Dρ10)⊤,1 0↓MI←(0,Δ)⊤MI÷10*T]
[5]   →0,ρNO←(L×1,|W)ρ(J,-W)↑G,MI,'E',NO
[((J,N)ρ13-×O),1+⌽(WIρ10)⊤|O]
[6]   E:'ΔET FIELD WIDTH PROBLEM'
      ∇
[7]   ∇
```

16.6 GRAPHIC OUTPUT

It is extremely useful to be able to plot the results of a computation. In the workspace PLOTFORMAT there is a function called PLOT which will enable you to produce a graph of one or more functions with a minimum of effort. By assigning the appropriate value to one of the variables in the function, you can get it to produce a histogram rather than a continuous curve.

The documentation of how the function works appears in the same workspace under a variable called HOWPLOT. If you typed the name of this variable, this is what you would see displayed:

HOWPLOT

THE FUNCTION PLOT WILL GRAPH ONE OR MORE FUNCTIONS SIMULTANEOUSLY,

AUTOMATICALLY SCALING THE VALUES TO FIT APPROXIMATELY WITHIN SCALE

DIMENSIONS SPECIFIED BY THE USER.   IT WILL WORK ONLY IN 1-ORIGIN INDEXING.

THE FORM IN WHICH PLOT IS USED IS:

SCALESIZE PLOT FUNCTION

LEFT ARGUMENT: ONE OR TWO NUMBERS.

THE FIRST NUMBER SPECIFIES THE APPROXIMATE SIZE OF THE VERTICAL AXIS AND

THE SECOND NUMBER DOES THE SAME FOR THE HORIZONTAL AXIS.

IF ONLY ONE NUMBER IS SUPPLIED, IT IS APPLIED TO BOTH AXES.

THERE IS NO BUILT-IN LIMIT TO THE DIMENSIONS, AND A HORIZONTAL AXIS LARGER THAN THE WORKSPACE WIDTH WILL CAUSE SOME POINTS TO BE PRINTED ON THE NEXT LOWER LINE.

RIGHT ARGUMENT: A RECTANGULAR ARRAY WITH RANK <3.

SCALAR: WILL BE TREATED AS A VECTOR OF LENGTH ONE.

VECTOR: WILL BE PLOTTED AS ORDINATE AGAINST ITS OWN INDICES AS ABSCISSA.

MATRIX: THE LEFTMOST COLUMN WILL BE TAKEN AS THE ABSCISSA AND ALL OTHER COLUMNS WILL BE PLOTTED AS ORDINATES.   A DIFFERENT PLOTTING SYMBOL UP TO THE NUMBER OF SYMBOLS AVAILABLE WILL BE USED FOR EACH COLUMN.   IN CASE TWO ORDINATES HAVE A COMMON POINT, THE SYMBOL FOR THE COLUMN FURTHEST TO THE RIGHT WILL BE USED.

3-DIMENSIONAL ARRAY: THE FIRST PLANE WILL BE PLOTTED AS A MATRIX, AND ALL OTHER PLANES WILL BE DISREGARDED.

PLOT CHARACTERS: THE SYMBOLS USED ARE ASSIGNED TO THE VARIABLE PC IN LINE 1 OF PLOT.   THE ALPHABET SUPPLIED IS 'O∗□∘'.   THIS ALPHABET MAY BE EXTENDED AND MODIFIED AS DESIRED, USING THE NORMAL FUNCTION-EDITING PROCEDURES: EITHER CHANGE LINE 1 OF THE FUNCTION, OR DELETE IT AND INDEPENDENTLY SPECIFY A VALUE FOR PC.

HISTOGRAMS: PLOT CAN BE USED TO GENERATE HISTOGRAMS BY SETTING THE VARIABLE HS TO 1 IN LINE 2 OF THE FUNCTION.   ALTERNATELY, LINE 2 CAN BE DELETED, AND HS CAN BE SET EXTERNALLY.

To demonstrate the use of the plot function, we shall plot the sine and cosine functions for all angles between 0 and 360° at intervals of 10° on the same graph.

```
        ∇ DEMOPLOT
[1]     ⍝THIS FUNCTION DEMONSTRATES THE USE OF THE PLOT
[2]     ⍝ROUTINE.  IT PLOTS THE FUNCTIONS SINE X AND COS X
[3]     ⍝FOR ALL ANGLES BETWEEN ZERO AND 360 DEGREES AT
[4]     ⍝INTERVALS OF TEN DEGREES. THE SCALE USED IN THE
[5]     ⍝PLOT IS 50 50.
[6]     T←1○(0,10×⍳36)×○1÷180
[7]     W←2○(0,10×⍳36)×○1÷180
[8]     R←0,10×⍳36
[9]     50 50 PLOT Z←R AND W AND T
[10] ∇
```

Fig. 16.6.1 The Function DEMOPLOT

The function DEMOPLOT shown in Figure 16.6.1 computes the
sine and cosine function for all of the angles that we want to plot. To
do so, it calls on the function AND. On completion, the data is
passed to the PLOT function with the indicated scale size. The results are shown in Figure 16.6.2.

To make the PLOT function produce a histogram, we set the variable HS to 1 in line 2 of the function.

The binomial probabilities,

$$\frac{\binom{10}{x}}{2^{10}} \text{ for } x = 0, 1, 2, \ldots, 10$$

plotted in the form of a histogram are shown in Figure 16.6.3.
The parenthesis denotes the combinatorial symbol. Many sophisticated
plotting routines have been developed by vendors and greater resolution
has been made possible by the introduction of a new golf ball. CRT type
displays with APL character sets are being made by a number of
manufacturers.

EXERCISES

1. Construct a function called TAB which tabulates a given function
whose header is $∇Z←CASE\ X$. The range over which the function is to be
tabulated and the increment are to be entered from the terminal.

2. Use the function TAB to evaluate a function that interests you.

3. Plot the functions sin X and sin(x + π/2) on the same graph from
x = 0° to x = 360° , at 15° intervals.

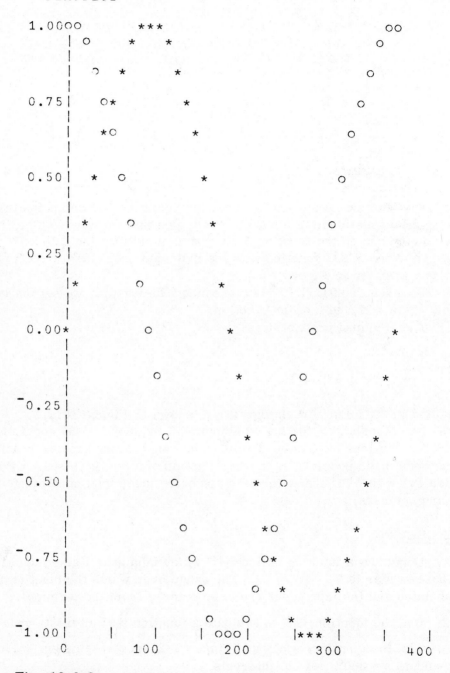

Fig. 16.6.2

```
   40 40 PLOT Q

0.25|                    o
    |                    o
    |                    o
    |                    o
    |               o  o  o
0.20|               o  o  o
    |               o  o  o
    |               o  o  o
    |               o  o  o
    |               o  o  o
0.15|               o  o  o
    |               o  o  o
    |               o  o  o
    |            o  o  o  o  o
    |            o  o  o  o  o
0.10|            o  o  o  o  o
    |            o  o  o  o  o
    |            o  o  o  o  o
    |            o  o  o  o  o
    |            o  o  o  o  o
0.05|            o  o  o  o  o
    |         o  o  o  o  o  o  o
    |         o  o  o  o  o  o  o
    |         o  o  o  o  o  o  o
    |      o  o  o  o  o  o  o  o  o
0.00| o    |        |        |  o  |        |
    0           5          10          15
```

Fig. 16.6.3

17.1 INTRODUCTION

It is one thing to write a function, another to get it to work properly. The process of getting a function to work properly is called error analysis, which is the primary concern of this chapter. We begin by categorizing the situations which tell us that our function is not working properly. The chapter discusses in detail the various error reports that may be produced and the action that will correct them. It describes facilities within the language which allow you to execute the function, one statement at a time, displaying the results as you go and stopping at predetermined statements. The concepts of suspended and pendant functions are introduced, and the use of the state indicator as a way of obtaining information about these functions is described.

17.2 ERROR ANALYSIS

How are we going to verify that a function we have written works properly? We might wonder if there is a function A which will operate on a given function B and tell us whether B is working properly. If there were such a function B, however, we would then require a third function C to know if B is working properly, etc. Therefore we have to rely on what might best be called a common-sense approach.

In order to know that a function is doing what it was intended to do, you must have obtained results by some other method, and you must know that they are correct. Furthermore, you must take into consideration all the different results that might be produced when different branches in the function are exercised and different options are exercised. If the paths the function takes are dependent on data, you must make sure that you have exercised the function for different sets of data. It is a good idea to try random sets of data. When your results agree in every case and you have exercised the function over a

period of time, then you can assume with a high degree of probability
that your function is working properly. We say "a high degree of
probability" since even functions thought to be free of errors have occasionally produced incorrect results. This occurs because some
path in the function or some set of data with special characteristics
was not tested previously. We cannot stress too strongly, especially
for the computer novice, that functions must be checked carefully and
thoroughly before they are certified as correct.

17.3 THREE CATEGORIES OF ERRORS

Although it is difficult to know that a function works properly, it is
easy to tell when the function is doing something wrong. Every error—and a function may contain many errors—falls into one of the
following three categories.

17.3.1 The Infinite Loop

Some sequence of statements within a function may be executed endlessly because there is no way of exiting from it. Consider the following sequence.

```
[5] K←20
[6] I←1
[7] BEGIN:→(K<I)/NEXT
[8] A←I FUN K
[9] →BEGIN
```

The programmer who wrote statement 7 intended to write

```
[7] BEGIN:→(K<I←I+1)/NEXT
```

This would have ensured that the sequence of statements 7 to 9 would
be executed exactly 20 times. The function would then have executed
the statement whose label is NEXT. Instead, statements 7 to 9 will
be executed endlessly because there is no way of escaping.

You will realize that something is wrong when you fail to get output. If you expect the function to run for a long time before output is
produced, i.e., on the order of minutes, it is good practice to ar-
range for the function to print out an indication of how far you are
from getting the real output. Then if you get no output or the same

output over and over again, you should consider the possibility that the function is in an infinite loop. The TRACE and STOP commands, which will be discussed in the next section, will help you find the loop.

17.3.2 Output Which Is Incorrect

The second kind of error is output that is incorrect. Once you recognize that the output is incorrect you need to determine which statement or statements are not doing what you think they are doing. For example, statement 11 of a function was written

    [11] $X \leftarrow C,10A,20A$

when we intended to write

    [11] $X \leftarrow C,(10A),20A$

We can expect, as a rule, to get an incorrect result.

It is a good idea to have a copy of the function at hand. When an error such as this occurs, you will sometimes be able to determine rapidly what the source of trouble is, and your ability to do so should increase with experience. If that should fail, there are two commands which will help you to track the error down systematically.

The Trace Command

Let F be any function. The command

    $T \Delta F \leftarrow V$

where V is a vector of integers corresponding to statement numbers in F, causes the results produced by the statements in F to be displayed when the function is executed. For a branch command, the result is the number of the statement which will be executed next.

The function $TRIG$ in Fig. 17.3.1 calculates the angles and their sines and cosines of a triangle given in terms of its sides. The angles and their trigonometric functions are they displayed.

    $T \Delta TRIG \leftarrow \iota 16$

```
        ∇TRIG[□]
      ∇ TRIG X;A;B;C
[1]     ⍝THIS FUNCTION CALCULATES THE ANGLES OF A TRIANGLE GIVEN IN TER
        MS
[2]     ⍝OF ITS THREE SIDES. IT ALSO CALCULATES THE SINE AND COSINE OF
[3]     ⍝EACH OF THE ANGLES. THE ANGLE A IS OPPOSITE TO X[1], B TO X[2]
        AND
[4]     ⍝C TO X[3]. IF THE GIVEN SIDES OF A TRIANGLE ARE INCONSISTENT,
        THE
[5]     ⍝FUNCTION WILL TELL YOU THIS AND STOP.
[6]     X←|X
[7]     →((X[1]<X[2]+X[3])∧(X[2]<X[1]+X[3])∧(X[3]<X[1]+X[2]))/BEGIN
[8]     'THE SIDES YOU HAVE SELECTED ARE INCONSISTENT'
[9]     →0
[10]    BEGIN:A←¯2○((+/X*2)-2×X[1]*2)÷2×X[2]×X[3]
[11]    B←¯2○((+/X*2)-2×X[2]*2)÷2×X[1]×X[3]
[12]    C←¯2○((+/X*2)-2×X[3]*2)÷2×X[1]×X[2]
[13]    '               ANGLE(DEGREES)                SINE                    COSINE'
[14]    20 3 20 3 20 3 DFT((A×180÷○1),(1○A),(2○A))
[15]    20 3 20 3 20 3 DFT((B×180÷○1),(1○B),(2○B))
[16]    20 3 20 3 20 3 DFT((C×180÷○1),(1○C),(2○C))
      ∇
[17]    ∇
```

Fig. 17.3.1

then every time we invoke TRIG we will print out the result of each statement executed by TRIG. This will enable us to see how the output is built up. In Figure 17.3.2 we see what happens when the trace command is issued and the function is invoked.

By examining each of the statements, we can see how the output is built up. This enables us to track down a single statement or group of statements whose output is not what it should be. We have traced the function with a set of inconsistent data to make sure that the function can properly handle that case. Here we have traced all the statements, but it will often be possible to confine the trace to a small number of them.

The trace function can also be used dynamically; i.e., a trace command may be inserted in the body of the function.

```
    [9] T∆FUN←5+I=J
```

```
     ∆TRIG←ι16
       TRIG 1 3 5
TRIG[6] 1   3   5
TRIG[7]
TRIG[8] THE SIDES YOU HAVE SELECTED ARE INCONSISTENT
TRIG[9] 0

       TRIG 3 4 5
TRIG[6] 3   4   5
TRIG[7] 10
TRIG[10] 0.6435011088
TRIG[11] 0.927295218
TRIG[12] 1.570796327
TRIG[13]           ANGLE(DEGREES)            SINE           COSIN
TRIG[14]              36.870               0.600           0.800
TRIG[15]              53.130               0.800           0.600
TRIG[16]              90.000               1.000           0.00(
```

Fig. 17.3.2

This command says that statement 5 is to be traced when I is not equal to J, statement 6 when I is equal to J. When we have no further use for the command we can delete it.

Stop Command

The stop command works like the trace command, except that the execution of the function is halted just prior to the execution of the statement specified. For example,

S∆TRIG←13

causes the function to stop execution just before statement 13 is to be executed. The carriage is spaced up one line and the statement number to be executed next is printed out.

```
        S∆TRIG←13
        TRIG 3 4 5

    TRIG[13]
```

Now you may display variables or expressions or the output produced so far. The advantage of the stop command is that you can examine the function when it has reached the state you are interested in.

Under control of the stop statement, the function is in what is called a suspended state, about which we shall have more to say shortly. To resume execution of the function, you issue the command

$\rightarrow S$

where S is the statement number of the function you want executed. It is not required that execution be continued where it left off.

To remove the stop control vector we write

$S \Delta TRIG \leftarrow 0$

The stop command, like the trace command, may be used dynamically, inserted in the body of a function.

17.3.3 Reported Errors

The third class of errors consists of those detected and reported by the computer. We have seen that a function caught in an infinite loop will remain in execution mode forever. A function which has produced all of its output, even if incorrect, has terminated. When a statement in the function violates the syntax of the language or contains some other error the computer recognizes, execution of the function halts, and the function is placed in a suspended state. An error report indicating what went wrong will then be printed out.

The state indicator will tell you the functions that are in a suspended state and the line number of the statement that would have been executed next. To display the contents of the state indicator, you issue the system command

$)SI$

and you will see, for example,

```
RF[8] *
GT[11] *
FUN[12]
  GT[9] *
  RF[11]
```

The functions are listed in the reverse order of suspension, the most recent first. In the example above, the function RF was suspended most recently. The asterisk indicates that the function is in a suspended state. Suspension applies only to a particular execution of the function. A new execution of it may begin at any time. The function FUN, which is said to be pendant, is listed because it has called on a suspended function, GT. A pendant function cannot be invoked, edited, or erased. Note that the same function (here RF) can be pendant and suspended simultaneously. The function is pendant because it called on a suspended function in its first execution. When it was invoked again, some error within RF caused it to be suspended. Since RF is in a pendant state, it cannot be invoked, edited, or erased.

Clearing the State Indicator

The state indicator can be cleared of suspended and pendant functions by use of the branch command with a vacuous statement number, that is, →. Each time this command is issued the suspended function at the head of the list is removed. By continuous execution of this command the state indicator is cleared. When the state indicator is empty and you attempt to display it, it will print out as a blank line. As a rule you should clear the state indicator of a suspended function before you attempt to execute it again.

State Indicator with Local Variables

If you issue the command

```
)SIV
```

you will get a list of the suspended and pendant functions, together with those local variables and labels which appear in the function header.

```
      )SIV
NETWORK[8] * J L T U1
  INPUT[11] * I J K M
   TEST[6]   K P Q
```

If you attempt to display the variable J, you will get the value assigned to J by the function NETWORK because the local variables of the function NETWORK are dominant. If the function is terminated or if the state indicator is cleared by the empty branch command, then the value of J will be the value assigned by the function INPUT. In other words, the current value of a local variable is the value assigned by the most recently suspended function containing that variable as a local variable. If a variable does not appear in the SIV list, its value, if any, is global.

17.4 A SUMMARY OF ERROR REPORTS

In previous sections we examined the three classes of errors. Here we concentrate on the third class, errors which result in an accompanying printout. We will consider in detail all the different error reports that are printed. We discuss their meaning, illustrate them by example, and describe some of the corrective actions which will remove detected errors.

1. Error Type: VALUE ERROR

Meaning: A variable in some statement has not been assigned a value.

EXAMPLE 1

No value has been assigned to V.

```
       X←V+2×Y
VALUE ERROR
       X←V+2×Y
       ∧
```

Corrective action:

1) Assign a value to the variable.
2) Determine if the variable is misspelled and was intended to be something else.

3) A function with an explicit result has not assigned a value to the dummy variable in the header. Assign a value to the dummy variable.

2. Error Type: DOMAIN

Meaning: The agrument or arguments of some function are not acceptable arguments for that function.

EXAMPLE 1

A logical function requires arguments which are 0 or 1.

```
      Y←6∨7
DOMAIN ERROR
      Y←6∨7
        ∧
```

Corrective action: Reassign to the argument of the function values that are acceptable.

3. Error Type: CHARACTER ERROR

Meaning: A character has been overstruck resulting in a character that is not permissible.

EXAMPLE 1

```
      Y←P×▨
CHARACTER ERROR
      Y←P×
        ∧
```

Corrective action: Rewrite the statement.

4. Error Type: DEFN

Meaning: You are attempting to define, modify, delete, display, or edit a function in an improper way.

EXAMPLE 1

The name of a function may be in use.

```
          Y←9
          ∇Z←Y A
     DEFN ERROR
          ∇Z←Y A
            ∧
```

EXAMPLE 2

Only the delta character and function name may be used to display
a function.

```
          ∇INTERPOLY X [□]
     DEFN ERROR
          ∇INTERPOLY X [□]
                      ∧
```

EXAMPLE 3

The delta character may not appear in the function name.

```
          ∇TES∇T
     DEFN ERROR
          ∇TES
             ∧
```

EXAMPLE 4

A pendant function cannot be displayed.

```
          )SI
     AND[13] *
     DEMOPLOT[5]
          ∇DEMOPLOT[□]
     DEFN ERROR
          ∇DEMOPLOT
                  ∧
```

EXAMPLE 5

A locked function cannot be displayed.

```
          ∇̰FUN X
     [1]   G←(X*2)+2×X-1
     [2]   ∇
          ∇FUN[□]
     DEFN ERROR
          ∇FUN
             ∧
```

Corrective action:

1) The function syntax may be violated.

 a) If ∇ symbol is misplaced, position it correctly.
 b) Move to the right a single argument which is to the left of the function name.
 c) If a name for the function is already in use as a global variable or as an indexed identifier, rename the function.
 d) If more than the function name is used to reopen the function, rewrite using only the del symbol ∇ and the function name.

2) You may be attempting to edit a pendant function. Use the empty branch → to clear the state indicator.

3) You may be attempting to violate the rule that locked functions cannot be edited or displayed.

5. Error Type: RANK

Meaning: The ranks of the variables involved are not conformable.

EXAMPLE 1

A vector and matrix cannot be added.

```
        V←5 6 7 8
        P←2 3ρι6
        V+R
RANK ERROR
        V+R
        ʌ
```

Corrective action: Reformulate the statement.

6. Error Type: LENGTH

Meaning: Two variables of the same rank differ in the dimension over which they are being combined.

EXAMPLE 1

Two vectors of different length cannot be added.

```
        V←5 6 7 9
        R←8 6
        V+R
LENGTH ERROR
        V+R
        ∧
```

EXAMPLE 2

```
        A←6 5ρ?ι30
        B←6 7ρ?ι42
        A+B
LENGTH ERROR
        A+B
        ∧
```

Corrective action: Reformulate the statement.

7. Error Type: INDEX

Meaning: You are attempting to retrieve a nonexistent element from an array.

EXAMPLE 1

```
        R

    1   2   3
    4   5   6

        R[2;4]
INDEX ERROR
        R[2;4]
        ∧
```

Corrective action: Reformulate the statement.

8. Error Type: SYNTAX

Meaning: You have violated the grammatical rules for forming state-ments, e.g., unmatched parentheses, juxtaposition of variables, use of a function with arguments that do not conform to the header.

EXAMPLE 1

In a monadic function the argument must appear to the right of the function.

```
        G←2×
SYNTAX ERROR
        G←2×
            ∧
```

EXAMPLE 2

A function must be inserted between the 2 and the quad.

```
        Y←9
        Z←2□+Y
□ :
        6
SYNTAX ERROR
        Z←2□+Y
            ∧
```

Corrective action: Reformulate the statement.

9. Error Type: DEPTH

Meaning: There are too many levels of defined functions within de-fined functions.

Corrective action:

1) Use the empty branch → to clear the state indicator.

2) Use the system commands SAVE, CLEAR, and COPY, to be explained in Chapter 18.

10. Error Type: LABEL

Meaning: You have made improper use of the colon or the name of a defined function as a label.

EXAMPLE 1

The statement label does not appear to the left of the colon.

```
        ∇ TRY
  [1]    :Y←101
  LABEL ERROR
  [1]
         ∧
```

Corrective action: Position colon correctly; change name of label.

11. Error Type: SYMBOL TABLE FULL

Meaning: There are too many names in use in the workspace.

Corrective action: Erase the least important functions, variables, etc. Then use the system commands SAVE, CLEAR, COPY, to be explained in Chapter 18.

12. Error Type: WS FULL

Meaning: The workspace is filled to capacity.

EXAMPLE 1

The matrix being defined is too large to be contained in the WS.

```
        B←100 100ρι10000
  WS FULL
        B← 100 100 ρι10000
              ∧
```

Corrective action: Clear the state indicator; erase any unwanted variables or functions; revise some calculations so that less space is required. Request a larger workspace.

13. Error Type: SI DAMAGE

Meaning: You have attempted to edit the label line of a suspended function.

Corrective action: Clear the state indicator.

14. Error Type: RESEND

Meaning: Message has not been transmitted properly.

Corrective action: Retransmit message. If error keeps occurring, check phone lines and terminal.

15. Error Type: SYSTEM

Meaning: There is an error internal to the computer.

Corrective action: A clear workspace is automatically entered and no action is required.

EXERCISES

1. Use the trace and stop commands on any of the functions shown in this book.

2. Execution of each of the following statements would result in an error. Describe the nature of the error.

A. $Z \leftarrow {}^{-}1 *.5$

B. $\leftarrow Y \leftarrow A + 2$

C. $A \leftarrow 2\ 2 \rho \iota 4$

   $B \leftarrow 3\ 5$

   $C \leftarrow A + B$

D. A user's state indicator appears as follows:

   $)SI$

   $RF[8]\ \star$

   $GT[11]\ \star$

   $RF[11]\ \star$

   What happens if the command below is issued?

$\nabla RF[\square]$

E. $G \leftarrow 3 \wedge A \leftarrow 1$

F. $G \leftarrow\ 1\ 3\ 5$

   $H \leftarrow 2\ 4\ 1\ 2$

   $Z \leftarrow G + H$

G. $Y \leftarrow 3\ 5\ 7$

   $G \leftarrow \phi / Y$

H. $Y \leftarrow 3\ 8\ 7$

   $G \leftarrow Y[4]$

I. $Y \leftarrow 2 + 7A \leftarrow 3.5$

J. $\rightarrow (Z < Y \leftarrow Y + 1)/NEXT$

18.1 INTRODUCTION

The emphasis until now has been on the APL language. We have concentrated on the different primitive functions that are available and
we have learned how to compose functions of our own. We now focus
our attention on the system commands, the commands which allow us
to use the system in an efficient and economical way. These commands are functionally grouped into five different categories, each of
which touches on a different aspect of the system.

Unlike the language commands, most of the system commands
cannot be used dynamically, i.e., as part of a user-defined function.
Instead, they must be individually entered from the keyboard. The
system commands dealing with signing on and off were introduced in
Chapter 1 so that you could get started. At various points in the text
we have touched on other system commands, indicating that a detailed
discussion would be deferred until this chapter. It is our intention
here to provide a detailed and systematic discussion of these commands which may serve as a convenient reference.

Intelligent use of the system does not demand that you be thoroughly familiar with all these commands. In the early stages, know-
ing how to use one or two commands in each of the five categories will
be sufficient for most work. As you use the system and as your curiosity begins to grow, you will want to add more of these commands to
your working knowledge.

Like the language commands, the system commands are concise,
containing only what is necessary to carry out their function. What
is important to the user is the syntax of the command and what the
command does functionally.

18.2 THE ANATOMY OF A SYSTEM COMMAND

Each system command begins with a right parenthesis,), immediately followed by one or more command words, which determine what

function will be carried out. Some of the command words are SAVE, COPY, LOAD, etc. Each takes one or more user-supplied arguments, although sometimes the argument is implied. Some of the command statements allow for certain optional pieces of information. Such information is always separated from the information preceding it by a colon.

When a system command is issued, there are two kinds of responses which may be elicited. The normal response, which varies from command to command, indicates that the command was executed successfully. A system command that is properly executed is usually followed by a printout giving some kind of information about what took place. When the command fails of execution, a trouble report is issued indicating the reason. The trouble report is usually self-explanatory and the necessary corrective action apparent. As we examine the different commands, we will point out what the normal responses are and what trouble reports may be issued. The trouble reports are summarized in two tables near the end of this chapter.

18.3 WORKSPACES AND LIBRARIES

Since most of the system commands are directly or indirectly concerned with workspaces, it is important to understand what a workspace is, what information it contains, and how a collection of workspaces is organized as a library. The discussion of workspaces and libraries in Chapter 1 was adequate to get started, but now we need to examine these concepts in more detail.

The workspace is the logical unit of storage in which all computations are performed. It is where all your constants, functions and variables reside. A portion of the workspace is used by the system for keeping track of what the workspace contains and is not available to the user. The size of your workspace is variable and will depend on the installation at which you are working. Most installations give the user a workspace of approximately 32,000 bytes (a byte is 8 binary digits).

When a user is admitted to the system, he is allocated a certain number of workspaces. A workspace is always in one of two states, active—i.e., the one you are working in—or inactive. Only one workspace may be active at a given time. System commands enable you to name a workspace, to make any workspace active, to pass data between workspaces, to eliminate data from a workspace, etc.

18.3.1 Continue Workspace

Included in each user's quota of workspaces is one that plays a special
role. This workspace is named CONTINUE. It is used by the system
to store the contents of your active workspace whenever certain difficulties are encountered. If the transmission lines are faulty or if
your data set connection is broken, the computer, on detecting either
of these conditions, immediately transfers the contents of your active
workspace to the CONTINUE workspace so that they are not lost.
Whatever was previously in the CONTINUE workspace is lost. When
you sign on again, with one exception, the contents of the CONTINUE
workspace will automatically be loaded into what would normally be a
clear workspace. At the time you sign on, there will be a printout to
indicate that the contents of the CONTINUE workspace are being
loaded into your active workspace. You may use the CONTINUE workspace as you would any other, but you risk losing its contents, and so
you should not plan to keep anything there for very long.

18.3.2 Libraries

Each user's collection of workspaces is referred to as his library and
is associated with his account number. There are two kinds of libraries within the APL\360 system, private and public. The private
library of a user cannot be accessed without knowledge of his account
number, and even that may not be sufficient if the user has protected
his account number with a password. The public libraries are those
to which every user in the system has access. The purpose of a public library is to provide a wide variety of functions that have general
applicability. It is good practice to familiarize yourself with the public libraries at your installation. In Chapter 17 we discussed the
functions DFT, EFT, and PLOT. All these functions are contained
in a workspace called PLOTFORMAT in Public Library 1, which is
delivered with the system. Most of the workspaces in a public library
contain a function called DESCRIBE, which indicates what the functions in that workspace do. Our description of the functions DFT and
EFT was obtained by invoking the DESCRIBE function in the workspace called PLOTFORMAT.

The public libraries also serve another purpose. If space is
available, you may store the contents of your workspace in a public
library. By attaching a password to the name of your workspace, you

may prevent other users from accessing it. In any event, only the person who has stored the workspace can modify its contents. Public libraries are always numbered from 1 to 1000. The flow of information between the user's terminal and the different workspaces and libraries is shown in Figure 18.3.1.

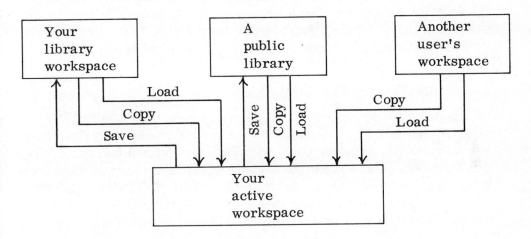

Fig. 18.3.1 The flow of information between workspaces

18.4 LOCKS AND KEYS

A lock is a password for protecting something that belongs to you against accidental or unauthorized use. In a time-sharing system accidental use is a problem because many persons are simultaneously using the system. APL\360 provides you with locks (passwords) to protect your account number or a workspace or a function belonging to you.

Names for passwords follow the same rules as for other variables, but only the first eight digits are significant. In any system command where a lock can appear, the lock follows the information it is protecting and is separated by a colon. For example, the system command you use to sign off allows you to specify a password (lock), which then becomes part of your account number. When you sign on again, you must supply the password before you can be admitted to the system. The password which acts as a lock in one system command functions as a key in another.

As noted above, you may also put a lock on a workspace. Thus, even if someone knows your account number, he cannot access your workspace if he does not know the password associated with it.

On still another level of security, you may lock individual functions within a workspace by overstriking the ∇ in the function header with the tilde $\sim$. Once a function has been locked it cannot be displayed or edited, but it can continue to be used and it can be erased.

18.5 DYNAMIC SYSTEM COMMANDS

In Chapter 1 we described the three system commands ORIGIN, DIGITS, and WIDTH. These three commands are the only ones that can be used dynamically, i.e., within a user-defined function. When you first sign on and are given a clear workspace, each of these system variables is assigned a value. The values of ORIGIN, DIGITS, and WIDTH are always associated with the workspace in which they appear, and they may have different values in different workspaces.

18.5.1 Origin

The ORIGIN may assume a value of 0 or 1 but is initially 1 when you sign on. This means that the first component of a vector has index 1. The first component of a matrix has index [1;1], etc. If A is an array, the index of the last component of any coordinate is $\rho\rho A$.

When the ORIGIN is given the value of 0, the index of the first component of a vector is 0, the index of the first element of a matrix is [0;0], etc. The last numbered component of any coordinate of an array A is $^{-}1+\rho\rho A$.

The system command (with response) is either

)ORIGIN 1

  WAS 0

or

)ORIGIN 0

  WAS 1

The primitive functions that are affected by the setting of the ORIGIN are shown in Table 18.5.1.*

TABLE 18.5.1
Functions Affected by the Setting of Origin

Function	Symbol	Example	Value (Origin 1)	Value (Origin 0)
Iota (monadic)	ι	$\iota 3$	1 2 3	0 1 2
Iota (dyadic)	ι	1 7 8ι1 8	1 3	0 2
Index*	$V[A]$	$V\leftarrow 1\ 3\ 5$		
		$V[2]$	3	5
Random	?	?5	_AN INTEGER SELECTED AT RANDOM FROM_ 1 _TO_ 5	_FROM_ 0 _TO_ 4
Deal	?	3?5	3 _INTEGERS CHOSEN RANDOMLY FROM_ 1 _TO_ 5	_FROM_ 0 _TO_ 4

* Composite functions such as reduction, where a coordinate is given explicitly or assumed, are affected by the setting of the ORIGIN.

ORIGIN exists as a function with an explicit result and may be used within other functions. It can be found in a workspace called WSFNS in Public Library 1. A description of how the function works is as follows:

THE FUNCTIONS ORIGIN, WIDTH, AND DIGITS ARE EACH SIMILAR TO THE COMMAND OF THE SAME NAME, EXCEPT THAT EACH IS A FUNCTION RATHER THAN A COMMAND AND MAY THEREFORE BE USED WITHIN OTHER FUNCTIONS. EACH HAS AN EXPLICIT RESULT WHICH IS THE PREVIOUS VALUE OF THE RELEVANT SYSTEM PARAMETER.

FOR EXAMPLE, THE FOLLOWING FUNCTION:

```
      ∇ F X
[1]   X←ORIGIN X
[2]   G
[3]   X←ORIGIN X∇
```

WILL EXECUTE THE FUNCTION G WITH WHATEVER INDEX ORIGIN IS SPECIFIED BY THE ARGUMENT OF F, AND WILL RESTORE THE INDEX ORIGIN TO THE VALUE THAT IT HAD BEFORE THE EXECUTION OF F.

18.5.2 Digits

The system command

)DIGITS X

where X is an integer between 1 and 16, causes that many significant digits to be displayed. The last digit is rounded off.

Normal response: The response to the command is

   WAS Y

where Y is the previous value. In a clear workspace Y is 10.

Trouble report: *INCORRECT COMMAND*

EXAMPLE 1

          2÷7
     0.2857142857

)DIGITS 6
     WAS 10
          2÷7
     0.285714

The DIGITS command, like the ORIGIN command, exists as a function with an explicit result and may be used within other functions.

18.5.3 Width

The system command

)WIDTH X

where X is an integer between 30 and 130, determines the width of a line of output.

Normal response:

   WAS Y

where Y is the previous value of width. In a clear workspace Y = 120.

Trouble report: *INCORRECT COMMAND*

EXAMPLE 1

```
      )WIDTH 35
WAS 120

      L←'A LINE OF TEXT APPEARS DIFFERENTLY'
      L
A LINE OF TEXT APPEARS DIFFERENTLY
      )WIDTH 25
INCORRECT COMMAND
      )WIDTH 30
WAS 35
      L
A LINE OF TEXT APPEARS DIFFERE
      NTLY
```

18.6 CLASSIFYING SYSTEM COMMANDS

Every system command can be classified from a functional standpoint into one of five groups. These groups and the different kinds of functions they perform are shown in Figure 18.6.1 and are discussed in the next five major sections.

In explaining the system commands, we shall follow a specific format. First, we show the form of the command, indicating optional items in brackets. We then explain the meaning of the command and the purpose it serves. Every command elicits a response which indicates either that the command was successfully executed (normal response) or that it could not be executed (trouble report). For each command we give both the normal response and the trouble reports. (The trouble reports are summarized in Section 18.12.) Finally, examples show both the normal response and some of the possible errors.

18.7 TERMINAL CONTROL COMMANDS (TC)

The primary purpose of the terminal control commands is to enable the user to gain admittance to the system and to terminate a session. In addition, these commands permit you to lock your account number and to make use of the special workspace called CONTINUE.

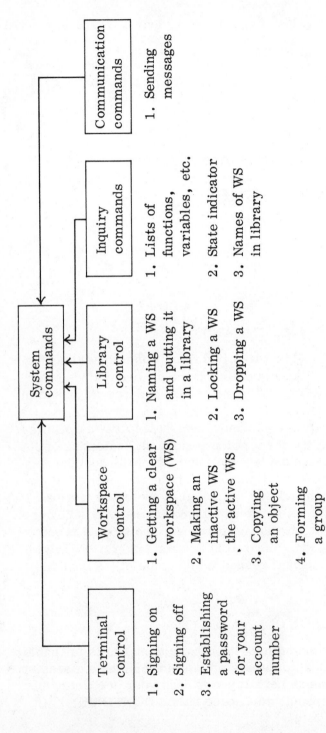

Fig. 18.6.1 Classification of the System Commands

18.7.1 TC 1

Form:)*NUMBER*[:*KEY*]

Meaning: This command is used to initiate a session. NUMBER re-
fers to your account number. KEY is a password previously established. Once such a password is established, it must be used each
time you sign on until it is either deleted or replaced.

Normal response:

1) You may or may not get a public address message sent by the
   operator, for example,

   OPR: SYSTEM WILL SHUT DOWN AT 2400 EST.

2) You will receive a typeout containing the following information.

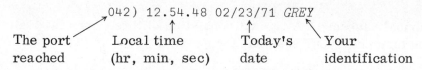

042) 12.54.48 02/23/71 *GREY*

| The port | Local time | Today's | Your |
| reached | (hr, min, sec) | date | identification |

3) You may or may not get the following information.

)*SAVED* 25.19.52 02/18/71

The SAVE report means that at your last session your unlocked active
workspace was stored (SAVED) in the workspace called CONTINUE by
an appropriate system command or automatically by the system itself.
If you do not get such a report, you have a clear workspace.

Trouble reports:

NUMBER NOT IN SYSTEM
INCORRECT SIGN ON
ALREADY SIGNED ON
NUMBER IN USE
NUMBER LOCKED OUT

EXAMPLE 1

Normal sign-on:

)2005:*GREY*
002) 26.36.06 02/24/71 *GREY*

   APL\3 6 0

EXAMPLE 2

```
)2007:GREY
NUMBER NOT IN SYSTEM
```

18.7.2 TC 2

Form:)OFF[:LOCK]

Meaning: This command is used to terminate a session. The contents of your active workspace are destroyed, accounting charges are terminated, and your port is relinquished. LOCK is a password to protect your account number, i.e., a name you must use with your account number when you sign in. You may establish a new password each time you sign off. A colon with nothing following it terminates the present lock.

Normal response: A typeout consisting of three lines is given when you terminate your session, for example,

```
002   24.49.12 02/26/71
CONNECTED      0.06.01  TO DATE  86.47.20
CPU TIME       0.00.02  TO DATE   1.07.00
```

The first line indicates the port number relinquished, the time you terminated, and the date. The next two lines are for accounting purposes. The first line indicates the total elapsed time between signing on and signing off at this session and also for the entire accounting period.

Trouble report: INCORRECT COMMAND

18.7.3 TC 3

Form:)OFF HOLD[:LOCK]

The only difference between this command and the previous one is that the data set connection is held for 60 seconds. This enables another user to sign on without redialing.

18.7.4 TC 4

Form:)CONTINUE

Meaning: This command is similar to the command)OFF[:LOCK].
Your active workspace is saved under the name CONTINUE, replacing
whatever was there previously. If the workspace does not have a lock
associated with it, it will be automatically loaded into the active workspace the next time you sign on. If the workspace does have a lock
associated with it, that lock will be applied to the workspace called
CONTINUE.

Normal response: The word SAVED followed by the date and time of
day.

Trouble report: *INCORRECT COMMAND*

EXAMPLE 1

```
     )CONTINUE
002   26.42.17 02/24/71 GREY
```

18.7.5 TC 5

Form: *)CONTINUE HOLD[:LOCK]*

Meaning: This command is identical with the previous one except that
the data set connection is held for 60 seconds to permit another user
to sign on without redialing.

18.8 WORKSPACE CONTROL COMMANDS (WC)

With the workspace control commands the user can retrieve an inactive workspace and transfer objects between the inactive and the
active workspace. They enable him to obtain a clear workspace,
eliminate unwanted variables, and form objects called groups. The
dynamic commands ORIGIN, WIDTH, and DIGITS discussed previously are classified as workspace control commands.

18.8.1 WC 1

Form: *)CLEAR*

Meaning: The contents of the active workspace are destroyed and the
workspace is made clear.

Normal response: The message C LEAR WS will be printed.

Trouble report: *INCORRECT COMMAND*

EXAMPLE 1

```
    )CLEAR
CLEAR WS
```

18.8.2 WC 2

Form: *)LOAD WSID[:KEY]*

Meaning: The workspace whose identification is given by WSID is brought into the active workspace. If the workspace belongs to another user, you must supply the account number as part of WSID. If the workspace is in a public library, you must supply the library number. For any locked workspace you must supply the password.

Normal response: The word SAVED will be printed, followed by the time of day and the date that the workspace was last saved.

Trouble reports:

```
WS NOT FOUND
WS LOCKED
INCORRECT COMMAND
```

EXAMPLE 1

```
    )LOAD COMM2
SAVED   25.19.52 02/18/71
```

18.8.3 WC 3

Form: *)COPY WSID[:KEY] NAME*

Meaning: The global object identified by name is copied from the workspace whose identity is WSID into the active workspace. If the workspace containing the object to be copied is locked, the password must be entered at the proper place in the command. Only global objects (i.e., functions, variables, etc., not local to a function) can be copied. An object in the active workspace is replaced by an object being copied which has the same name.

Normal response: The response consists of the word SAVED followed by the time and the date that the workspace being copied from was last saved.

Trouble reports:

```
NOT WITH OPEN DEFINITION
WS NOT FOUND
WS LOCKED
OBJECT NOT FOUND
WS FULL
INCORRECT COMMAND
```

EXAMPLE 1

```
    )COPY COMM1 DFT
SAVED   9.51.56 02/22/71
```

EXAMPLE 2

```
    )COPY 20 PLOTFORMAT PLOT
WS NOT FOUND
```

18.8.4 WC 4

Form:)COPY WSID[:KEY]

Meaning: Copy all global objects in the workspace whose name is given by WSID. The origin, width, digits, trace, stop, and seed are not copied.

Normal response: The word SAVED followed by the time and date the workspace was last saved.

Trouble reports:

```
NOT WITH OPEN DEFINITION
WS NOT FOUND
WS LOCKED
WS FULL
INCORRECT COMMAND
```

EXAMPLE 1

```
    )COPY COMM2
SAVED   23.47.44 3/23/71
```

EXAMPLE 2

```
    )COPY COMM1
WS LOCKED
```

18.8.5 WC 5

Form: *)PCOPY WSID [:KEY]NAME*

Meaning: This command is similar to the COPY command, except that an object will not be copied if a global object of the same name exists in the active workspace. By means of this command the user can protect against the accidental destruction of a global object by another global object of the same name. If a group is involved, only those referents which have no global homonyms in the active workspace will be copied.

Normal response: The word SAVED followed by the time and date the workspace being copied from was last saved.

Trouble reports:

> *NOT WITH OPEN DEFINITION*
> *WS NOT FOUND*
> *WS LOCKED*
> *OBJECT NOT FOUND*
> *WS FULL*
> *INCORRECT COMMAND*

EXAMPLE 1

```
        )PCOPY COMM1 DFT
SAVED    9.51.56 02/22/71
```

18.8.6 WC 6

Form: *)PCOPY WSID[:KEY]*

Meaning: Identical with the corresponding COPY command, except that any global object with the same name appearing in both the active and copied workspaces will not be copied.

Normal response: As for the corresponding COPY command.

Trouble report: As for the corresponding COPY command.

EXAMPLE 1

```
        )PCOPY COMM1
SAVED    9.51.56 03/26/71
```

18.8.7 WC 7

Form: *)GROUP NAME LIST*

Meaning: Form a group whose name is NAME and whose members are given by LIST. A group is a collection of names. If the name which appears in LIST is the name of an object in the workspace, i.e., a function, a variable, or another group, then the name is said to have a referent. It is not required that a name appearing in LIST have a referent. Furthermore, a name in LIST may have a referent at one time and not at another. Repeating the group name allows you to add names to the group.

Normal response: No printout is given. The carrier will space up one line and indent six spaces.

Trouble reports:

> *NOT GROUPED, NAME IN USE*
> *INCORRECT COMMAND*

EXAMPLE 1

> *)GROUP GRAPHIC PLOT DFT AND*

EXAMPLE 2

> *)GROUP OUTPUT DFT AND PLOT*
> *NOT GROUPED, NAME IN USE*

18.8.8 WC 8

Form: *)ERASE LIST*

Meaning: This command deletes the global referents of the names which appear in LIST, which is a list of names. If LIST contains the name of a group, then the referents of the names in the group are deleted. If a group, G, is a member of a group, H, and G is erased, then the group H will be dispersed, but the referents of the names in H will not be deleted. A pendant function or a function being edited cannot be erased.

Normal response: If all the objects in the list have been erased, no printout will be given. Any objects in the list that were not erased will be printed.

Trouble report: *INCORRECT COMMAND*

EXAMPLE 1

> *)ERASE INVERSE M N S*

EXAMPLE 2   )SI
          G[4]   *
          H[5]
)ERASE G H
          NOT ERASED: H

18.8.9 WC 9

Form:)WSID NAME

Meaning: This command requests the identification of the active workspace and allows the user to optionally change the name of the workspace if it belongs to him. NAME becomes the name of the new
workspace.

Normal response: The name of the active workspace is printed. If
it is part of a public library or belongs to another user, the public
library number or user account number is printed as part of the identification. If the user changes the name of a workspace belonging to
him, the message WAS PREV is printed out where PREV is the name
being replaced.

Trouble report: INCORRECT COMMAND

EXAMPLE 1

)WSID
     COMM2

EXAMPLE 2

)WSID TRIG
     WAS CLEAR WS

18.9 LIBRARY COMMANDS (LC)

The library commands enable the user to name a workspace, to establish a lock for the name, and to add and delete workspaces from
the library.

18.9.1 LC 1

Form:)SAVE WSID[:LOCK]

Meaning: The active workspace is given the name WSID and is stored
under that name. Only the first 11 characters of WSID are recog-
nized. Any previously established password with this identity will be
replaced. If the workspace is part of a public library or belongs to
another user, then WSID must include the library number or user account number.

Normal response: The word SAVED will be printed, followed by the time and date.

Trouble reports:

NOT WITH OPEN DEFINITION
NOT SAVED, WS QUOTA USED UP
NOT SAVED, THIS WS IS WSID
IMPROPER LIBRARY REFERENCE
INCORRECT COMMAND

EXAMPLE 1

*   )SAVE COMM2*
21.38.19 03/01/71

EXAMPLE 2

*   )SAVE TRIG:GREY*
NOT SAVED, WS QUOTA USED UP

18.9.2 LC 2

Form: *)SAVE*

Meaning: The active workspace is stored under the name previously assigned to it, replacing the workspace with the same identification. A password established previously remains in effect. If the workspace is new—i.e., no inactive workspace with the same identification exists—then the identification of the workspace must have been established by the command)WS WSID.

Normal response: The time and date are printed, followed by the identification of the workspace.

Trouble reports:

NOT WITH OPEN DEFINITION
NOT SAVED WS QUOTA USED UP
NOT SAVED, THIS WS IS WSID
IMPROPER LIBRARY REFERENCE
INCORRECT COMMAND

EXAMPLE 1

*   )SAVE*
21.38.39 03/01/71

EXAMPLE 2

>*SAVES*
INCORRECT COMMAND

18.9.3 LC 3

Form:)*DROP WSID*

Meaning: The workspace whose identification is given by WSID is removed from the library. If the workspace has a lock, you need not
know the password to drop it.

Normal response: The time and date are printed.

Trouble reports:

WS NOT FOUND
IMPROPER LIBRARY REFERENCE
INCORRECT COMMAND

EXAMPLE 1

>*DROP CONTINUE*
21.39.22 03/01/71

18.10 INQUIRY COMMANDS (IC)

The primary purpose of the inquiry commands is to obtain listings of
certain objects residing in the workspace. Included are the names of
functions, variables, groups, and suspended and pendant functions
that are currently in the active workspace.

18.10.1 IC 1

Form:)*FNS LETTER*

Meaning: All user-defined function names are listed alphabetically.
If LETTER is a letter of the alphabet, the listing begins with LETTER.
If there is no function whose name begins with that letter, all function
names will be listed.

Normal response: The list of user-defined functions is printed.

Trouble report:

INCORRECT COMMAND

EXAMPLE 1

```
      )FNS
DEL      DESCRIBE      ERASE    FACTOR
INITIALIZE      INV   LSTSQR   OFFSET
OUT      PLOT    SINE    SPLINE   STEP
SYMBOL   TTY     WHERE
```

18.10.2 IC 2

Form:)*VARS LETTER*

Meaning: All variable names in the workspace are listed alphabetically. If LETTER is a letter of the alphabet, the listing starts with LETTER. If no variable name begins with that letter, all variables are listed alphabetically.

Normal response: The list of variable names is printed.

Trouble report: *INCORRECT COMMAND*

EXAMPLE 1

```
      )VARS G
HT       IXY     JALPH   JSYM    PENP
S        STEPP   SYM     XF      XXYY
XYO      XYS     BKSP    BSKP    CR
PLOTC    Q
```

18.10.3 IC 3

Form:)*GRPS LETTER*

Meaning: All group names are listed alphabetically. If LETTER is a letter of the alphabet, the listing begins with that letter. If no group begins with that letter, all group names will be listed alphabetically.

Normal response: The list of group names is printed.

Trouble report: *INCORRECT COMMAND*

EXAMPLE 1

```
      )GRPS
CALCULUS          TRIG
```

18.10.4 IC 4

Form: *)GRP NAME*

Meaning: The names belonging to the group whose name is NAME are listed.

Normal response: The list of names belonging to the group whose name is NAME is printed.

Trouble report: *INCORRECT COMMAND*

EXAMPLE 1

```
     )GRP CALCULUS
DERF   INTEGRAL    LIMIT
```

18.10.5 IC 5

Form: *)SI*

Meaning: A request for a listing of all suspended and pendant functions, beginning with those suspended most recently. An asterisk next to a function name indicates that the function is suspended. No asterisk means it is pendant. For each function the line number where the function was halted is shown.

Normal response: A listing of all suspended and pendant functions in the active workspace, beginning with the function suspended most recently is printed. Also shown is the line number on which each function was halted.

EXAMPLE 1

```
     )SI
AND[12] *
DEMOPLOT[5]
HAMMING[11] *
HAMMINGL10] *
HAMMING[21] *
HAMMING[10] *
HAMMING[12] *
HAMMING[10] *
HAMMING[11] *
HAMMING[10] *
INTERPOLY[12] *
```

18.10.6 IC 6

Form:)*SIV*

Meaning: This command is identical with the previous one, except that the listing will also include the names of the variables local to the function.

EXAMPLE 1

```
      )SIV
AND[12] *        L      A      B      C      D
DEMOPLOT[5]
HAMMING[11] *    N
HAMMING[10] *    N
HAMMING[21] *    N
HAMMING[10] *    N
HAMMING[12] *    N
HAMMING[10] *    N
HAMMING[11] *    N
HAMMING[10] *    N
INTERPOLY[12] * P      V      X
```

18.10.7 IC 7

Form:)*LIB   NUMBER*

Meaning: A request for the names of all workspaces associated with a particular library. If the word LIB appears by itself, the library is assumed to be the library associated with the account number signed in at the terminal, i.e., the user's own library. NUMBER is a number designating the account number of another user or the number of a public library (1 to 1000). If a lock is attached to the workspace, it will not appear in the listing.

Normal response: A listing of the workspace names associated with the library is printed.

Trouble reports:

IMPROPER LIBRARY REFERENCE
INCORRECT COMMAND

EXAMPLE 1

```
     )LIB
BILL235
FRANK
WSFNS
BILL
FUN
BILMET
BILCO
```

18.10.8 IC 8

Form:)*PORTS*

Meaning: A request for the port numbers and user identification of those ports connected to the system.

Normal response: A listing of the port numbers and associated user codes.

Trouble report: *INCORRECT COMMAND*

18.10.9 IC 9

Form:)*PORT CODE*

Meaning: A request for all the port numbers associated with the user code CODE. A number of different users may have a common identification, e.g., the members of a particular department at a college.

Normal response: A listing of all active port numbers associated with the user identification CODE is printed.

Trouble report: *INCORRECT COMMAND*

18.11 COMMUNICATION COMMANDS (CC)

The purpose of the communication commands is to permit messages to be exchanged between different users and between each user and the central operator. The central operator's location at a privileged terminal permits him to carry out many supervisory functions, e.g., sending out broadcast messages. Questions concerning system problems or schedules and requests for additional workspaces are directed to him via the communication commands. The commands allow the user to specify whether a reply is expected or not. However, the central operator is not always physically present at the terminal, so you should check at your own installation to see how long you will have to wait for a reply or for some specific action.

18.11.1 CC 1

Form: *)MSGN PORT TEXT*

Meaning: The message whose text is TEXT, where TEXT is limited to 120 characters (WIDTH settings do not affect messages), is sent to the port number specified by PORT. The character N in MSGN indicates that no reply is expected. A message sent by any user other than the central operator can be received only when the receiving terminal keyboard is locked and the terminal is in the execution mode. A message sent to a nonexistent or inactive port is reflected back to the sender.

Normal response: The sender's port number, followed by a colon, followed by text, is sent to the receiving terminal. If the port number is inactive or nonexistent, the message is reflected back to the sender's terminal. When the message is received, the word SENT is printed out at the sender's terminal.

Trouble reports:

> *MESSAGE LOST*
> *INCORRECT COMMAND*

EXAMPLE 1

```
        )MSGN 002 JUST TESTING
041:  JUST TESTING
SENT
```

18.11.2 CC 2

Form: *)MSG PORT TEXT*

Meaning: The only difference between this command and the preceding one is that a reply is expected. The sender's keyboard is locked and remains locked until the reply is received or an ATTN signal is detected.

18.11.3 CC 3

Form: *)OPRN   TEXT*

Meaning: This command is identical with the previous one, except that the receiving terminal is the operator.

18.11.4 CC 4

Form: *)OPR   TEXT*

Meaning: In this case the reply is received from the operator.

EXAMPLE 1

> *)OPR WHAT IS THE SCHEDULE FOR TONIGHT?*
> *SENT*

18.12 A SUMMARY OF TROUBLE REPORTS

Tables 18.12.1 and 18.12.2 summarize the trouble reports referred to in previous sections. The problem that causes each report to be made and the appropriate corrective action are given.

TABLE 18.12.1
Trouble Reports, General

Report	Error condition	What to do
Not saved; WS quota used up	You have exceeded your quota of workspaces.	Use workspace CONTINUE, drop a WS no longer needed, or ask installation manager for more workspaces.
Not saved; this WS is WSID	The active workspace does not have the name WSID.	Use)WSID command to change name of the active workspace.

TABLE 18.12.1 continued

Report	Error condition	What to do
Number not in system	Either the number is not valid or the number has a lock and wrong key was used.	Check the number and/or lock.
Number in use	Another user has signed on using your account number.	Try again. If you cannot find out who it is, notify the installation manager.
Number locked out	Your number is no longer authorized for use.	Contact person who gives authorization.
Not with open definition	Terminal is in definition mode.	Close the definition with ∇.

TABLE 18.12.2
Trouble Reports Associated with the System Commands

Report	Error condition	What to do
Improper library reference	You attempted to)SAVE,)DROP, or)LIB for a private library other than that associated with your account number.	Do not repeat your mistake.
Already signed on	Work session at the terminal is proceeding.	Find whoever is using terminal.

TABLE 18.12.2 continued

Report	Error condition	What to do
WS full	Active workspace does not have space for all material requested. A variable is copied completely, but a partially copied function will cause active workspace to be in definition mode.	Erase unneeded objects and use SAVE, CLEAR, and COPY commands.
WS locked	Incorrect key (or no key) was used.	Locate proper key.
WS not found	No workspace with that name in this library.	Check name.
Incorrect sign on	Command syntax is incorrect.	Check and enter correctly.
Message lost	Attention key was struck before the message was sent.	Don't strike attention key until after SENT report appears.
Not erased: name(s)	Function is either pendant or being edited.	Clear state indicator if function is pendant; ∇ to end definition if function is being edited.
Not grouped; name in use	Another object in WS has that name.	Change group name or erase object with that name.
Object not found	Workspace does not contain the object.	Look elsewhere.

18.13 SYSTEM-DEPENDENT FUNCTIONS

An additional class of functions provides basic information about the state of the system. They are all dynamic and may appear in user-defined functions. Thus it is possible to design functions whose behavior depends on the state of the system. Each of the functions has the form

$R \leftarrow IS$

where the character I is formed by overstriking ⊥ and ⊤. Therefore they are referred to as the I beam functions. The variable S is a scalar which presently takes the values 19 through 29. The result R produced by the function is always a scalar with one exception: When S is equal to 27, R is a vector. The currently implemented functions are described below.

I19: The total accumulated time during the current session when the keyboard has been unlocked awaiting entry. Time is given in units of sec/60.

I20: The time of day in 60ths of a second.

EXAMPLE 1

To convert to hours, minutes, and seconds, we write

```
      ☐←3↑24 60 60 60⊤I20
10   41   18
```

I21: The central processing unit (CPU) time used since sign-on in 60ths of a second.

I22: The remaining storage in the active workspace in bytes. A byte is equal to 8 binary digits. The amount of storage required by different elements is as follows:

Element	Bytes requires
Character	1
Logical	0.125
Integer $< 2^{31}$	4
Other numbers	8

A small number of additional bytes should be allowed for over-head. A workspace of standard size usually contains 32,000 bytes.

EXAMPLE 1

To find out how much space is required by the function DFT

```
      )CLEAR
CLEAR WS
      I22
31868
      )COPY 30 FORMAT DFT
         9.44.04 03/30/71
      I22
30116
```

I23: The number of users currently signed on.

EXAMPLE 1

The I beam functions 20 and 23 are useful for obtaining statistics on the level of user activity. The function ACTIVITY gives the number of users at a particular time of day.

```
       ∇ ACTIVITY
[1]     ⍝THIS FUNCTION GIVES THE NUMBER OF USERS
[2]     ⍝SIGNED ON AT A PARTICULAR TIME. THE UNITS OF
[3]     ⍝TIME ARE HOURS:MINUTES:SECONDS.
[4]     'TIME ';3↑ 24 60 60 60 TI20
[5]     'NUMBER OF USERS ';□←I23
```

I24: The time at which you signed on in 60ths of a second.

EXAMPLE 1

Obtain sign-on time in hours, minutes, and seconds.

```
      I24
2220590
      □←3↑24 60 60 60TI24
10   16   49
```

I25: Today's date. The format is MMDDYY

EXAMPLE 1

```
      I25
41371
```

I26: Current value of the line counter, i.e., in a user–defined function, the statement number being executed. This information can be used for branching purposes.

EXAMPLE 1

If a function has been suspended, the statement number at which it was halted is given by I26. To resume execution at this point, we would write

→ I26

EXAMPLE 2

Branch to the statement whose number is five greater than this one.

→ 5+I26

I27: The vector of statement numbers in the state indicator. This vector consists of the statement numbers in which functions became suspended or pendant, starting with the one most recently suspended. If there are no suspended functions, the vector is empty.

EXAMPLE 1

```
        )SI
FR1[11] *
FR1[11] *
FR1[9] *
FR1[8] *

        I27
11  11  9  8
```

I28: The terminal device being used according to the following convention:

Code	Device
1	2741 ATS
2	2741 TSS
3	1050
4	Console typewriter

I29: The user sign-on number

EXAMPLE 1

```
                    I29
   2800030
```

EXERCISES

1. Write the system commands which will effect the following.

    A. Change. *ORIGIN* from 1 to 0
    B. Set *WIDTH* to 82
    C. Set *DIGITS* to 13

2. Write a command that will terminate your present session, hold the communication line for the next user, and establish *JAMES* as a password on your account number.

3. A. Make the workspace called *MATH* your active workspace. Assume that it has a lock whose name is *CALC* .
    B. Erase the contents of your active workspace.
    C. Bring the function called *TRIG* from *MATH* , which is part of Library 32, into your active workspace.

4. A. Form a group of objects whose name is *CHEMICALS* and whose members are *TIN* , *LEAD* , *GOLD* , and *SILVER* .
    B. Disperse the group.
    C. You have forgotten the name of your active workspace. Find out what it is and change it to *PROB* .

5. A. Assign the name *CALC* to your active workspace and store it, giving it a lock called *MINE* .
    B. Wipe out the workspace called *CALC*

6. Find out what in the following categories are stored in your active workspace.

    A. Functions
    B. Variables beginning with the letter *H*
    C. Names of all groups

    D. Names of all workspaces in library 120

    E. Users connected to the system

7. A. Send the message *HOW ARE YOU?* to the user on port 307. Ask for a response.

    B. Send the message *THANKS* to the central operator. No response is required.

8. Issue the proper ⊤ beam command for determining the following.

    A. The number of bytes left in your active workspace

    B. The amount of computer time you have accumulated in the current session

    C. The number of users currently signed on

PART FOUR
APL SHARED VARIABLES

At this stage, we have completed our discussion of APL\360. We have introduced all of the primitive functions, the system commands, and the various concepts which make up the language. We have aimed at giving the user a working knowledge of APL\360 and we have tried to achieve this through examples and by applications which we hope will be useful.

Apart from the mechanics of the language, there is, of course, a philosophy which has guided the design and development of APL. We have not said very much about it because we felt, from a pedagogical standpoint, that the philosophy would be better appreciated and more easily understood when the student had acquired a good knowledge of of the language and had spent sufficient time working examples and doing problems at a terminal. Hopefully, many of you have arrived at this stage.

In order not to get lost in the details of the language and lose sight of broader objectives, it is necessary to review the considerations which motivated APL. In doing this, we shall be preparing ourselves for the next stage in the development of the language. Let us remember that APL was defined by Iverson as a machine-independent programming language having sufficient power and breadth to concisely formulate algorithms without masking their operation with superfluous or irrelevant detail. Thurber and Myrna[1] have pointed out that APL has five basic characteristics.

1. It allows a clear and simple representation of the sequence in which steps of an algorithm are performed.

2. It provides a concise and consistent notation for the operations occurring in a wide range of processes.

3. It permits the description of a process to be independent of the choice of a particular representation for the data.

---

(1) K. J. Thurber and J. W. Myrna "System Design of a Cellular APL Computer." IEEE Transactions on Computers, Vol. C-19, No. 4, April 1970.

4. It allows economy in operation symbols.

5. It provides convenient subordination of detail without loss of detail.

To understand and fully appreciate APL, one must see it in the context of these objectives. In particular, APL\360 should be regarded as a first step toward attaining these objectives. It proved that the characteristics of a language designed as a tool for communication among people made it good for communication with a machine. It also provided a laboratory where ideas could be tested in the field and where their impact on various groups of users and in different application areas could be assessed.

Because a good many years elapsed between the design and conception of the language and its implementation, the designers had the freedom to make radical changes. It appears that the long lag between the design and implementation of the language was a blessing in disguise.

The experience gained from APL\360 also provided the basis for the next stage in the evolution of the language. As users acquired experience with the language, various modifications and enhancements suggested themselves. The most popular, if not the most important, enhancement centered about providing APL with the capabilities of dealing with large files of data and communicating with different peripheral devices. Since APL\360 was designed for both input and output from a remote terminal of the IBM 2741 type, it is not practical to have to enter or output large quantities of data. To remedy this deficiency and some others as well, it appeared that a new implementation would be required as well as a new set of concepts.

Because the designers of the language did not wish to introduce any new concepts that would be at variance with the integrity or structure of what had already been established, it was necessary that the concepts should be carefully thought through. The implementation of a new APL system with major enhancements was announced by IBM in

the summer of 1973 under the name APL SHARED VARIABLES (APLSV).
The most important enhancement in APLSV, as we have mentioned,
is the ability to operate on large files of data and to communicate with
peripheral devices. Some new and very powerful primitive functions,
as well as some dynamically executable system functions, have been
defined. A facility is provided for establishing a defined function as a
character matrix making possible the storage of functions as data and
the generation and application of defined functions under program control. A new set of variables (system variables) which makes the I beam
functions redundant is introduced. These variables make possible a
latent expression, i.e., one which is automatically executed when a
workspace is activated. In addition to the major changes, there are a
number of minor changes. Part Four of this book is concerned with
a discussion of the features of APLSV that will be of interest to most
users.

19.1 CHANGES IN KEYBOARD ENTRY AND OUTPUT

19.1.1 Automatic Closing of Open Quote

Should a carriage return be entered after the first quote but before the closing quote, the closing quote will automatically be typed in on the next line. The situation is identical to that in which the user strikes the carriage return key and then types in the closing quote. The quote may be erased by backspacing and using the attention sign.

19.1.2 Character Errors

Should a character error occur in an input line, the line will be printed out up to the first such error, at which point the keyboard will unlock to allow further entry. This is identical to what takes place when the printed line is entered from the keyboard.

19.2 SYSTEM COMMANDS IN FUNCTION DEFINITION

A system command entered as part of a functions definition will no longer be executed directly but will be stored as part of the functions definition. During execution, the line will be treated as an APL statement and will cause an appropriate error message.

19.3 EXTENDED PRINTING WIDTH

The printing width as set by the width command can now be set to 390.

19.4 BARE OUTPUT

Bare output denoted by expressions of the form $⎕←X$ if followed by another bare output or a character input of the form $X←⎕$ permits the entry to be typed on the same line immediately following the bare output just as though the user had spaced over to that position.

EXAMPLE 1

```
∇TEST[□]
      ∇ TEST
[1]     □←'TRUE OR FALSE: THE CUBE OF '
[2]     □←?6
[3]     □←' IS '
[4]     □←(?6)*3
[5]     X←□
      ∇
[6]     ∇


      TEST
TRUE OR FALSE: THE CUBE OF 6 IS 1FALSE
      X
                                   FALSE
```

Both the carriage returns occasioned by the page-width limitation and
the normal one following output are omitted when bare output is used.

19.5 HETEROGENEOUS OUTPUT

Heterogeneous output should no longer be used. The FORMAT function
to be described in Section 21.3 obviates the need for heterogeneous output. Heterogeneous output must now be regarded as a convenience
introduced at an earlier stage in the development of the language which
is no longer warranted.

19.6 CHANGES IN ERROR HANDLING

19.6.1 Depth Error

Depth errors no longer occur.

19.6.2 Errors in Locked Function

A locked function is essentially treated as a primitive function, and
its execution will invoke only a DOMAIN error. Execution will be
terminated by any error or by a double attention. Certain conditions
such as *WS FULL* will be reported.

19.6.3 Line Editing

An entry of the form [$N\Box$0] results in the carrier resting at the end of the line as though the line had been entered from the keyboard. At this point the line can be modified in whatever way is appropriate.

19.7 STOP AND TRACE IN LOCKED FUNCTIONS

When a function definition is locked, settings of Stop and Trace are automatically nullified.

19.8 DISPLAY OF COMMENTS

Like lines with labels, comment lines are extended one space to the left when the function definition is displayed.

19.9 MONADIC TRANSPOSE FUNCTION

Previously the monadic transpose function interchanged the last two coordinates. It now reverses the order of all coordinates.

```
        C←3 3 3ρι27
        C
 1    2    3
 4    5    6
 7    8    9

10   11   12
13   14   15
16   17   18

19   20   21
22   23   24
25   26   27

        ⍉C
 1   10   19
 4   13   22
 7   16   25

 2   11   20
 5   14   23
 8   17   26

 3   12   21
 6   15   24
 9   18   27
```

19.10   RESIDUE FUNCTION

The residue function is now defined as follows:

1.   If $C=0$ then $C|D$ is equal to D.

2.   If $C\neq0$ then $C|D$ is such that $0\leq(C|D)<C$.

EXAMPLE 1

```
          A←4 0 ¯4
          B← ¯8 ¯7 ¯6 ¯5 ¯4 ¯3 ¯2 ¯1 0 1 2 3 4 5 6 7 8
          A∘.|B
    0   1   2   3   0   1   2   3   0   1   2   3   0   1   2   3   0
   ¯8  ¯7  ¯6  ¯5  ¯4  ¯3  ¯2  ¯1   0   1   2   3   4   5   6   7   8
    0  ¯3  ¯2  ¯1   0  ¯3  ¯2  ¯1   0  ¯3  ¯2  ¯1   0  ¯3  ¯2  ¯1   0
```

```
          X←34.976
          .01|X
    0.006
```

19.11   ENCODE FUNCTION

The definition of the encode function ⊤ is based on the residue
function.   This dependence is given by the following function where
C is a vector and D a scalar.

<u>Encode.</u>   The definition of the encode function ⊤ is based on the
residue function in the manner specified by the following function
for vector A and scalar B :

```
          ∇Z←A E B
    [1]      Z←0×A
    [2]      I←ρA
    [3]   L:→(I=0)/0
    [4]      Z[I]←A[I]|B
    [5]      →(A[I]=0)/0
    [6]      B←(B-Z[I])÷A[I]
    [7]      I←I-1
    [8]      →L
          ∇
```

When the left argument of the encode function has one or more negative arguments, the result is affected by the change in the definition of the residue function.

EXAMPLE 1

```
        3 3 3⊤5
0 1 2
        ¯3 ¯3 ¯3⊤5
0 ¯2 ¯1
        3 3 3⊤¯15
1 1 0
        3 3 3⊤15
1 2 0
```

19.12 GENERALIZED MATRIX PRODUCT AND MATRIX DIVIDE

The domino function is now applicable to vector and scalar arguments as follows. A vector is treated as a one-column matrix and a scalar is treated as a 1×1 matrix. If Y is a scalar the expression $⌹Y$ is equivalent to $÷Y$. If X and Y are scalars the expression $X⌹Y$ is equivalent to $X÷Y$ except that it yields a $DOMAIN$ error for $0÷0$.

19.13 CHANGES IN SYSTEM COMMANDS

19.13.1 Communication commands

There are many occasions when a user may wish to be undisturbed by messages arriving at the terminal, for example, when producing finished output or while concentrating on a difficult problem. Even under such circumstances, however, it may be necessary to communicate briefly with another port.

The command $)MSG\ OFF$ blocks any message except one coming in response to a transmitted message which requested a reply (that is a message of the form $)OPR$ or $)MSG$ and arriving before the keyboard is again unlocked. Any blocked message is treated as if the keyboard were continuously unlocked and it will so appear to the sender.

The command $)MSG\ ON$ restores the acceptance of messages and causes the last public address message, if any, to be printed.

19.13.2 Copy Commands

The commands $)COPY$ and $)PCOPY$ now accept a multiplicity of object names. The response lists separately the objects not found (headed by $NOT\ FOUND$) and those found but not copied (headed by $NOT\ COPIED$).

19.13.3 Erase Command

The erase command now acts on any global object and no longer distinguishes between pendent functions and others. Problems that may possibly arise from erasing a pendent function are forestalled by the response *SI DAMAGE* , which warns the user to take appropriate action before resuming function execution.

19.13.4 Save Command

An attempt to save a workspace during execution of a function (as was possible by an explicit command during a ⎕ input request or a forced ⎕ input disconnect) will result in interruption of the function prior to the execution of the command. Therefore, function execution will not automatically resume. Such automatic resumption can be invoked by the system variable ⎕*LX* defined in Table 1 of Section 22.8.

19.13.5 Symbol Table Size

The command)*SYMBOLS* without a number prints the current number of names accommodated.

19.13.6 Workspace Identification

The command)*WSID* can be used to set a lock as well as the workspace name, using the same form as the)*SAVE* command. Used as an inquiry,)*WSID* will continue to return only the workspace identification.

19.13.7 Privacy

In the interest of privacy, a workspace saved with the name *CONTINUE* cannot be activated or copied by a user other than the one in whose library it has been saved.

19.13.8 Public Libraries

Workspaces named *CONTINUE* cannot be stored in public libraries.

19.13.9 Local Function Names

As a result of the introduction of the system function ⎕*FX* (defined in Section 21.3) local names may now refer to functions as well as to variables. Consequently, the phrase "functions and global variables" occurring in the <u>APL 360 User's Manual</u> should now be read as "global functions and variables."

EXERCISES

1. Design a function using bare output to test whether a student under
stands multiplication.

2. Before evaluating the following expressions on your terminal, try
predicting the results.

   A. $\phi M \leftarrow 3\ \ 3\ \ 3 \rho \iota 27$

   B. ⊟1.7

   C. $(4 \rho\ ^-3) \tau 17$

NEW PRIMITIVE FUNCTIONS

20.1 SCAN FUNCTION

Let α be a dyadic function and X a vector. We speak of the α scan of X, that is:

$R \leftarrow \alpha \backslash X$

The result R is a vector such that $R[I]$ is equal to $\alpha / I \uparrow X$, for example:

```
      ×\1 2 3 5
1 2 6 30
```

The operation may be extended to any array as follows. If $R \leftarrow \alpha \backslash [I] A$ then ρR is equal to ρA and the vectors along the Ith coordinate of R are α scans over the vectors along the Ith coordinate of A.

EXAMPLE 1

```
      A←3 5 2 9 4 8
      A
3 5 2 9 4 8
      +\A
3 8 10 19 23 31
      ×\A
3 15 30 270 1080 8640
```

EXAMPLE 2

```
      A←2 1 2 1
      *\A
2 2 2 2


      A←1 0 0 1 1
      ∧\A
1 0 0 0 0

      ∨\A
1 1 1 1 1
```

20.2 EXECUTE FUNCTION

The monadic function $\pmb{\iota}$ formed by overstriking the characters $\bot$ and $\circ$ takes as its argument a character vector or scalar which it attempts to execute as though the argument were a well-formed APL statement. When the argument is not a well-formed APL statement an error will result. There are several major uses of the function:

1. In many cases it is desirable to use the name of a defined function rather than its **value** as an argument. For example, in a numerical integration routine, the arguments might be the name of the function to integrated and grid of points at which the function is defined.

EXAMPLE 1

```
        ∇INT[☐]
     ∇ Z←L INT X;Y
[1]    Z←(1↓X-¯1ϕX)+.×0.5×1↓Y+¯1ϕY←⍎L,' X'
     ∇
[2]    ∇


        ∇FUN[☐]
     ∇ Z←FUN X
[1]    Z←X*2
     ∇
[2]    ∇


        'FUN' INT 0,ι10
335


        'FUN' INT 0,(.01×ι100)
0.33335
```

2. When the execute function takes a vector of characters representing numerical constants as its argument, the result is a vector of numerical values.

EXAMPLE 1

```
        1+A←⍎'3254'
3255
```

3. The execute function may be used to select a set of data from a collection which cannot be combined into a single array. This can be accomplished by selecting one of a set of names from a character matrix

4. By use of the construction $\pm$⍞ input may be examined by the function prior to execution.

5. Conditional expressions can be constructed in which execution is applied only to the expression selected by the condition, thus avoiding unnecessary computation, that is, a recursive conditional statement defining the factorial function.

```
        ∇FACT[⎕]
      ∇ Z←FACT N
[1]     ±3 ¯12[1+N≠0]↑'Z←1 Z←N×FACT N-1'
      ∇
[2]   ∇
```

20.3 FORMAT FUNCTION

The format function is denoted by ⍕ (the characters ⊤ and ∘ overstruck) and allows the user to convert numerical arrays to character arrays. In addition to its obvious use for composing tabular output it has a number of other important uses as well. The monadic format function has as its result a character array identical to that which would result if the argument were printed.

EXAMPLE 1

```
        MAT←3=?4 4ρ3
        R←⍕MAT
        MAT
0 0 0 1
0 0 1 0
1 1 1 0
0 1 1 0
        ρMAT
4 4
```

(continued)

```
              R
    0  0  0  1
    0  0  1  0
    1  1  1  0
    0  1  1  0
              ρR
    4  8
              R[;2×ι4]
```



```
              R[;(2×ι4)-1]
    0001
    0010
    1110
    0110
```

```
              ρ⍕8 9 6 2
    7
              ∧/,R=⍕R
    1
              ⍕'ABCDEGHT'
    ABCDEGHT
```

The dyadic format function takes a numerical array as its argument. The left argument is used to control the format of the right
argument when it is displayed. The left argument may be a scalar,
a pair of numbers or a vector of length $2 \times {}^{-}1\uparrow1,\rho A$ (where A is the
right argument). When a pair of numbers is used as the left argument,
the first determines the width of the field and the second the precision.
In the case of decimal output, precision means the number of digits to
the right of the decimal point. If the sign of the argument used to
indicate precision is negative, the output will be in exponential form;
if the sign is positive, the output will be in decimal form. In the
former case, precision means the number of digits in the multiplier.

EXAMPLE 1

```
       A←3 3ρ19.25 ⁻65.879 22 0 ⁻.98 0.0 ⁻0.89 1456.3
       ρ□←A
   19.25              ⁻65.879              22
    0                  ⁻0.98                0
   ⁻0.89              1456.3               79
 3 3
```

```
        ρ□←12 3▼A
        19.250          ¯65.879         22.000
         0.000           ¯0.980          0.000
        ¯0.890         1456.300         79.000
 3  36


        R←9  2▼A
        S←9 ¯2▼A


        ρ□←R
     19.25    ¯65.88      22.00
      0.00     ¯0.98       0.00
     ¯0.89   1456.30      79.00
 3  27



        ρ□←S
    1.9E01    ¯6.6E01     2.2E01
    0.0E00    ¯9.8E¯01    0.0E00
   ¯8.9E¯01    1.5E03     7.9E01
 3  27



        ρ□←6  0▼A
     19    ¯66      22
      0     ¯1       0
     ¯1    1456      79
 3  18
```

If the width indicator of the control pair is zero, a field width is chosen
such that there will be at least one space between adjacent numbers. If
a single number is used, it is interpreted as the precision specification
and the width control is treated as though zero were specified. In the
case of a matrix, each column may be individually specified by a pair of
arguments. In conjunction with other APL functions the format function
is a very powerful report generator.

EXAMPLE 2

```
        ρ□←7 ¯1▼A
    2E01     ¯7E01     2E01
    0E00     ¯1E00     0E00
   ¯9E¯01     1E03     8E01
 3  21
```

(continued)

```
      ρ⎕←2⍕A
   19.25      ⁻65.88       22.00
    0.00      ⁻0.98         0.00
   ⁻0.89    1456.30        79.00
3  27


      ρ⎕←0 2⍕A
   19.25      ⁻65.88       22.00
    0.00      ⁻0.98         0.00
   ⁻0.89    1456.30        79.00
3  27



      ρ⎕←⁻2⍕A
   1.9E01    ⁻6.6E01      2.2E01
   0.0E00    ⁻9.8E⁻01     0.0E00
  ⁻8.9E⁻01    1.5E03      7.9E01
3  27



      ρ⎕←0 ⁻2⍕A
   1.9E01    ⁻6.6E01      2.2E01
   0.0E00    ⁻9.8E⁻01     0.0E00
  ⁻8.9E⁻01    1.5E03      7.9E01
3  27
```

The two rows of literal matrix M are the names of two functions for producing even and odd random integers, respectively, on the integers one to one hundred (assuming the $ORIGIN$ is 1). The appropriate function is selected on the basis of the computed variable ROW.

```
      M←2 3ρ'ODDEVN'
      M
ODD
EVN

      ∇EVN[⎕]
    ∇ Z←EVN
[1]    Z←2×?50
    ∇
[2]    ∇
```

```
        ∇ODD[☐]
      ∇  Z←ODD
[1]      Z←EVN-1
      ∇
[2]      ∇


      ROW←1
      ⍕M[ROW;]
99

      ROW←2
      ⍕M[ROW;]
90
```

XERCISES

1. Using the array M←3 3ρ1.0257 1.0572 3.97865 572.6889 7.125 16.21 173.21 994.2 1.078, format the array according) the following specifications:

 A. field width 9, 3 digits in the multiplier, and E notation,

 B. field width 11 and 3 decimal places.

2. Show how the 9 × 9 identity matrix may be displayed without paces between elements.

3. Let L be the literal vector 'THE ANSWER IS' and N a numeric ariable. Show how both variables may be put on the same line of utput without using the semicolon.

4. Before trying to evaluate the following expressions on your ter-ninal, try predicting the results.

 A. ⍕'B←ι9'
   ⍕'R←B+3'

 B. ⍕'3+5'

 C. ÷\1 2 4 8

 D. -\1 2 4 8

5. If a variable X has a value (integer) from one to ten, a new varia-le Y is to be specified with the same value as X; otherwise, no new ariable is to be created. Write an APL expression to accomplish his.

21.1 INTRODUCTION

The purpose of the system variables and system functions is to provide
us with a capability for managing the environment of the system in
which APL operates. This is accomplished by singling out certain
variables and designating them as elements of the interface between
APL and its host system. While these variables are abstract objects t
APL, their values have special meaning for the host system. System
functions are functions based on the use of system variables. Both
system variables and system functions have distinguished names that
always begin with a quad. They cannot be applied to user-defined objects nor can they be copied, grouped, or erased. In APL statements
the normal rules of syntax apply. The system functions have many of
the properties of ordinary functions, i.e., they are monadic or dyadic
and have explicit results. There are thirteen system functions of which
seven will be described in this chapter and six in the following chapter.

21.2 CANONICAL REPRESENTATION

By a canonical representation we mean a representation in some stan-
dardized form. With respect to a defined function there are certain
advantages to be gained by being able to represent the definition which
is displayed as a character matrix. The monadic function $\Box CR$ where F
is an unlocked defined function produces as an explicit result a canonic
representation of the function. The canonical representation is obtained from the definition printed in displaying the function by the execu
tion of the following operations:

1. removal of the ∇ symbol, line numbers, and brackets;

2. shifting of rows containing line labels to the right so there is no
exdenting;

3. padding rows with spaces on the right whenever necessary so that
all rows are of equal length.

The resulting character matrix is called the canonical representation of *F*.

EXAMPLE 1

```
        M←□CR 'MEDIAN'
        M
Z←MEDIAN V;V1
ΑTHIS FUNCTION COMPUTES THE MEDIAN OF A SET OF DATA
ΑGIVEN IN THE FORM OF A VECTOR V
V1←V[▲V]
→(((2|(ρV))=0))/EVEN
Z←V1[((ρV1)+1)÷2]
→0
EVEN:Z←(V1[(ρV1)÷2]+V1[((ρV1)+2)÷2])÷2
→0
```

If the function □*CR* is applied to any argument other than the name of an unlocked defined function, it will yield a matrix of dimension 0 × 0.

21.3 FUNCTION ESTABLISHMENT

The system function □*FX M*, where *M* is the canonical representation of a function, fixes or established the definition of the function. The explicit result produced is the vector of characters representing the name of the function being fixed.

EXAMPLE 1

```
        M[9;2]←'9'

        □FX M
MEDIAN

        ∇MEDIAN[□]
     ∇ Z←MEDIAN V;V1
[1]    ΑTHIS FUNCTION COMPUTES THE MEDIAN OF A SET OF DATA
[2]    ΑGIVEN IN THE FORM OF A VECTOR V
[3]     V1←V[▲V]
[4]     →(((2|(ρV))=0))/EVEN
[5]     Z←V1[((ρV1)+1)÷2]
[6]     →0
[7]    EVEN:Z←(V1[(ρV1)÷2]+V1[((ρV1)+2)÷2])÷2
[8]     →0
     ∇
[9]    ∇

        MEDIAN 1 3 5 7
```

4

The function $\Box FX$ M will result in a function being established if:

1. M is a canonical representation or if it differs from a canonical representation by the addition of nonsignificant spaces (excluding rows consisting wholly of spaces).

2. The name of the function being established is not the name of a halted function, label, group, or variable. If the function cannot be established the result returned will be the scalar index of the row in the argument where the fault was found.

21.4 DYNAMIC ERASURE

The expunge function $\Box EX$ M allows the user to dynamically eliminate the existing use of a name. The argument is a matrix of names but it must not include the name of a label, group, pendant, or suspended function. The explicit result returned is a logical vector where a 1 indicates that the corresponding object has been erased leaving the name free for use and a 0 that the name is still in use or that the argument is not a well-formed name.

EXAMPLE 1

```
        )VARS
B         C         CRMEDIAN          M          R
        []EX  'M'
1

        []EX  'S'
1
```

21.5 NAME LIST

The monadic function $\Box NL$ V, where V is either a vector restricted to the integers 1, 2, and 3 or a scalar, will result in a matrix of names of objects in the dynamic environment according to the following scheme:

1. labels
2. variables
3. functions

EXAMPLE 1

```
        ⎕NL  3
ILLUS
NEW
EVN
ODD
MEDIAN
        ⎕NL  1

        ⎕NL  2
B
C
CRMEDIAN
R
S
```

The dyadic function S ⎕NL V works the same way except that the list of names is restricted to those whose initial letter is specified by S where S is a scalar or vector of alphabetic characters.

EXAMPLE 1

```
        'N'  ⎕NL  3
NEW
```

21.6 NAME CLASSIFICATION

The monadic function ⎕NC M is the companion function to the name list function. The argument M is a vector or a matrix of characters. The explicit result produced is the class of the name represented by each row of the argument. The class is denoted by one of the integers 0 to 4 as follows:

0 -- the name is available for any use;
1 -- the name of a label;
2 -- variables;
3 -- functions;
4 -- the name is not available for use.

EXAMPLE 1

```
        ⎕NC  'NEW'
   3
        ⎕NC  'C'
   2
        ⎕NC  'OLD'
   0
        ⎕NC  'ILLUS'
   3
```

Name	Purpose	Value in Clear Workspace	Meaningful Range	Alternate Facility ⌶11
⎕CT	Comparison tolerance (relative): used in ⌈ ⌊ < ≤ = ≥ > ≠	1E¯13	0-1	SETFUZZ
⎕IO	Index origin: used in indexing and in ? and ⍳	1	0 1	ORIGIN
⎕LX	Latent expression executed on activation of workspace	' '	Characters	None
⎕PP	Printing precision: affects numeric output and monadic ⍕	10	⍳16	DIGITS
⎕PW	Printing width: affects all but bare output	120	29+⍳361	WIDTH
⎕RL	Random link: used in ?	7*5	¯1+2*31	SETLINK
⎕AI	Account information: identification, computer time, connect time, keying time (All times are in milliseconds and are cumulative during session.)			⌶29 21 24 19
⎕AV	Atomic vector			None
⎕LC	Line counter: line numbers of functions in execution, innermost first	⍳0		⌶27 26
⎕TS	Time stamp: year, month, day, hour, minute, second, millisecond			⌶25 20

⎕TT	Terminal type: 0 for 1050; 1 for Selectric; 2 for PTTC/BCD	ι28
⎕UL	User load	ι23
⎕WA	Working area available	ι22

Note 1: The old definitions of the workspace functions will no longer work. See text for corrective action.

Table 1. System Variables

(Reprinted by permission from APL Shared Variables (APLSV) Programming RPQ WE1191-- Users' Guide, copyright © 1973 by International Business Machine Corporation.

21.7 DELAY FUNCTION

The monadic function $\Box DL$ M causes a pause in the execution of any statement in which it appears. The scalar or vector V is the pause time in seconds.   This function is useful where some test is required at repeated intervals to determine if an event has taken place. The delay can be aborted by pressing the ATTN key.

21.8 SYSTEM VARIABLES

System variables are a special instance of shared variables. Sharing takes place automatically between the workspace and the APL processor. when the workspace is activated. If the variable is localized in a function, sharing takes place each time the function is invoked. Table 1 lists all of the system variables, what they provide, the value of the variable in a clear workspace, the allowable range, and the facility in APL\360 which they are intended to replace.

In the case of the first six system variables, the value specified by the user or the default value is used by the APL processor when it carries out the function to which the system variable applies. Any value outside the appropriate range, no value in the case of a localized variable, or a nonscalar value will result in an implicit error at execution time. In the case of the last six system variables in the table, settings by the user or localization have no effect since the APL processor will always reset the variable before it can be used again. The atomic vector $\Box AV$ requires some explanation. This vector consists of 256 elements representing all possible characters. Let V be any eight-element logical vector in 0 origin the character in $\Box AV$ whose internal representation is V is given by $\Box AV[2\perp V]$.

EXAMPLE 1

```
        V←0 1 1 0 0 1 1 1
        C←2⊥V
        C
   103

        ⊔AV[2⊥V]
  B

        V←0 0 0 0 1 1 1 1
        C←2⊥V
        C
   15
        ⊔AV[2⊥V]
  L
```

22.1 INTRODUCTION

The concept of shared variables is crucial to an understanding of
how communication between different elements in an APL system
works. These elements, or processors as we shall call them,
may be two active workspaces, a workspace and a peripheral device,
the parent APL system, and some other system running on the same
computer, etc. In every case, we may think of the interface between
the two processors as consisting of a common set of variables which
each processor shares with the other, hence the name, shared variables.
To illustrate the sharing, let us first concentrate on communication
between two active workspaces, i.e., between two different users. The
communication process is initiated when one of the users makes an offer
to share a variable in his workspace with another user.

22.2 OFFERS TO SHARE

The offer to share information is made using the dyadic function

$P \ \Box SVO \ N$

where P is the identification for another processor. For the moment,
let us think of P as a user identification number. N is a character
vector representing a pair of names or a matrix whose rows are name
pairs. The first name in the pair is the name of the variable being offered for sharing. The second name is a surrogate name offered to
match a name offered by the other processor, i.e., the other user.
A surrogate name need not be explicitly offered, in which case N consists of a single name. In this case, the name of the variable is its
own surrogate. To make these matters a little clearer, suppose we
have two users whose user identification numbers are 36841 and 92654
respectively. Figure 22.2 illustrates the use of surrogate names when
user 36841 initiates an offer to share information with user 92654. In

every instance, the variable known as $MY1$ to user 36841 and known as $MY2$ to 92654 is being offered for sharing.

$$USER\ 36841 \qquad\qquad USER\ 92654$$

92654 $\square SVO$ 'MY1 X'

1

92654 $\square SVO$ 'MY1 MY2'

1

92654 $\square SVO$ 'MY1'

1

36841 $\square SVO$ 'MY2 X'

2

36841 $\square SVO$ 'MY2'

2

36841 $\square SVO$ 'MY2 MY1'

2

Fig. 22.2.1

All that the surrogate names do is control the matching. each processor need not be concerned with the variable name used by the other. The use of the dyadic $\square SVO$ function produces an explicit result. In the case of the user initiating the offer, the result is 1. When a counter off is made (which is tantamount to acceptance of the initial offer), the resu produced is a 2. We have said nothing yet of the means by which user 92654 becomes aware that an offer to share has been extended. We shall make this clear shortly. For the moment, we shall assume that users are aware of any offers they have made or which have been made to them. Let us take a closer look now at the explicit result of using the dyadic $\square SVO$ function. This result is called the degree of coupling of the name or name pair in N.

22.3 DEGREE OF COUPLING

The degree of coupling of a name or name pair N with respect to a processor whose identification is given by P is defined as:

0   if N has not been offered for sharing by P or offered to P for sharing;

1   if an offer to share N has been made by P or extended to P but not matched;

2   if an offer to share N has been made by P or extended to P and matched.

The monadic function $\square SVO$ N reports the degree of coupling of N as
its explicit result. When the degree of coupling is 1 or 2, either the
monadic or dyadic function $\square SVO$ may be used to inquire about the
degree of coupling. The dyadic function may be used because a repeated offer does not affect the degree of coupling. If the name has a
coupling of 0 then an offer to share will increase the coupling provided the name is not the name of a label, a function, or a group.

22.4 REQUIREMENTS FOR SHARING

Shared variables in an APL workspace may be local or global and are
syntactically indistinguishable from ordinary variables. Sharing is a
bilateral process, i.e., each shared variable may have only two
owners. This is not a real restriction, however, because a variable
shared by two processors, that is, 1 and 2 may be shared between 2
and 3, between 3 and 4, etc. In this way, various arrangements may
be carried out. Furthermore, a given processor may simultaneously
share variables with many other processors. In making multiple share
offers, to a processor, the surrogate can be repeated. In this event
they are matched in sequence by appropriate counter offers. As a
practical matter, each user is given a quota alloted by the host system.
If an attempt is made to exceed this quota, an error report will be received, i.e., *INTERFACE QUOTA EXHAUSTED*. If the shared variable
facility is inoperative, the error report will be *NO SHARES*. When a
processor is not available, an offer to share will still be tendered.

22.5 BECOMING AWARE OF OFFERS

Once a processor is aware that another processor wishes to share information, appropriate action may be taken. As we have said before,
making a counter offer to share is tantamount to acceptance of the
original offer. Failing this, the degree of coupling of the offered
variable remains at 1. In order to determine whether an offer to
share has been extended, a user will made use of the monadic function
$\square SVO$ V. If V is an empty vector, the result will be the identification
of each user who has tendered an offer to share. If V is the identification of another processor, the result will be a matrix of names offered for sharing by that processor excluding any names for which a
counter offer has been made.

22.6 THE ACCESS MATRIX

With respect to any shared variable, there are only two actions that
an owner may take -- to either assign or reassign a value to that

variable. In that case, we shall say that its value has been set. Or
the owner may make use of the value, in which case we shall say that
it has been used. Either of these actions will be referred to as an
access. In a shared variable environment, it is usually desirable
to impose some discipline on the accessing of a variable. For example,
if processor 1 has set a variable, it might be desirable that he or she
not be allowed to set the variable again until processor 2 has been able
to read it and vice versa. Or it might be desirable to prevent processor
1 from using a variable until processor 2 has set it. What we require
is an accessing discipline consistent with each of the owner's needs.

An accessing discipline is imposed by means of the dyadic system
function $\Box SVC$. The right argument is a vector or row matrix of names
of shared variables whose access protocol is being specified. The left
argument is a logical vector containing four elements defined as shown
in Fig. 22.6.1. In reading the table, you are user 1. The user you are
sharing with is user 2.

Element Number	Value	Meaning
1	1	User 2 must access the variable before user 1 can reassign it.
2	1	User 1 must access the variable before user 2 can reassign it.
3	1	User 1 cannot read the variable twice unless user 2 has reassigned it.
4	1	User 2 cannot read the variable twice unless twice unless user 1 has reass it.

Fig. 22.6.1

When the value of any element is zero, the corresponding restriction does not apply. When invoking the $\Box SVC$ command, a user imposes
an access discipline on each shared variable in the argument list.
However, life is not a one-way street. Since the co-owner of the shared
variable is also free to impose an access discipline on the shared variables, we have to consider what the net effect will be. The answer is
that the resulting applicable access discipline is given by the logical
union of the two access-discipline vectors. Thus the resulting pre-

vailing discipline is always more restrictive. Any restriction you
have set cannot be negated; but in cases where you have set no restrictions, you may find restrictions imposed. The result returned by
the $\Box SVC$ function is the resulting access protocol for each of the variables in the argument list.

The monadic $\Box SVC$ function allows you to inquire about the access
protocol currently in effect for the shared variables specified. The
right argument is the vector or row matrix of variable names and the
result returned is the access protocol in effect.

The initial value of a shared variable is determined by the following rules:

1. If both owners had assigned values, the value is that specified by
   the owner making the original offer.

2. If only a single owner had specified a value, then the value is
   assigned.

3. If neither owner had made an assignment, the variable had no
   value.

22.7 RETRACTION OF OFFERS

If for any reason a co-owner of a shared variable wishes to retract an
offer to share, he or she may exercise the option to do so. The mechanism by which a retraction is effected is the monadic function $\Box SVR \ N$
where N is a character or matrix of names. The result returned is
the degree of coupling immediately prior to the retraction. The effect
of the retraction is to reduce the coupling to zero. Just as an offer
may be retracted at any time, so may it be reinstituted.

Certain other conditions will cause retraction to take place automatically. These conditions include failure of the communication
lines, signing off, loading a new workspace, erasure of the variable,
and for local variables completion of the function in which they appear.

When a co-owner of a shared variable attempts to access the variable,
variable, his or her execution will be deferred if there is an action
required on the part of the other owner. When that action has been
taken, execution will continue. Pressing the ATTN key twice will abort
the access and unlock the keyboard.

FILE MANAGEMENT

23.1 INTRODUCTION

The ability to access files, expecially large files, is an integral part
of many applications. The way in which files are structured, organized
and accessed is an important part of data management. It is a topic
which has received considerable attention from both a theoretical and
practical standpoint. A thorough discussion of files and file concepts is
beyond the scope of this book. Our concern here will be with the way in
which APLSV allows the user access to files and the various storage
devices on which they reside. We shall be concerned here with the
essential features of file management within APLSV. For a more thorough discussion the reader is advised to consult IBM publication SH-20-
1463, "TSIO Reference Guide" and IBM publication GC-26-3783,
"OS/VS Data Management Service Guide."

23.2 DATA SETS

What we want to discuss now is the establishment and use of files outside of an APL workspace as well as peripheral devices concerned with
high-speed data input and output. To do this we must first introduce
some definitions. By a data set we shall mean a collection of data to
which a name has been assigned and which is already in existence or
which is to be created on a storage device. Any input or output operation (I/O) makes reference to a data set. Prior to accessing, that is,
reading or writing a data set, certain preliminary operations are required. When these operations have been performed we shall say that
the data set has been opened. When the data transfer has been completed and the facility is once again available, the data set is closed.
All of the information required to effect data transfer is provided by
the APLSV user in the form of a character vector. The vector is trans-
lated by an auxiliary processor TSIO into a form which the system understands. Responses from the system are accepted by TSIO which

translates them for the APLSV user. This two-way communication takes place through a <u>control variable</u> which is in fact a shared variable.

After the data set is opened, transfer of data may take place at any time using the control variable or an associated shared <u>data variable</u>. During the data transfer TSIO carrys out a number of functions. It may remove or supply the header or control information that is part of the internal representation of all APL data. It searches for an empty vector which signals the end-of-data transmission as well as a retraction of the control variable. Such a retraction ends the data transfer operation immediately and forces the data set to be closed.

23.3 COMMUNICATION WITH TSIO

To communicate with the TSIO processor it is necessary to use a control variable whose surrogate name begins with the characters CTL. Should a data variable we required, its surrogate name must begin with the characters DAT and conclude with the same suffix used in the name for the control variable. The TSIO processor will have an identification number assigned to it which may differ from installation to installation. Let this identification number be assigned to a variable ID. Communication will be initiated as follows:

```
     ID □SVO                    (The user offers to share.)
 1
        1 1 1 1 □SVC 'CTL'
 1 1 1 1                        (The variable is interlocked.)
```

The acceptance of the offer to share by TSIO results in a full interlock on the control variable CTL. Since the acceptance of the offer is not immediate, however, it is necessary for the user to establish the interlock before further action is taken.

23.4 CONTROL VARIABLE MODES

Because a control variable is used both to initiate data-transfer operations and for data transfer itself, it is necessary for the TSIO processor to know what mode is intended. We shall say that the control variable either in a command mode or in a data-transfer mode. In the command mode the value of the variable is interpreted by the processor as a command. The control variable is in a command mode when one of the following conditions occurs:

1. After TSIO matches the users offer to share the control variable;

2. Immediately following commands which request a one-step operation such as renaming or deleting a data set.

3. At the conclusion of data access when the control variable is in the data transfer mode. Termination of data access may be brought about by the APLSV user or by TSIO; any of the following conditions will result in termination of data access.

a) The user indicates termination of data access by assigning an empty vector to the control variable.

b) TSIO normally concludes data transfer in a sequential-read operation. When the empty vector is detected, the following use results in a numeric return code which puts the control variable in the command mode.

c) During a sequential-write operation, data transfer will be terminated if certain errors are encountered. In this case, the control variable immediately yields a numeric return code which places it in the command mode.

For the moment let us concentrate on the command mode and examine the kinds of commands which TSIO can carry out. Prior to this, a few words about data sets are in order. Data sets are composed of one or more records grouped in blocks which are the units of data actually transferred between the storage device and the computer memory. When the block consists of a single record it is said to be unblocked.

23.5 DATA MANAGEMENT COMMANDS [1]

A data management command is a character vector having a special format. The command begins with a word designating the main action to be taken. The rest of the command deals with the parameters of the set that govern the usage of the set. These parameters may appear in any order. The following six data-management operations are available to all users of TSIO.

SW	(Sequential Write) to create a new data set and to sequentially write records into, append to, or modify an existing data set;
SR	(Sequential Read) to read records sequentially from an existing data set;

---

1 Reprinted by permission from APL Shared Variables (APLSV) programming RPQ WE-1191-TSIO Program Reference Manual. Copyright © 1973 by International Business Machines Corporation.

IRW	(Indexed Read and Write) to read and write records in arbitrary sequence from or to an existing data set.
IR	(Indexed Read) to read records in arbitrary sequence from an existing data set.
RENAME	to change the name of an existing data set.
DELETE	to delete an existing data set.

The data-set parameters which follow the action item may appear in any order. We shall summarize the essential characteristics of these parameters here:

DSN	The value associated with this variable is the name of a new or existing set. A name can have at most eight characters starting with an alphabetic character and including numerals.
DISP	The possible values associated with this variable are:

(NEW) -- A data set is to be created
(OLD) -- A data set exists and access starts at the first record
(MOD) -- A data set exists and access starts after the last record.

All of the above imply exclusive use of the data set by the APLSV user. If simultaneous access is to be granted to another user, the value associated with the variable must be SHR.

BLKSIZE	The largest blocksize to be used in the data set. This parameter must be specified when a new data set is created.
LRECL	The record length
SPACE	Storage area to be allocated to the data set
RECFM	The format of the data set. The following are the allowable values for this variable.

U -- variable-length unblocked records without explicit length information as part of each record and block.

F -- <u>f</u>ixed length not blocked.

V -- <u>v</u>ariable length not blocked.

FB -- <u>f</u>ixed length <u>b</u>locked.

VB -- <u>v</u>ariable length blocked.

CODE   The header of the internal representation is either:

1. supplied and removed as the data goes to and
    from an APL workspace. In this case, the
    variable may take on any of the following values:

    B -- <u>B</u>oolean

    I -- <u>i</u>nteger

    F -- <u>f</u>loating point

    C -- <u>c</u>haracter

    E -- character type with translation between APL
        and EBCDIC

    These codes can be used to read any record what-
    soever but writing is restricted to values of the
    indicated type.

2. the representation is to be transferred as a whole.
    In this case the code must be A. It can be used to
    write any value but only records written with an A
    can be read with this code.

23.6 RESPONSE CODES

When the control variable is in the command mode, each specification
of the variable results in a response code which indicates that the command has been successfully executed or that it has failed. A response
of 0 indicates successful execution. A complete description of all
response codes is given in the TSIO Reference Guide.

23.7 AN EXAMPLE OF SEQUENTIAL READING AND WRITING

To illustrate some of the concepts we have been discussing, we shall
give an example of a sequential read and write

ID □SVO 'CTL'   (An offer to share the variable 'CTL'
                       is made to TSIO.)

1   (The offer is accepted.)

1 1 1 1 □SVC 'CTL'   (A full interlock is placed on the variable.)

CTL←'SW DSN=TESTDATA,BLKSIZE=615,DISP=NEW'

Sequential write.   Filename is TESTDATA.   There are 615 bytes per block.   A new file is created.

CTL
0   (The access command has been successfully executed.)

CTL←3 5 11   (The variable CTL is now in data transfer mode and
                       data for the first record is transferred.)
CTL
0   (The record has been written successfully.)

CTL←'ABC'   (The second record is transferred.)

CTL
0   (Writing is successful.)

CTL←' '   (The empty vector is detected by TSIO and the variable
                       CTL is placed in command mode.)

CTL
0   (Writing has terminated and the data set is closed.)

Assume now that we want to read what was just written.

$CTL\leftarrow$'SR $DSN=TESTDATA$' (Open $TESTDATA$ for sequential reading.)

CTL

0   (Response to command.)

CTL

3 5 11   (First record is read and displayed.)

$X\leftarrow CTL$

X

ABC (Second record is read.)

CTL (An empty vector is returned -- this indicates that
                         reading has terminated and the control variable is
                         in the command mode.)

We shall now show how a record can be appended to the file.

$CTL\leftarrow$'SW $DSN=TESTDATA,DISP=MOD$'

CTL

0   (the file command to open the file is)
                         (successfully executed)

$CTL\leftarrow \iota 5$ (a record is appended)

CTL

0

$CTL\leftarrow$' '   (return to command mode)

0   (the control variable is returned to)
                         (command mode)

The command

$CTL\leftarrow$'SW $DSN=TEST$ $DATA$'   erases all records in the
CTL data set but the data set
0   identity is retained. The
                                             next record written will be
                                             the first record.

In the above examples, the parameters $SPACE,LRECL,$
$RECFM$ and $CODE$ took on default values assigned by
TSIO.

In the above examples, the parameters $SPACE,LRECL,RECFM,$ and $CODE$
took on default values assigned by TSIO.

For a sequential data set liek *TESTDATA* the following are a simple set of command forms:

SW DSN=TESTDATA,DISP=NEW,BLKSIZE=615	Create data set
SW DSN=TESTDATA,DISP=MOD	Extend data set
SW DSN=TESTDATA	Rewrite data set
SR DSN=TESTDATA	Read data set
RENAME DSN=TESTDATA,NEWNAME=B1	Change name of data set
DELETE DSN=TESTDATA	Destroy data set

23.8 PERIPHERAL DEVICES

The use of peripheral devices such as the high-speed printer and magnetic tape requires the intervention of the system operator. This is because direct control of a device such as a high-speed printer or a magnetic tape from a remote terminal is neither practical or economical. Since the systems operator's function is to service the APL user, it is a matter of communicating with the operator and letting him or her know what is desired. In the case of the high-speed printer, it is necessary to specify the data set that is to be printed together with the appropriate parameters. A data set produced with a sequential write command *SW* with the following parameter values:

CODE= E, RECFM = VB, LRECL = 137 BLKSIZE = 689,
SPACE = (1061 **(120, 11)**

will print one record per line automatically skipping over the perforated page break. The rationale for this choice is explained in the TSIO Reference Guide.

In the case of a magnetic tape having standard tape labels, an appropriate read command would be:

CTL←'SR DSN=NNN,CODE=C,UNIT=2400,VOLUME=ABC02P'

The manual "OS/VS Tape Labels" (IBM Publication GC26-3795) discusses standard tape labels in detail.

To effective master the concepts of TSIO requires a good deal of practice, but fortunately this can be done at the terminal

MANUALS AND PRIMERS

APL\360 Primer, Prog. Nos. 5734-XM1, 5736-XM1, Form No. GH20-0689-1, White Plains, N.Y.:IBM, January, 1970.

APL\360-OS and APL\360-DOS User's Manual, Prog. Nos. 5734-XM6, 5736-XM6, Form No. GH20-0906-1, White Plains, N.Y.:IBM, January, 1973.

APL Shared Variables (APLSV), Programming RPQ WE1191, User's Guide, Program No. 5799-AJF SH20-1460-0, White Plains, N.Y.: IBM, January, 1974.

APL Shared Variable (APLSV), Programming RPQ WE1191, TSIO Program Reference Manual, Program No. 5799-AJF SH20-1463-0, White Plains, N.Y.: IBM, January, 1974.

APL/CMS User's Manual, Programming RPQ MF2608, Prog. No. 5799-ALK SC20-1846-1, File No. S370-22, Palo Alto, Calif.: IBM, March, 1975.

General Information Manual, APL\360-OS(5734 XM6) and APL\360-DOS(5736-XM6), Form No. GH 20-0830, White Plains, N.Y.: IBM.

Pakin, S., APL\360 Reference Manual, 2nd ed., Chicago: Science Research Associates, 1972.

BOOKS

Buckley, J.W., D.L. Sharp, J. Nagara, J. Schenck, Management Problem Solving With APL, New York: Wiley/Becker and Hayes, 1974.

Gilman, L., and A. Rose. APL\360: An Interactive Approach, 2nd ed., New York: Wiley, 1974.

Hellerman, H., Digital Computer System Principles, 2nd ed., New York: McGraw-Hill, 1974.

Iverson, K.E., A Programming Language, New York: Wiley, 1962.

Iverson, K.E., Elementary Functions: An Algorithmic Treatment, Chicago: Science Research Associates, 1966.

Iverson, K.E., Algebra. An Algorithmic Treatment, Reading, Mass.: Addison-Wesley, 1973.

Katzan, H., Jr., APL Programming and Computer Techniques, New York: Van Nostrand-Reinhold, 1970.

Katzan, H., Jr., APL User's Guide, New York: Van Nostrand-Reinhold, 1971.

Mock, T.J., and M.A. Vasahbely, APL for Management, New York: Becker & Hayes, 1972.

Pakin: S., APL -- A Short Course, Englewood Cliffs, N.J.: Prentice-Hall, 1975.

Polivka, R., and S. Pakin, APL -- The Language and Its Usage, Englewood Cliffs, N.J.: Prentice-Hall, 1975.

Prager, W., An Introduction to APL, Boston: Allyn & Bacon, 1971.

Smillie, K., APL\360 With Statistical Examples, Reading, Mass.: Addison-Wesley Publishing Co., 1975.

Wiedman, C., Handbook of APL Programming, New York: Petrocelli, 1974.

CONFERENCES & PROCEEDINGS

APL Congress 75 -- Facility of Engineering, University of Pisa, Pisa, Italy.

Proceedings of the Sixth International APL User's Conference, Anaheim, May, 1974.

APL Congress 73, New York: American Elsevier, 1973.

Proceedings of the Fifth International APL User's Conference, Toronto, Canada, May, 1973.

Proceedings of the Fourth International APL User's Conference, At
Atlanta, June, 1972.[1]

APL Quote Quad, Published by the STAPL/SIGPLAN of the ACM. This
informal quarterly publication contains articles, algorithms, announce-
ments, problems, book reviews, and other materials of interest to AP
users.

---

(1) The article by J.C. Rault and G. Dewars "Is APL Epidemic? or A
Study of Its Growth Through an Extended Bibliography" in these proceedings contains an excellent bibliography of articles dealing with AP
up to 1972.

A SUMMARY OF APL FUNCTION SYMBOLS

The following is a summary of all of the APL function symbols discussed in this book, with appropriate page references. The symbols d and f are used to denote any of the primitive scalar dyadic functions.

Symbol	M = Monadic D = Dyadic	Meaning	Page Reference
←	D	assign to	19
×	M	the sign of	26–27
×	D	multiplication	26
÷	M	reciprocal	27
÷	D	division	27
+	M	identity	28
+	D	addition	27
−	M	negation	28
−	D	subtraction	28
=	D	equals	34
≤	D	less than or equal to	34
<	D	less than	34
≥	D	greater than or equal to	34
>	D	greater than	34
≠	D	not equal	34
∨	D	logical or	36
∧	D	logical and	36
~	D	logical not	36
⍲	D	logical nand (not and)	36
⍱	D	logical nor (not or)	36
⋆	M	exponential (base e)	41
⋆	D	power	42
⍟	M	natural logarithm	42
⍟	D	logarithm to a base	43
⌊	M	floor	45

Symbol	Mode M=Monadic D=Dyadic	Meaning	Page Reference
⌊	D	minimum	45
⌈	M	ceiling	46
⌈	D	maximum	46
|	M	absolute value	46–6
|	D	residue	47–4
○	M	times π	49
○	D	trigonometric functions	49
!	M	factorial	52–5
!	D	combinational	53–5
?	M	roll	54
ρ	D	restructure	68
ρ	M	dimension	70
ι	M	index generator	72
ι	D	index of	85
[ ]	D	indexing	79
,	M	ravel	89
,	D	catenate	91
,	M	laminate	94
f/	D	reduction	123
⌹	M	matrix inverse	135
⌹	D	matrix divide	137
f.d	D	inner product	137
o.f	D	outer product	140
⍋	M	grade up	151–
⍒	M	grade down	151–
↑	D	take	154
↓	D	drop	157
⍉	M	transpose (last two coordinates)	160
⍉	D	transpose	163
⌽	M	reversal	165
⌽	D	rotate	166
/	D	compression	171
\	D	expansion	174
∈	D	membership	176
?	D	deal	181
⊥	D	decode	184

Symbol	Mode M=Monadic D=Dyadic	Meaning	Page Reference
⊤	D	encode	187
⎕	D	input	193
⍞	D	literal input	196
⍞	D	bare output	264
⎕	M	display	198
f\	M	scan	271
⍎	M	execute	272
⍕	D	format	274
⍕	M	format	273

Table B.1 Systems Command Summary (A PL\360) [1]

Reference and Purpose COMMAND FORM 1,2,3	NORMAL RESPONSE	TROUBLE REPORTS [4]
TC1 Sign on designated user and start a work session.		
)NUMBER [PASSWORD]	[TEXT]; PORT,TIME,DATE,USER;SYSTEM; [SAVED,TIME,DATE]	1 2 3 4
TC2 End work session.		
)OFF [PASSWORD]	PORT,TIME,DATE,USER CODE;TIME USED	16
TC3 End work session and hold dial-up connection.		
)OFF HOLD [PASSWORD]	PORT,TIME,DATE,USER CODE;TIME USED	16
TC4 End work session and store active workspace.		
)CONTINUE [PASSWORD]	[TIME,DATE,CONTINUE]; PORT,TIME,DATE,USER CODE; TIME USED	6 16
TC5 End work session, store active workspace, and hold dial-up connection.		
)CONTINUE HOLD [PASSWORD]	[TIME,DATE,CONTINUE]; PORT,TIME,DATE,USER CODE; TIME USED	6 16
WC1 Activate a clear workspace.		
)CLEAR	CLEAR WS	16
WC2 Activate a copy of a stored workspace.		
)LOAD WSID [PASSWORD]	SAVED,TIME,DATE	7 8 16
WC3 Copy a global object from a stored workspace.		
)COPY WSID [PASSWORD] NAME SAVED,TIME,DATE		6 7 8 9 10 16
WC3a Copy all global objects from a stored workspace.		
)COPY WSID [PASSWORD]	SAVED,TIME,DATE	6 7 8 10 16
WC4 Copy a global object from a stored workspace, protecting active workspace.		
)PCOPY WSID [PASSWORD] NAME SAVED,TIME,DATE		6 7 8 9 10 16
WC4a Copy all global objects from a stored workspace, protecting active workspace.		
)PCOPY WSID [PASSWORD]	SAVED,TIME,DATE	6 7 8 10 16
WC5 Gather objects into a group.		
)GROUP NAME[S]	NONE	11 16
WC6 Erase global objects.		
)ERASE NAME[S]		16
WC7 Set index origin for array operations.		
)ORIGIN INTEGER,0-1	WAS,FORMER ORIGIN	16
WC8 Set maximum for significant digits in output.		
)DIGITS INTEGER,1-6	WAS,FORMER MAXIMUM	16
WC9 Set maximum width for an output line.		
)WIDTH INTEGER,30-130	WAS,FORMER WIDTH	16
WC10 Change workspace identification.		
)WSID WSID	WAS,FORMER WSID	16
WC11 Change quantity of permitted symbols.		
)SYMBOLS INTEGER,26-4241	WAS,FORMER SYMBOL TABLE SIZE	16
LC1 Re-store a copy of the active workspace.		
)SAVE	TIME,DATE,WSID	6 12 13 14 16
LC1a Store a copy of the active workspace.		
)SAVE WSID [LOCK]	TIME,DATE	6 12 13 14 16
LC2 Erase a stored workspace.		
)DROP WSID	TIME,DATE	7 14 16
IQ1 List names of defined functions.		
)FNS [LETTER]	FUNCTION NAMES	16
IQ2 List names of global variables.		
)VARS [LETTER]	VARIABLE NAMES	16
IQ3 List names of groups.		
)GRPS [LETTER]	GROUP NAMES	16

TROUBLE REPORT FORMS

1 NUMBER NOT IN SYSTEM
2 INCORRECT SIGN-ON
3 ALREADY SIGNED ON
4 NUMBER IN USE
5 NUMBER LOCKED OUT
6 NOT WITH OPEN DEFINITION
7 WS NOT FOUND
8 WS LOCKED
9 OBJECT NOT FOUND
10 WS FULL
11 NOT GROUPED, NAME IN USE
12 NOT SAVED, WS QUOTA USED UP
13 NOT SAVED, THIS WS IS WSID
14 IMPROPER LIBRARY REFERENCE
15 MESSAGE LOST
16 INCORRECT COMMAND

(1) Reprinted by permission from A PL\360–OS and A PL\360–DOS Users
Manual, Copyright © 1973 by international Business Machines
Corporation.

```
Q4  List membership of designated group.
  )GRP NAME                      FUNCTION NAMES,VARIABLE NAMES                    16
Q5  List halted functions (state indicator).
  )SI                            SEQUENCE OF HALTED FUNCTIONS                     16
Q6  List halted functions and associated local variables (augmented state indicator).
  )SIV                           SEQUENCE OF HALTED FUNCTIONS WITH NAMES OF LOCAL VARIABLES  16
Q7  Give identification of active workspace.
  )WSID                          WSID                                             16
Q8  List names of workspaces in designated library.
  )LIB [NUMBER]                  NAMES OF STORED WORKSPACES                    14 16
Q9  List ports in use and codes of connected users.
  )PORTS                         PORT NUMBERS AND ASSOCIATED USER CODES           16
Q10 List port numbers associated with designated user code.
  )PORTS CODE                    PORT NUMBERS                                     16
M1  Address text to designated port.
  )MSGN PORT [TEXT]              SENT                                          15 16
M2  Address text to designated port, and lock keyboard.
  )MSG PORT [TEXT]               SENT                                          15 16
M3  Address text to recording terminal (APL Operator).
  )OPRN [TEXT]                   SENT                                          15 16
M4  Address text to recording terminal (APL Operator), and lock keyboard.
  )OPR [TEXT]                    SENT                                          15 16
Notes:  1. Items in brackets are optional.
        2. PASSWORD: a password set off from preceding text by a colon.
        3. WSID: library number and workspace name, or workspace name alone, as required.
        4. See insert table of trouble report forms.
```

Table B.2 Changes in Systems Commands (APLSV) [2]

__Communication commands.__   There are many occasions when a user
may wish to be undisturbed by messages arriving at the terminal; for
example, when producing finished output or while concentrating on a
difficult problem. Even under such circumstances, however, it may
be necessary to communicate briefly with another port.

The command)MSG OFF blocks any message except one coming
in response to a transmitted message in which a reply was requested
(that is, a message of the form)OPR or)MSG and arriving before
the keyboard is again unlocked. Any blocked message is treated as if
the keyboard were continuously unlocked, and it will so appear to the
sender.

The command)MSG ON restores the acceptance of messages and
causes the last public address message, if any, to be printed.

__Copy commands.__   The commands)COPY and)PCOPY now accept a
multiplicity of object names. The response lists separately the objects
not found (headed by NOT FOUND) and those found but not copied (headed
by NOT COPIED).

(2) Reprinted by permission from APL Shared Variables (APLSV) Programming RPQ WE1191-- Users' Guide, Copyright © 1973 by
International Business Machines Coporation.

Erase command. The erase command now acts on any global object, and no longer distinguishes between pendent functions and others. Problems that may possibly arise from erasing a pendent function are forestalled by the response *SI DAMAGE* , which warns the user to take appropriate action before resuming function execution.

Save command. An attempt to save a workspace during execution of a function, as had been possible through an explicit command during a request for ⎕ input or a forced disconnect in ⍞ input, will result in the function's being interrupted prior to the execution of the command.
   When the workspace is next activated, therefore, function execution will not automatically resume. Such automatic resumption can be invoked by the system variable *⎕LX* defined in Part 4.

Symbol table size. The command)*SYMBOLS* without a number prints the current number of names accommodated.

Workspace identification. The command)*WSID* can be used to set a lock as well as the workspace name, using the same form as the)*SAVE* command. Used as an inquiry,)*WSID* will continue to return only the workspace identification.

Privacy. In the interest of privacy, a workspace saved with the name *CONTINUE* cannot be activated or copied by a user other than the one in whose library it has been saved.

Public libraries. Workspaces named *CONTINUE* cannot be stored in public libraries.

Local function names. As a result of the introduction of the system function *⎕FX* (defined in Part 4), local names may now refer to functions as well as variables. Consequently, the phrase "functions and global variables" occurring in the APL 360 User's Manual should now be read as "global functions and variables."

Table B.5 System Functions (APL?)

Function	Requirements			Effect on Environment	Explicit result
	Rank	Length	Domain		
$\square CR$ A	$1 \geq \rho\rho A$		Array of characters.	None	Canonical representation of object named by A. The result for anything other than an unlocked defined function is of dimension 0 0.
$\square FX$ M	$2 = \rho\rho M$		Matrix of characters.	Fix (extablish) definition of the function represented by M, unless its name is already in use for an object other than a function which is not halted.	A vector representing the name of the function established, or the scalar row index of the fault which prevented establishment.
$\square EX$ A	$2 \geq \rho\rho A$		Array of characters.	Expunge (erase) objects named by rows of A, except groups, labels, or halted functions	A Boolean vector whose I th element is 1 if the I th name is now free.
$\square NL$ N	$1 \geq \rho\rho N$ $1 \geq \rho$	$,S$	$\wedge/N \in 1$ 2 3	None	A matrix of rows (in accidental order) representing names of designated kinds in the dynamic environment: $1,2,3$ for labels, variables, functions.
A $\square NL$ N	$1 \geq \rho\rho N$ $1 \geq \rho A$		$\wedge/N \in 1$ 2 3 Elements of must be alphabetic.	None	The same as for the monadic form, except that only names beginning with letters in A will be included.

Table B3. System Functions (APLSV) (continued)

Function	Requirements			Effect on Environment	Explicit result
	Rank	Length	Characters		
$\Box NC\ A$	$2 \geq \rho\rho M$		Array of characters.	None	A vector giving the usage of the name in each row of A: $0,1,2,3,4$ for name is available, a label, a variable, a function, other.
$\Box DL\ S$	$1 \geq \rho\rho S$		Numeric value.	None, but requires S seconds to complete	scalar value of actual delay.

Table B.4 System Variables (APLSV)

Name	Purpose	Value in Clear WS	Meaningful Range	Alternate Facility
⎕CT	Comparison tolerance (relative): used in ⌈ ¦ < ≤ = ≥ > ≠ .	$1E^{-}13$	0-1	SETFUZZ
⎕IO	Index origin: used in indexing and in ? and ⍳ .	1	0 1	ORIGIN
⎕LX	Latent expression executed on activation of workspace.	''	Characters	None
⎕PP	Printing precision: affects numeric output and monadic ⍕ .	10	⍳16	DIGITS
⎕PW	Printing width: affects all but bare output.	120	29+⍳361	WIDTH
⎕RL	Random link: used in ? .	7*5	⍳¯1+2*31	SETLINK
⎕AI	Account information: identification, computer time, connect time, keying time (all times in milliseconds and cumulative during session).			⍳29 21 24 19
⎕AV	Atomic vector			None
⎕LC	Line counter: line numbers of functions in execution, innermost first.	⍳0		⍳27 26
⎕TS	Time stamp: year, month, day, hour, minute, second, millisecond.			⍳25 20
⎕TT	Terminal type: 0 for 1050; 1 for Selectric; 2 for PTTC/BCD.			⍳28

(continued)

TABLE B4. System Variables (APLSV) (continued)

Name	Purpose	Value in Clear WS	Meaningful Range	Alternate Facility
□UL	User load			I23
□WA	Working area available.			I22

Note 1: The old definitions of the workspace functions will no longer work. See test for corrective action.

Table C.1 lists major commercial sources providing APL service. If
If you do not have access to a computer or if economic considerations
do not warrant the use of your computer, a commercial source may be
the answer for you. All vendors listed provide continuous and reliable
operation. Because they are dedicated almost exclusively to APL, they
are continually updating both hardware and software, thus providing
their customers with a relatively sophisticated environment. All the
vendors have the capability of handling large files, although their
implementation methods vary. They are thus playing an active role in
the development and extension of the language. Each vendor makes
available to its customers a large library of APL functions for a great
variety of applications and will usually supply a free catalog on request.

Table C.1 Major Commercial Sources of APL

APL Service, Inc.
865 Lower Ferry Road
Trenton, N.J. 08628
(609) 883-0050

Boeing Computer Services Inc.
825 Third Avenue
New York, N.Y. 10022
(212) 486-7240

Computer Company
Seventh and Franklin Building
Richmond, Va. 23219
(703) 648-5823

Computer Innovations
10225 Southwestern Avenue
Chicago, Ill. 60643
(312) 445-0626

L.P. Sharpe Associates, Ltd.
P.O. Box 71
Toronto Dominion Center
Toronto 1, Ontario, Canada

Scientific Time Sharing Corp.
2101 S. Street, N.W.
Washington, D.C. 20008
(202) 462-1165

Shared Educational Computer
  System, Inc.
50 Market Street
Poughkeepsie, N.Y. 12601
(914) 485-8770

Time Sharing Resources Inc.
Great Neck, New York
(516) 487-0101

In September of 1975 IBM announced the IBM 5100 portable computer, a desk-top computer utilizing A PLSV and BASIC with 16,384 to 65,536 storage positions, a display screen showing 1024 characters in sixteen 64-character lines, a data cartridge holding 204,000 characters, and an optional printer, tape unit, and communications adapter. A picture of the IBM 5100 provides an A PL capability at a cost of between $10,000 and $30,000 depending on the options selected. For many installations, this may be an attractive way of gaining an A PL capability.

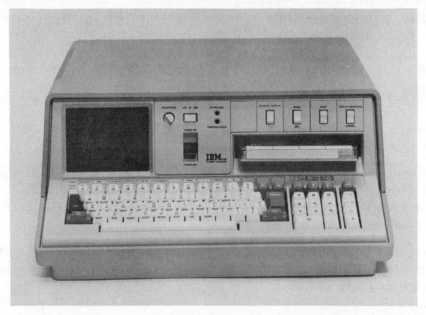

(Photo courtesy of IBM)

Fig. D.1 The IBM 5100 Portable Computer

Specifications

IBM 5100 Portable Computer
- **Dimensions:** 8" x 17-1/2" x 24" (20 cm x 45 cm x 61 cm)
- **Weight:** 46-50 lbs. (20.9 kg-22.7 kg) depending on configuration
- **Power:** AC, grounded 115 volts
- **Read-only storage:** 48K bits per chip, for language implementation. Input/output microcode in functional storage unit maximizes main storage work space while executing read-only storage programs
- **MOSFET main storage:** Four increments available, from 16,384 to 65,536 storage positions
- **Display screen:** Shows 1024 characters in sixteen 64-character lines. Faceplate of high-impact plastic
- **Covers:** High-impact, structured foam plastic provides high strength-to-weight ratio in a tough, dent-resistant material

Communications Adapter (Optional)
- Start/stop line discipline
- 134.5 or 300 bits-per-second line rates (EBCD line code)
- EIA RS-232C standard interface
- Emulates an IBM 2741 Communications Terminal to a remote system

5103 Printer (Optional)
- Dimensions: 12-1/4" x 13-1/4" x 23" (31 cm x 34 cm x 59 cm)
- Weight: 56 lbs. (25.4 kg)
- Bidirectional printing at 80 characters per second (cps)
- 132-character print line
- Standard forms tractor
- Handles multipart forms

5106 Auxiliary Tape Unit (Optional)
- Dimensions: 7-1/4" x 10" x 12" (19 cm x 26 cm x 31 cm)
- Weight: 18 lbs. (8.2 kg)
- Reads up to 2850 characters per second
- Writes and checks up to 950 cps
- Searches or rewinds at 40 inches per second

IBM Data Cartridge
- Holds up to 204,000 characters
- File protect feature
- Highly reliable, quarter-inch magnetic tape

Fig. D.2 Specifications for the IBM 5100 Portable Computer

CHAPTER 2

1. A. $2.96853E2$ D. $7.592E{}^{-}4$
       296.853 0.0007592

   B. ${}^{-}1.07596E0$ E. ${}^{-}9.5217E{}^{-}2$
       ${}^{-}1.07596$ ${}^{-}0.095217$

   C. $1.62128E4$
       16212.8

2. A.   The comma is not a legitimate character in naming a constant.
   C.   No spaces are permitted between successive digits.
   E.   Exceeds the magnitude of numbers which can be represented.
   G.   At most 16 significant digits can be represented.
   H.   The right quotation mark is missing.

3. B.   A space character may not be part of a name.
   D.   A variable name must begin with an alphabetic character.
   F.   A function symbol cannot be part of a name.

CHAPTER 3

1.
         $\times 7$
   1

         $\times{}^{-}4$
  ${}^{-}1$

       ${}^{-}45\div{}^{-}9$
   5

(continued)

	$-^-5$		$^-5×6$
5		$^-30$	
	$9×8$		$×0$
72		0	
	$7+^-10$		$2+6÷+2×3××2$
$^-3$		3	
	$^-5+^-1$		$2÷6×^-1+5$
$^-6$		0.08333333333	
	$+^-10$		$×1+4+5×2.E1$
$^-10$		1	

2.

$$X←7$$
$$Y←8$$
$$Z←2$$

$$(X×Y)÷Z$$
28

$$(Y÷Z)+X$$
11

$$(X+Y)*2$$
225

3.   A.   The function × requires an argument on its right.
   C.   The term 3U is not allowed. There must be a function be-
        tween 3 and U.
   D.   The term 4¯5H is not allowed. A function is required betwee
        4 and ¯5 and between ¯5 and H.
   E.   A right parenthesis is missing.

4.

$$X←3$$
$$Y←2$$
$$Z←^-1$$

$$W←××X+Y×-Z$$
$$W$$
1

$$W←Z+X×Y÷Z$$
$$W$$
$^-7$

$$W \leftarrow 3 \times X - Y - Z$$
$$W$$

0

$$W \leftarrow X + Y + Z - 3 \div Z$$
$$W$$

7

5. A.
$$(.03 \times 1000) + (.02 \times 3000) \div .01 \times 3000$$
    120

$$(.03 \times 1000) + (.02 \times 3000) + (.01 \times 4000) + .005 \times 2000$$
    B. 140

CHAPTER 4

1. A, C, and D

2. A, E, G, H - Tautology
    D, F - Contradiction
    B, C - Neither

3.
$$X \leftarrow (10 \times (Y < Z)) + (2 \times (Z \geq Y))$$
$$X \leftarrow ((\times Y) = (\times Z)) + (3 \times ((\times Y) \neq (\times Z)))$$
$$W \leftarrow 6 \times ((X = Y) \wedge (X = Z)) + 3 \times ((X \neq Y) \vee (X \neq Z))$$
$$Y \leftarrow ((.2 \times Z) \times (X < 1.7)) + ((.25 \times Z) \times (X \geq 1.7))$$

$$Z \leftarrow ((X > 0) \wedge (Y > 0)) + (2 \times ((X < 0) \wedge (Y > 0))) +$$
$$(3 \times ((X < 0) \wedge (Y < 0))) + (4 \times ((X > 0) \wedge (Y < 0)))$$

4.
$$P \wedge Q$$

5. A. $Z \leftarrow A1 \lfloor A2 \lfloor A3$

    B. $Z \leftarrow A1 \lceil A2 \lceil A3$

CHAPTER 5

1.

```
      ⌈0.5
1

      ¯6⌊¯3
¯6

      ¯6*2
36

      *0
1

      3|¯10
2

      20090÷180
1.743934249E¯16

      |¯5
5

      ~1∨30090÷360
0

      !6
720

      4!8
70
```

2.

```
         *○1
23.14069263

         **1
15.15426224

         (○1)*.5
1.772453851

         10⍟3
0.4771212547

         ⍟3
1.098612289
```

3.

A. Z*(M+N)
B. (Z-1)*(M-N)
C. ((C+D)÷(Y+A×X))-3
D. X*-Y

E. 1÷(1+X*.5)
F. ((X-Y)*.5)÷Z
G. (⍟(X-Y))÷10⍟(X+Y)
H. ?100

4.

A. Z←⌊U⌊V⌊W⌊Y
B. Z←Y|X
C. Z←?51

5.
$$C \leftarrow (5 \div 9) \times (F - 3 2)$$

6.

A.
```
A←3
B←4
C←5
S←(A+B+C)÷2
AREA←(S×(S-A)×(S-B)×(S-C))*.5
AREA
```
    6

B.
```
A←1
B←2
C←2
S←(A+B+C)÷2
AREA←(S×(S-A)×(S-B)×(S-C))*.5
AREA
```
0.9682458366

C.
```
A←7
B←11
C←13
S←(A+B+C)÷2
AREA←(S×(S-A)×(S-B)×(S-C))*.5
AREA
```
38.4991883

7.
```
S←16×T*2
S←16×3*2
S
```
A. 144
```
S←16×6*2
S
```
B. 576

C. no.

8.

```
          3296|18325
     1845

          3296|6594
     2

          3296|12111
     2223


          A←24×(1.01)*730
          A
     34262.10984


          1.01*20
     1.22019004
```

9.

$$P←A×I×((I+1)*N)÷(((I+1)*N)-1)$$

10.

```
          24×1.005*1464
     35589.80867
```

CHAPTER 6

1. A.   `Z←(2×ι50)-1`

    B.   `M←3 5ρ?15ρ73`

    C.   `Z←M⌈N`

    D.   `Z←M⌊N`

    E.   `Z←2*ι30`

    F.   `X←1+(.1÷ι40)`
         `Z←(*X)×(1+X+X*2)`

    G.   `A←(77ρ X)*(7 7ρ⌈((ι49)÷7)`

2.   `C←(A=B)×A`

3. $A \leftarrow 2\ 3\ 5\ 7$
                $B \leftarrow \iota 4$
                $C \leftarrow 2\ 2\rho 1\ 3\ 5$

   A. $A+B$
        3   5   8   11

   B. $A \star B$
        2   9   125   2401

   C. $2 \times A-B$
        2   2   4   6

   D. $5\rho C$
        1   3   5   1   1

   E. $A+7$
        9   10   12   14

   F. $3\ 2\rho C$

        1   3
        5   1
        1   3

   G. ρC
        2   2

   H. $\rho 5$

   I. $8-\iota 8$
        7   6   5   4   3   2   1   0

   J. $3 \times \iota 0$

   K. $A \lceil B$
        2   3   5   7

   L. $A \lfloor B$
        1   2   3   4

   M. $200 \lceil B$
        ‾1   1   ‾1   1

   N. $A \leq B$
        0   0   0   0

4.
```
     Z←10 10ρ1 0 0 0 0 0 0 0 0 0 0
     Z
```
```
1 0 0 0 0 0 0 0 0 0
0 1 0 0 0 0 0 0 0 0
0 0 1 0 0 0 0 0 0 0
0 0 0 1 0 0 0 0 0 0
0 0 0 0 1 0 0 0 0 0
0 0 0 0 0 1 0 0 0 0
0 0 0 0 0 0 1 0 0 0
0 0 0 0 0 0 0 1 0 0
0 0 0 0 0 0 0 0 1 0
0 0 0 0 0 0 0 0 0 1
```

5.
```
     E←12 19 110 220
     R←3.6 5.2 20.3 18.6
     I←E÷R
     I
3.333333333  3.653846154  5.418719212
11.82795699
```

6.
```
          X←ι41
     P←41+X+X*2
     P
43  47  53  61  71  83  97  113  131
        151  173  197  223  251  281
        313  347  383  421  461  503
        547  593  641  691  743  797
        853  911  971  1033  1097  1163
        1231  1301  1373  1447  1523
        1601  1681  1763
```

7.
```
     D←(C←(B←(A←(ι100)*2)*.25)*6)*(1÷9)
     D
1  1.25992105  1.44224957  1.587401052
        1.709975947  1.817120593  1.912931183
        2  2.080083823  2.15443469  2.223980091
        2.289428485  2.351334688  2.410142264
        2.466212074  2.5198421  2.571281591
        2.620741394  2.668401649  2.714417617
        2.758924176  2.802039331  2.84386698
        2.884499141  2.924017738  2.962496068
```

```
3   3.036588972   3.072316826
3.107232506   3.141380652   3.174802104
3.20753433   3.239611801   3.27106631
3.301927249   3.332221852   3.361975407
3.391211443   3.419951893   3.44821724
3.476026645   3.50339806   3.530348335
3.556893304   3.583047871   3.60882608
3.634241186   3.65930571   3.684031499
3.708429769   3.732511157   3.756285754
3.77976315   3.802952461   3.825862366
3.848501131   3.870876641   3.892996416
3.914867641   3.936497183   3.95789161
3.979057208   4   4.020725759
4.041240021   4.0615481   4.081655102
4.10156593   4.1212853   4.140817749
4.160167646   4.179339196   4.198336454
4.217163327   4.235823584   4.254320865
4.272658682   4.290840427   4.30886938
4.326748711   4.344481486   4.362070671
4.37951914   4.396829672   4.414004962
4.431047622   4.447960181   4.464745096
4.481404747   4.497941445   4.514357435
4.530654896   4.546835944   4.562902635
4.57885697   4.594700892   4.610436292
4.626065009   4.641588834
```

8.
```
D←ρV←5.975+.025×ι41
D
```
```
41
```

9.
```
X←3 2 1 ‾8 4
Y←2 3 ‾1 7 6
```

A.
```
Z←X≥Y
Z
```
```
1   0   1   0   0
```

B.
```
Z←(3=Y)>Y
Z
```
```
0   0   0   1   0
```

C.
```
Z←(X+Y)*Z
Z
```
```
1   1   1   ‾1   1
```

D.

```
Z←(X×Y)+1
Z
7   7   0   ‾55   25
```

10.

```
Z←2⊕ι100
Y←⊕ι100
X←10⊕ι100
⌈/|((Z-(X+Y))÷Z)
```
```
1
```

CHAPTER 7

1.

```
A←2 3 5 7
B←ι4
P←2 2ρ1 3 5
G←'AEFHWO'
H←3 5 7ρι30
```

A. $A[B[3]]$
```
5
```

B. $G[A[B[3]]]$
```
W
```

C. $P[;1]$
```
1   5
```

D. $G[5 4 6]$
```
WHO
```

E. $A[ι2]$
```
2   3
```

F. $H[1; ;2]$
```
2   9   16   23   30
```

G. $G[P]$
```
AF
WA
```

H. $H[;1 2;]$

```
1    2    3    4    5    6
8    9   10   11   12   13

6    7    8    9   10   11
13   14   15   16   17   18

11   12   13   14   15   16
18   19   20   21   22   23
```

2. **A.**
$\qquad \rho A$
4
$\qquad\qquad\qquad\qquad \rho P$
2 2

B.
$\qquad \rho \rho A$
1
$\qquad\qquad\qquad\qquad \rho \rho P$
2

C.
$\qquad \rho B$
4
$\qquad\qquad\qquad\qquad \rho G$
6

D.
$\qquad \rho \rho B$
1
$\qquad\qquad\qquad\qquad \rho \rho G$
1

$\qquad\qquad\qquad\qquad \rho H$
3 5 7

$\qquad\qquad\qquad\qquad \rho \rho H$
3

3.

```
        M←3 3ρ5 2 1 7 7 9 4 5 8
        M

  5   2   1
  7   7   9
  4   5   8

        M[1;]
  5   2   1

        ML;2]
  2   7   5

        M[1 2;]

  5   2   1
  7   7   9

        M[1 2;1 2]

  5   2
  7   7

        M[1 3;1 3]

  5   1
  4   8
```

4.

$$B \iota A$$

2   3   5   5

$$G \iota (P-1)$$

7   7
7   7

$$A \iota B[3]$$

2

$$B \iota H$$

1	2	3	4	5	5	5
5	5	5	5	5	5	5
5	5	5	5	5	5	5
5	5	5	5	5	5	5
5	5	1	2	3	4	5

5	5	5	5	5	5	5
5	5	5	5	5	5	5
5	5	5	5	5	5	5
5	5	5	5	1	2	3
4	5	5	5	5	5	5

5	5	5	5	5	5	5
5	5	5	5	5	5	5
5	5	5	5	5	5	1
2	3	4	5	5	5	5
5	5	5	5	5	5	5

5. A. $Y \leftarrow X[5 + \iota 5]$
   B. $Y \leftarrow X[5 \times \iota 5]$

CHAPTER 8

1.

$$V \leftarrow 3 \quad 5 \quad 9 \quad 1$$
$$M \leftarrow 4 \quad 4 \rho \iota 16$$
$$A \leftarrow 3 \quad 2 \quad 5 \rho \iota 30$$

$$,M$$

A. 1   2   3   4   5   6   7   8   9   10   11   12
        13   14   15   16

B. $,A$
  1 2 3 4 5 6 7 8 9 10 11 12
       13 14 15 16 17 18 19 20
       21 22 23 24 25 26 27 28
       29 30

       $,V*2$
C. 9 25 81 1

       $V,2*V$
D. 3 5 9 1 8 32 512 2

2.
  $Z \leftarrow ((\iota 50)-51),\iota 50$

3.
```
R1←1 19.6 31.12 1612
R2←2 21.3 26.8 811
R3←3 34.8 41.7 616
R4←4 39.7 52.1 512
R5←5 65.2 85.99 432
M←5 4ρR1,R2,R3,R4,R5
M
```

1   19.6
    31.12   1612
2   21.3
    26.8   811
3   34.8
    41.7   616
4   39.7
    52.1   512
5   65.2
    85.99   432

4.
```
R1←3 3ρ1 0 0 0
R2←3 3ρ0 0 1 0 1 0 1
M←(R1,R2),[1](R2,R1)
M
```
```
1 0 0 0 0 1
0 1 0 0 1 0
0 0 1 1 0 0
0 0 1 1 0 0
0 1 0 0 1 0
1 0 0 0 0 1
```

5.
```
X← ¯5 3 1 ¯2 4
Y←7 ¯8 ¯5 1
X,Y
```
```
¯5  3  1  ¯2  4  7  ¯8  ¯5  1
Y,X
```
```
7  ¯8  ¯5  1  ¯5  3  1  ¯2  4
Y,(ι3),X
```
```
7  ¯8  ¯5  1  1  2  3  ¯5  3  1  ¯2  4
```

6.
```
V←ι80
A←ι5
V←V[ι63],A,V[63+ι(ρV)-63]
V
```
```
 1   2   3   4   5   6   7   8   9  10  11  12
13  14  15  16  17  18  19  20
21  22  23  24  25  26  27  28
29  30  31  32  33  34  35· 36
37  38  39  40  41  42  43  44
45  46  47  48  49  50  51  52
53  54  55  56  57  58  59  60
61  62  63   1   2   3   4   5  64  65
66  67  68  69  70  71  72  73
74  75  76  77  78  79  80
```

7.
```
J←4
K←5
V←ι79
V[ιJ],V[J+K+ι(ρV)-J+K]
```

```
1   2   3   4   10  11  12  13  14  15  16
        17  18  19  20  21  22  23  24
        25  26  27  28  29  30  31  32
        33  34  35  36  37  38  39  40
        41  42  43  44  45  46  47  48
        49  50  51  52  53  54  55  56
        57  58  59  60  61  62  63  64
        65  66  67  68  69  70  71  72
        73  74  75  76  77  78  79
```

CHAPTER 9

1. A, B, and F are correct.
    C. Quad sign is missing.
    D. A function name cannot begin with a numeric.
    E. Quad sign is missing.

2.
```
        ∇TRIANGLE[□]
     ∇ TRIANGLE S;A;B;C
[1]     AS IS A VECTOR WITH 3 COMPONENTS REPRESENTING THE LENGTHS OF
[2]     A THE 3 SIDES OF A TRIANGLE
[3]     A←¯2○((S[1]*2)-(S[2]*2)+(S[3]*))÷¯2×S[2]×S[3]
[4]     B←¯2○((S[2]*2)-(S[1]*2)+(S[3]*))÷¯2×S[1]×S[3]
[5]     C←(○1)-A+B
[6]     'ANGLES A,B AND C IN DEGREES'
[7]     (A,B,C)×(180÷○1)
[8]     'SINES OF ANGLES A,B AND C'
[9]     1○(A,B,C)
[10]    'COSINES OF ANGLES A,B AND C'
[11]    2○(A,B,C)
[12]    'TANGENTS OF ANGLES A,B,C'
[13]    3○(A,B,C)
[14]    'AREA OF TRIANGLE'
[15]    0.5×S[2]×S[3]×1○A
     ∇
[16]    ∇
```

3.
```
        ∇D←PRIMES N;X
[1]     D←2,X←3
[2]     →(N<X←X+2)/0
[3]     →(∨/0=D|X)/2
[4]     D←D,X
[5]     →2
[6]     ∇
```

4.
```
        ∇RP[□]
     ∇ Z←X RP Y
[1]    Z←(0=ZMY)/Z←(0=(ι|X))/ι|X
     ∇
[2]    ∇
```

5.
```
        ∇TAXES[□]
     ∇ TAXES I
[1]    →((I-88)<0)/C1
[2]    →((I-183)<0)/C2
[3]    →((I-333)<0)/C3
[4]    →((I-708)<0)/C4
[5]    →((I-1167)<0)/C5
[6]    →((I-1667)<0)/C6
[7]    TAX←291.01+0.25×(I-1667)
[8]    →0
[9]    C1:TAX←0
[10]   →0
[11]   C2:TAX←0.14×(I-88)
[12]   →0
[13]   C3:TAX←13.3+0.17×(I-183)
[14]   →0
[15]   C4:TAX←38.8+0.16×(I-333)
[16]   →0
[17]   C5:TAX←98.8+0.19×(I-708)
[18]   →0
[19]   C6:TAX←186.01+0.21×(I-1167)
[20]   →0
     ∇
[21]   ∇
```

6.
```
        ∇ROLL[□]
     ∇ Z←ROLL N
[1]    ⍝ASSUMES ORIGIN IS ONE
[2]    ⍝OUTPUT VECTOR IS V WHERE
[3]    ⍝V[1] IS HEADS AND V[2] TAILS.
[4]    I←0
[5]    V← 0 0
[6]    FIRST:→((I←I+1)>N)/0
[7]    T←?2
[8]    V[T]←V[T]+1
[9]    →FIRST
[10]   Z←V
     ∇
[11]   ∇
```

7.
```
        ∇RUNGEKUTTA[□]
      ∇ RUNGEKUTTA V;K1;K2;K3;K4;X;Y
[1]     '              X              Y'
[2]     X←V[1]
[3]     Y←V[2]
[4]     LOOP:K1←V[3]×(X FUN Y)
[5]     K2←V[3]×((X+V[3]÷2) FUN(Y+K1÷2))
[6]     K3←V[3]×((X+V[3]÷2) FUN(Y+K2÷2))
[7]     K ←V[4]×((X+V[3]) FUN(Y+K3))
[8]     Y←Y+(K1+(2XK2)+(2XK3)+K4)÷6
[9]     →(V[4]<X←X+V[3])/0
[10]    14 4 14 4 DFT X,Y
[11]    →LOOP
      ∇
[12]  ∇
```

A. $V←.5\ .8825\ .01\ .6$
        RUNGEKUTTA V

X	Y
.5100	.8781
.5200	.8735
.5300	.8690
.5400	.8643
.5500	.8596
.5600	.8549
.5700	.8501
.5800	.8452
.5900	.8403
.6000	.8353

B. $V←1\ 1\ .1\ 2$

        RUNGEKUTTA V

X	Y
1.1000	1.2100
1.2000	1.4400
1.3000	1.6900
1.4000	1.9600
1.5000	2.2500
1.6000	2.5600
1.7000	2.8900
1.8000	3.2400
1.9000	3.6100
2.0000	4.0000

8.   ∇CHEB[☐]
        ∇ Z←N CHEB X
    [1]   ⍝COMPUTATION OF THE CHEBYSHEV POLYNOMIALS
    [2]   ⍝USING THE RECURSION FORMULA. N IS THE ORDER
    [3]   ⍝OF THE POLYNOMIAL EVALUATED AT X
    [4]   →(N=0)/CASE1
    [5]   →(N=1)/CASE2
    [6]   Z←(2×X×((N-1) CHEB X))-(N-2) CHEB X
    [7]   →0
    [8] CASE1:Z←1
    [9]   →0
   [10] CASE2:Z←X
        ∇
   [11]   ∇

9. A. ∇Z←A COMPADD B
        Z←A+B

    B. ∇Z←A COMPSUB B
        Z←A-B

    C. ∇Z←A COMPMULT B
        Z←(ρA)ρ(,-/[1]A×B),,+/[1]A×⌽[1]B

    D. ∇Z←MOD A
        Z←(+/[1]A×A)*.5

CHAPTER 10

1.

```
      ∇FOURIER[□]
    ∇ FOURIER V;A;B;J;T;ZZ;L
[1]   ⍝CALCULATION OF FOURIER SERIES COEFFICIENTS FOR A FUNCTION
[2]   ⍝DEFINED AT 2N DISCRETE POINTS
[3]   ⍝REFERENCE: R. HAMMING,'NUMERICAL METHODS FOR SCIENTISTS AND ENGINEERS',
[4]   ⍝MCGRAW-HILL PUBLISHING CO.;1962-P67-71
[5]   ⍝REQUIRES FUNCTION 'DFT'
[6]   13ρ' ';'CALCULATION OF FOURIER SERIES COEFFICIENTS'
[7]   2 2 ρ' '
[8]   T←2×N←(ρV)÷2
[9]   4ρ' ';'K';7ρ' ';'A(K)';9ρ' ';'B(K)'
[10]  K←¯1
[11]  →(N<K←K+1)/0
[12]  A←(+/V×2○K×((⍳T)-1)÷N)÷N
[13]  B←(+/V×1○K×((⍳T)+1)÷N)÷N
[14]  ZZ←K,A,B
[15]  5 0 12 5 12 5 DFT ZZ
[16]  →11
    ∇
[17]  ∇
```

The function DFT, which is not shown here, specifies the format of the
printout and is discussed in Chapter 16.

2.   *FOURIER G*
                CALCULATION OF FOURIER SERIES COEFFICIENTS

K	A(K)	B(K)
0	0.00000	0.00000
1	0.00000	1.27062
2	0.00000	0.00000
3	0.00000	0.41653
4	0.00000	0.00000
5	0.00000	0.24142
6	0.00000	0.00000
7	0.00000	0.16319
8	0.00000	0.00000
9	0.00000	0.11708
10	0.00000	0.00000
11	0.00000	0.08541
12	0.00000	0.00000
13	0.00000	0.06128
14	0.00000	0.00000
15	0.00000	0.04142

(continued)

```
16    0.00000    0.00000
17    0.00000    0.02401
18    0.00000    0.00000
19    0.00000    0.00787
20    0.00000    0.00000
```

3.

```
      ∇INTERPOLY[□]
    ∇ P←V INTERPOLY X;G;H;T
[1]   ATHIS FUNCTION GIVES THE VALUE OF THE LAGRANGE INTERPOLATING POLYNOMIAL
[2]   AAT THE POINT X. THE POLYNOMIAL PASSES THROUGH THE N+1 POINTS X(0),X(1),...X(N)
[3]   A AND ASSUMES THE VALUES Y(0),Y(1),...Y(N) AT THESE POINTS. THESE POINTS ARE
[4]   A REPRESENTED IN THE FORM OF A MATRIX  M WITH THE FIRST ROW OF THE MATRIX
[5]   A REPRESENTING THE X'S AND THE SECOND ROW THE Y'S.
[6]   A REFERENCE: 'NUMERICAL CALCULUS'; W.E. MILNE,PRINCETON UNIVERSITY PRESS 1949 P
[7]   G←(ρV)[2]
[8]   T←,V[2;]∘.-V[2;]
[9]   T←×/T←(G,(G-1))ρT[(((G+1)|ι(G*2))≠1)/ι(G*2)]
[10]  H←GρX
[11]  H←,H∘.-V[2;]
[12]  H←×/H←(G,(G-1))ρH[(((G+1)|ι(G*2))≠1)/ι(G*2)]
[13]  P←+/(H÷T)×V[1;]
    ∇
[14]  ∇
```

4. A. $DIST←(+/(X-Y)*2)*.5$

    B. $DIST←(+/(|X-Y)*P)*1÷P$

    C. $DIST←⌈/|X-Y$

5. $M←3$ $3ρ2$ 7 5 5 2 1 7 7 9

    A.   +/M
          14   8   23

    B.   ×/M
          70   10   441

    C. |/M
           1   1   2

    D.   ⌈/M
           7   5   9

    E.   ⌊/M
           2   1   7

6.

        ITEM←ι5
        CP←12.4 18.21 62.5 112.3 1060
        SP←14.25 21.74 78.61 145.82 1200
        NIS←212 611 74 12 86
A.   *PP*←((*SP-CP*)÷*SP*)×100
B.   *AVG*←(+/*PP*)÷ρ*PP*

7.

A. $A←(+/R)÷ρR$

B. $G←(×/R)*1÷(ρR)$

C. $H←(ρR)÷(+/1÷R)$

8.

A. $(|+/R)≤+/|R$

B. $((|+/R×S)*2)≤(+/R*2)×(+/S*2)$

C. $(|+/R×S)≤((+/(|R)*P)*1÷P)×((+/(|S)*P)*1÷P)$

D. $((+/R)×(+/S))≤(ρR)×(+/R×S)$

E. $((+/(R+S)*P)*1÷P)≤((+/R*P)*1÷P)+((+/S*P)*1÷P$

9.

A. $∧/A>B$

B. $∨/A>B$

C. $∨/A=B$

10.

        $+/+/A=B$

11.

A. $+/M$

B. $⌈/M[;2]$

C. $⌊/⌊/M[1 2;]$

12.   ∇*SIMPSON*[☐]
       ∇ *Z←N SIMPSON R;N*
[1]   ⍝*R IS A VECTOR WITH 2 COMPONENTS CONTAINING THE LIMITS*
[2]   ⍝*OF INTEGRATION. N IS THE NUMBER OF INTERVALS.*
[3]   ⍝*Y IS A VECTOR VARIABLE CONTAINING THE FUNCTION VALUES*
       NUMBER OF VALUES)
[4]   *H←(R[2]-R[1])÷N*
[5]   *Z←(+/(1,((¯1+1)ρ 4 2),1)×Y)×H÷3*
       ∇
[6]   ∇

A.   *X←(0,⍳10)÷10*
                        Y←1+X⋆4
                        10 *SIMPSON* 0 1
             1.200013333

B.   *X←(0,2×⍳14)÷10*
                        Y←(1+X⋆3)⋆.5
                        14 *SIMPSON* 0 2.8
             6.333468623

13.
VAR←+/((V-MEAN←(+/V)÷ρV)⋆2)÷((ρV)-1)

14.
(+/M)÷(ρM)[1]

AVG←+/M×(12 5ρ.15 .15 .20 .30 .30)

CHAPTER 11

1.   A.   *S+.×R*
            64   54   50   64   54
            59   44   77   59   44
            84   46   62   84   46
            64   54   50   64   54
            59   44   77   59   44

      B.

      S⌈.⋆R
   6561   65536   256   65
            65536
      256   6561   65536   2
            6561

```
65536                    256              6561              65536
          256                                   256
6561                 65536                256                 6561
      65536
256                    6561          65536                    256
      6561
```

C. $R+.\times S$

```
44   54   46   44   54
59   64   84   59   64
77   50   62   77   50
44   54   46   44   54
59   64   84   59   64
```

D. $R+.\neq S$

```
5   3   5   5   3
5   5   3   5   5
4   5   5   4   5
5   3   5   5   3
5   5   3   5   5
```

E. $S\times.\div R$

```
0.25                 2              0.75        0.25
          2
0.3333333333     2.666666667        1           0.3333333333
      2.666666667
0.5                  4              1.5         0.5
          4
0.25                 2              0.75        0.25
          2
0.3333333333     2.666666667        1           0.3333333333
      2.666666667
```

F. $S+.\times G$

```
130   144
158   172

127   142
157   172

148   164
180   196

130   144
158   172

127   142
157   172
```

2.
```
      K←3 3ρ3 7 3 7 8 4 3 2 1
      ⌹K
   4.091011093E⁻16    ⁻2.000000000E⁻1    8.000000000E⁻1
  ⁻1.000000000E0     ⁻1.200000000E0      1.800000000E0
  ⁻2.000000000E0      3.000000000E0     ⁻5.000000000E0


      K+.×(⌹K)
   1.000000000E0      2.858824288E⁻15   ⁻3.330669074E⁻1⁵
  ⁻4.241719593E⁻15    1.000000000E0     ⁻7.105427358E⁻1⁵
  ⁻5.490535115E⁻16    8.604228441E⁻16    1.000000000E0
```

3.
```
      Y←V+.×U←(ιR)∘.≤ιR←(ρV)[ρρV]
```

4.
```
         ∇LSQ[□]
      ∇ Z←N LSQ M
  [1]    ⍝N IS THE DEGREE OF THE POLYNOMIAL
  [2]    ⍝TO BE FITTED. M IS A MATRIX OF DATA
  [3]    ⍝WITH EACH ROW REPRESENTING AN
  [4]    ⍝OBSERVATION.
  [5]    ⍝COL 1 IS THE INDEPENDENT VARIABLE
  [6]    X AND THE REMAINING COLUMNS ARE
  [7]    ⍝ALTERNATE SETS OF THE DEPENDENT
  [8]    ⍝VARIABLE Y.
  [9]    Z←(0 1 ↓M)⌹M[;1]∘.*0,ιN
         ∇
  [10]   ∇
```

5.
```
      ∇LINT[□]
      ∇ Z←X LINT V;M;P
  [1]    ⍝THE VARIABLE V DESIGNATES THE N POINTS AT WHICH
  [2]    ⍝THE FUNCTION IS KNOWN. THESE POINTS ARE WRITTEN
  [3]    ⍝ X[1],X[2],...X[N],Y[1],Y[2],...Y[N].
  [4]    ⍝ X IS THE VECTOR OF POINTS AT WHICH WE WISH
  [5]    ⍝TO EVALUATE Y
  [6]    ⍝REF:APL QUOTE-QUAD JAN 1970
  [7]    Z←V[M+P]+(V[M+1+P]-V[M+P])×(X-V[P])÷V[P+1]-V[
         P←1⌈(⁻1+M)⌊+/X∘.≥V[ιM←0.5×ρV←,V]]
         ∇
  [8]    ∇
```

6.
```
        ∇PATH[]]
      ∇ M PATH V
[1]     ⍝M IS THE N×N MATRIX DEFINING
[2]     ⍝THE EDGES OF THE GRAPH. V IS
[3]     ⍝A VECTOR SUCH THAT V[1] IS J
[4]     ⍝AND V[2] IS K.
[5]     K←0
[6]     Z←M
[7]     BEGIN:→((K←K+1)=(ρM)[1])/NCON
[8]     →(M[V[1];V[2]]≠0)/ANS
[9]     Z←Z+.×M
[10]    →BEGIN
[11]    ANS:'SHORETEST PATH HAS LENGTH'
[12]    K
[13]    →0
[14]    NCON:'NO CONNECTION'
[15]    →0
        ∇
[16]    ∇
```

7. A.   0 BESX 2
   0.2238907791

   B.   8 BESX ¯1.75
   7.824199624E¯6

   C.   3.2 FRACBES 6.2
   0.1249727139

   D.   4.1 FRACBES 5
   0.3819859524

   E.   .75 FRACBESL 8.25
   0.2780327568

   F.   .5 SPHRBES 6.34
   ¯0.09839936235

   G.   1 FRACBESL 2
   0.5767248078

8. A.   ERF 0
   0

   B.   ERF 3.5
   0.9999997111

   C.   ERF .6
   0.6038560908

9. A.   1 HERMITE 5
   10

   B.   7 HERMITE ¯3.2
   ¯93557.56503

   C.   5 HERMITE 1.2
   ¯52.85376

10. A.   0 *LAGUERRE* 1   C.   6 *LAGUERRE* 3.25
              1   ⁻0.4721757677

    B.   5 *LAGUERRE* ⁻2.1
       53.37702925

11. A.   0 *LEGENDRE* 3   C.   6 *LEGENDRE* 3.25
              1   14885.98143

    B.   5 *LEGENDRE* ⁻2.1
       ⁻244.5267037

12.
```
        ∇MAXEIGEN[□]
     ∇ Z←V MAXEIGEN M;INIT;EIGVAL;AEIGVAL;C;NINIT
[1]     ⋒THIS FUNCTION GIVES THE LARGEST EIGENVALUE
[2]     ⋒IN ABSOLUTE VALUE AND THE ASSOCIATED EIGENVECTOR
[3]     ⋒OF A MATRIX M WHICH HAS REAL DISTINCT EIGENVALUES.
[4]     ⋒V IS A VECTOR SUCH THAT V[ι((ρV)-1)] IS AN INITIAL
[5]     ⋒GUESS AT THE EIGENVECTOR AND V[ρV] IS THE CONVERGEN
[6]     ⋒CRITERIA. REF:'NUMERICAL CALCULATIONS AND ALGORITHM
[7]     ⋒R. BECKETT AND J. HURT;MCGRAW-HILL PUBLISHING CO.
[8]     ⋒P124-127
[9]     INIT←M+.×⍉V[ι((ρV)-1)]
[10]    C←(|INIT)ι C←⌈/|INIT
[11]    AEIGVAL←INIT[C]
[12]    NINIT←M+.×⍉(INIT)÷(INIT[C])
[13]    EIGVAL←NINIT[C]
[14]    →((|(EIGVAL-AEIGVAL))<V[ρV])/END
[15]    INIT←NINIT
[16]    AEIGVAL←EIGVAL
[17]    →12
[18]    Z←EIGVAL,NINIT÷NINIT[C]
     ∇
[19]    ∇
```


13.
```
        ∇GAUSEID[□]
     ∇ Z←E GAUSEID C;R;X
[1]     ⋒ THIS FUNCTION IMPLEMENTS THE GAUSS-SEIDEL METHOD
[2]     ⋒FOR SOLVING A SYSTEM OF LINEAR EQUATIONS. C  IS THE AUGMEN
        MATRIX
[3]     ⋒OF COEFFICIENTS WITH THE CONSTANTS APPENDED AS THE LAST
[4]     ⋒COLUMN.E IS THE VECTOR OF ALLOWABLE RESIDUES.
[5]     ⋒REFERENCE-'DIGITAL COMPUTER SYSTEM PRINCIPLES'-
[6]     ⋒ H. HELLERMAN-MCGRAW-HILL PUBLISHING CO.-1967; P63-64
```

```
[7]     R←(ρC)[1]ρ0
[8]     X←(ρC)[1]ρ0
[9]     J←0
[10]    →((ρC)[1]<J←J+1)/TEST
[11]    R[J]←C[J;(ρC)[2]]-C[J;ι(ρC)[2]-1]+.×X
[12]    X[J]←X[J]+R[J]÷C[J;J]
[13]    →10
[14]    TEST:→((∧/(|E≥|R))≠1)/9
[15]    Z←X
[16]    →0
     ∇
[17]    ∇
```

```
        C

   10    2    6   28
    1   10    9    7
    2   ‾7  ‾10  ‾17
```

```
     .02 GAUSEID C
1.000479189  ‾2.998533922  3.999069584
```

CHAPTER 12

1. A. $V1←V[\boxed{↓}V]$ C. $V1←V[\boxed{↑}|V]$

    B. $V1←V[\boxed{↓}]$

2.   ∇MEDIAN[□]
            ∇ Z←MEDIAN V;V1
```
    [1]     ⍝THIS FUNCTION COMPUTES THE MEDIAN OF A SET OF DATA
    [2]     ⍝GIVEN IN THE FORM OF A VECTOR V
    [3]     V1←V[⍋V]
    [4]     →(((2|(ρV))=0))/EVEN
    [5]     Z←V1[((ρV1)+1)÷2]
    [6]     →0
    [7]     EVEN:Z←(V1[(ρV1)÷2]+V1[((ρV1)+2)÷2])÷2
    [8]     →0
         ∇
    [9]     ∇
```

3.   ∇AMP[□]
            ∇ Z←AMP M
```
    [1]     Z←V[⍋V←(+/[1] T←M*2)*0.5]
         ∇
    [2]     ∇
```

4.
```
        V←1 9 8 2 6 5
        M←5 5ρι25
```

  A.   `W←⍋¯3↑V`   C.   `W←,1 ¯2↑M`
                   `W`   `W`
      1 3 2   4 5

  B.   `W←⍒¯1↓V`
               `W`
     2 3 5 4 1

5.
```
        ∇CHARSORT[☐]
      ∇ Z←CHARSORT M;D
  [1]   D←'ABCDEFGHIJKLMNOPQRSTUVWXYZ0123456789'
  [2]   Z←M[⍋(2+ρD)⊥⍉D⍳M;]
      ∇
  [3]   ∇
```

6.
```
        ∇ADDQUEUE[☐]
      ∇ ADDQUEUE A
  [1]   Q←Q,A
      ∇
  [2]   ∇
```

```
        ∇DELQUEUE[☐]
      ∇ Z←DELQUEUE
  [1]   Z←1↑Q
  [2]   Q←1↓Q
      ∇
  [3]   ∇
```

7.
```
        ∇DIFF[☐]
      ∇ Z←Y DIFF N
  [1]   J←0
  [2]   BEGIN:→((J←J+1)>N)/PRINT
  [3]   D←(1↓Y)-(¯1↓Y)
  [4]   Y←D
  [5]   →BEGIN
  [6]   PRINT:'THE ';N;'    DIFFERENCES ARE ';D
      ∇
  [7]   ∇
```

8.
```
         ∇PUSH[☐]
       ∇ STACK PUSH A
[1]      STACK←A,STACK
       ∇
[2]    ∇
```

```
         ∇POP[☐]
       ∇ Z←STACK POP A
[1]      Z←1↑STACK
[2]      STACK←1↓STACK
       ∇
[3]    ∇
```

CHAPTER 13

1. $U←{}^{-}1↓(V+1\phi V)÷2$

2.   A.
```
              ∇ SYMMETRIC[☐]
            ∇ Z←SYMMETRIC M
   [1]        Z←∧/∧/M=⍉M
            ∇
   [2]      ∇
```

   B.   This matrix is always symmetric.

3. $T←+/1\ 1\phi M$

4.   Only B is a permutation vector. In each of the others a number is
      missing (A, 2; C, 1; D, 4).

CHAPTER 14

1. A. $V \leftarrow (V>0)/V$ C. $V \leftarrow (V>11)/V$

   B. $V \leftarrow (V<0)/V$ D. $V \leftarrow 1\ 0\ 1\ 0\ 0\ 0\ 0/V$

2. $B \leftarrow (52\rho 1,0)\backslash A$

3. $U \leftarrow +/+/M \epsilon N$

4. A. $(V \epsilon U)/V$ C. $(U \epsilon V)/U$

   B. $V,(\sim V \epsilon U))/V$ D. $(\sim(V \epsilon U))/V$

5.
```
∇BRIDGE
Z←4 13ρ52?52
N←Z[1;]
S←Z[2;]
W←Z[3;]
E←Z[4;]
∇
```

6.
```
       ∇RANDOM[□]
   ∇  Z←RANDOM N
[1]    Z←ι0
[2]    I←0
[3]    FIRST:→((I←I+1)>N)/0
[4]    Z←Z,D[?(ρD)]
[5]    →FIRST
   ∇
[6]    ∇
```

Answers   345

CHAPTER 15

1. **A.** $A \leftarrow 1\ ^-16\ 9$ **C.** $A \leftarrow 1\ 0\ 3\ ^-6\ 11$
   $X \leftarrow 3.1$ $X \leftarrow .07$
   $X \perp A$ $X \perp A$
   $^-30.99$ 10.59472401

   B. $A \leftarrow 2\ 0\ 0\ 5\ ^-13\ 11\ 2$
   $X \leftarrow 6.2$
   $X \perp A$
   114362.5912

2. **A.** $V \leftarrow 360\ 60\ 60$ **B.** $V \leftarrow 360\ 60\ 60$
   $T \leftarrow 26\ 10\ 13$ $T \leftarrow 105\ 38\ 15$
   $DEG \leftarrow (V \perp T) \div 3600$ $DEG \leftarrow (V \perp T) \div 3600$
   DEG DEG
   26.17027778   105.6375
   $RAD \leftarrow DEG \times (O \div 180)$ $RAD \leftarrow DEG \times (O \div 180)$
   RAD RAD
   0.4567575134   1.843722189

3. **A.** $S \leftarrow 15911$
   $V \leftarrow 15\rho 2$
   $V \top S$
   0 1 1 1 1 1 0 0 0 1 0 0 1 1 1

   B. $S \leftarrow 3716$ **C.** $S \leftarrow 1612$
   $V \leftarrow 8\ 8\ 8\ 8$ $V \leftarrow 8\rho 5$
   $V \top S$ $V \top S$
   7 2 0 4   0 0 0 2 2 4 2 2

4. $\nabla HEX[\Box]$
   ∇ $Z \leftarrow HEX\ X$
   [1] $Z \leftarrow '0123456789ABCDEF'[1+(4\rho 16)\top X]$
   ∇
   [2] ∇

5. **A.** $\nabla INDEX[\Box]$
   ∇ $INDEX\ D$
   [1] $((\rho D)\top((1\uparrow \Psi,D)-1))+1$
   ∇
   [2] ∇

   B. $\nabla INDEX1[\Box]$
   ∇ $INDEX1\ D$
   [1] $((\rho D)\top((1\uparrow \spadesuit,D)-1))+1$
   ∇
   [2] ∇

CHAPTER 16

1.

```
      ∇TAB[□]
   ∇ Z←TAB;LIM;NPTS;X;Y;U;H
[1]   ⍝THIS FUNCTION TABULATES A GIVEN FUNCTION WHOSE
      NAME IS ∇Z←CASE X
[2]   'ENTER LIMITS OF TABULATION'
[3]   LIM←□
[4]   'ENTER INTERVAL'
[5]   H←□
[6]   Y←X←⍳0
[7]   ARG←LIM[1]
[8]   START:→(ARG>LIM[2])/NEXT
[9]   U←CASE ARG
[10]  Y←Y,U
[11]  X←X,ARG
[12]  ARG←ARG+H
[13]  →START
[14]  NEXT:Z←X AND Y
   ∇
[15]  ∇
```

3.

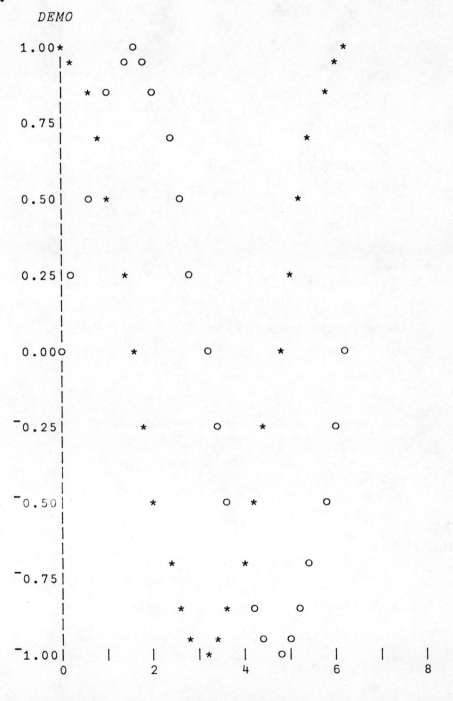

CHAPTER 17

2.

```
        ←(
```

A.
```
            Z←¯1*.5
DOMAIN ERROR
            Z←¯1*0.5
                 ∧
```

B.
```
            ←Y←A+2
SYNTAX ERROR
            ←Y←A+2
             ∧
```

C.
```
            A←2 2ρι4
            B←3 5
            C←A+B
RANK ERROR
            C←A+B
                ∧
```

D.
```
            DEFN ERROR
```

E.
```
            G←3∧A←1
DOMAIN ERROR
            G←3∧A←1
                 ∧
```

F.
```
            G←1 3 5
            H←2 4 1 2
            Z←G+H
LENGTH ERROR
            Z←G+H
                ∧
```

G.
```
            Y←3 5 7
            G←⌽/Y
SYNTAX ERROR
            G←⌽/Y
                ∧
```

H.
```
            Y←3 8 7
            G←Y[4]
INDEX ERROR
            G←Y[4]
                 ∧
```

I.
```
            Y←2+7A←3.5
SYNTAX ERROR
            Y←2+7 A←3.5
                  ∧
```

J.
```
            →(Z<Y←Y+1)/NEXT
VALUE ERROR
            →(Z<Y←Y+1)/NEXT
                 ∧
```

CHAPTER 18

1. A.   `)ORIGIN 0`

   B.   `)WIDTH 82`

   C.   `)DIGITS 13`

2.   `)OFF HOLD:JAMES`

3. A.)*LOAD MATH:CALC*

   B.)*ERASE MATH*

   C.)*COPY TRIG MATH* 32

4. A.)*CHEMICALS TIN LEAD GOLD SILVER*

   B.)*ERASE CHEMICALS*

   C.
```
      )WSID PROB
WAS MATH
```

5. A.)*SAVE CALC:MINE*

   B.)*DROP CALC*

6. A.)*FNS*

   B.)*VARS H*

   C.)*GRPS*

   D.)*LIB* 120

   E.)*PORTS*

7. A.)*MSG* 307 *HOW ARE YOU?*

   B.)*OPRN THANKS*

8. A.)I22

   B.)I21

   C.)I23

CHAPTER 19

2.A. ⌽*M*←3 3 3⍴⍳27

```
3   2   1
6   5   4
9   8   7
```

(continued)

```
       12   11   10
       15   14   13
       18   17   16

       21   20   19
       24   23   22
       27   26   25
```

B.   囷1.7
       0.5882352941

C.   (4ρ⁻3)τ17
       ⁻1 ⁻1 0 ⁻1

CHAPTER 20

1.
       M←1.0257 1.0572 3.97865 572.6889 ⁻7.125
       M←M,16.21 173.21 994.2 1.078
       M←3 3ρM
       M

        1.0257   ⁻1.0572   3.97865
      572.6889   ⁻7.125   16.21
      173.21   994.2   1.078

   A.   9 ⁻3▼M
        1.03E00   1.06E00   3.98E00
        5.73E02 ⁻7.12E00   1.62E01
        1.73E02   9.94E02   1.08E00

   B.   9 3▼M
         1.026   ⁻1.057   3.979
       572.689   ⁻7.125   16.210
       173.210   994.200   1.078

2.
         Z←9 9ρ1 0 0 0 0 0 0 0 0
         Z

     1 0 0 0 0 0 0 0 0
     0 1 0 0 0 0 0 0 0
     0 0 1 0 0 0 0 0 0
     0 0 0 1 0 0 0 0 0
```
```

```
0 0 0 0 1 0 0 0 0
0 0 0 0 0 1 0 0 0
0 0 0 0 0 0 1 0 0
0 0 0 0 0 0 0 1 0
0 0 0 0 0 0 0 0 1
```

```
        R←⍭Z
        ρZ
9   9
        ρR
9  18
        R[;(2×⍳9)-1]
100000000
010000000
001000000
000100000
000010000
000001000
000000100
000000010
000000001
```

3.

A.

```
        ⍕'B←⍳9'
        ⍕R←B+3'
        B
1 2 3 4
        R
4 5 6 7 8 9 10 11 12
```

B.
```
        ⍕'3+5'
8
```

C.
```
        ÷\1 2 4 8
1 0.5 2 0.25
```

D.
```
        -\1 2 4 8
1 ‾1 3 ‾5
```

4.   ⍕((X∊⍳10)=1)/'Y←X'